MIDDLE ENGLISH TEXTS · 31

The Three Kings of Cologne

Edited from London,
Lambeth Palace MS 491
by FRANK SCHAER

Universitätsverlag
C. WINTER
Heidelberg

Die Deutsche Bibliothek – CIP-Einheitsaufnahme

The three kings of Cologne: ed. from London, Lambeth Palace MS 491 / by Frank Schaer. – Heidelberg: Winter, 2000

(Middle English texts; 31)
ISBN 3-8253-1122-8

ISBN 3-8253-1122-8

Imprimé en Allemagne · Printed in Germany
Druck: Strauss Offsetdruck GmbH, 69509 Mörlenbach

CONTENTS

LIST OF FIGURES

ACKNOWLEDGEMENTS

This edition has followed many years of work at the University of Adelaide on the better known English prose version of the *Three Kings of Cologne* and its Latin original, and was completed during a period as honorary research follow at the University of Sheffield and finally at the Central European University, Budapest. I should like to thank those who have helped me in the task: Professor Manfred Görlach (who kindly supplied notes for the Language section) and Dr Oliver Pickering; the members of the Department of English Language and Literature at the University of Adelaide and the Department of English Language and Linguistics at the University of Sheffield, particularly Mr Brian Donaghey and Dr Geoff Lester; and at the Central European University, Professor J. M. Bak. I would like to thank William Marx for seeing this volume through to publication, and Karen Jankulak for technical help and proof-reading. A grant generously provided by the Huntington allowed me to spend a month at their library examining HM 114, and I should like to thank the Trustees for permission to reproduce a page of the manuscript. I should also like to thank the Trustees of Lambeth Palace Library for permission to use MS 491 as base text for the present work and to reproduce a page of the manuscript.

Frank Schaer
Department of Medieval Studies
Central European University, Budapest
Epiphany 2000

I am grateful to Karen Jankulak for serving as Assistant to the General Editor in the preparation of this volume.

William Marx
Department of English
University of Wales, Lampeter
2000

ABBREVIATIONS

This volume uses the conventional abbreviations for the *Oxford English Dictionary* (*OED*), *Middle English Dictionary* (*MED*) and Early English Text Society (EETS). Square brackets enclose conventional titles.

BC	[*Book of Cologne*], ed. by Reinhold Röhricht and Heinrich Meisner, 'Ein niederrheinischer Bericht über den Orient', *Zeitschrift für deutsche Philologie*, 19 (1887), 1–86
BL	British Library
ERE	*Encyclopaedia of Religion and Ethics*, ed. by James Hastings, 13 vols (New York, 1908)
H	San Marino, Huntington Library MS 114
Hm.	*The Three Kings of Cologne*, ed. by C. Horstmann, EETS OS 85 (1886)
HTR	*Historia Trium Regum*
IMEV	C. Brown and R. H. Robbins, *The Index of Middle English Verse* (New York, 1943)
IMEV(S)	R. H. Robbins and J. L. Cutler, *Supplement to the Index of Middle English Verse* (Lexington, 1965)
IPMEP	R. E. Lewis, N. F. Blake, and A. S. G. Edwards, *Index of Printed Middle English Prose* (New York and London, 1985)
L	London, Lambeth Palace Library MS 491
LALME	A. McIntosh, M. L. Samuels, and M. Benskin, *A Linguistic Atlas of Late Medieval English*, 4 vols (Aberdeen, 1986)
Ludolf	Ludolf of Sudheim, *Description of the Holy Land, and of the Way Thither*, trans. by Aubrey Stewart (London, 1897)
Manual	J. Burke Severs and Albert E. Hartung, eds, *A Manual of the Writings in Middle English 1050–1500*, 10 volumes published to date (New Haven, Conn., 1967–98)
MV	Ugo Monneret de Villard, *Le leggende orientali sui Magi evangelici*, Studi e Testi, 163 (Vatican City, 1952)
ODCC	F. L. Cross and E. A. Livingstone, eds, *The Oxford Dictionary of the Christian Church*, 2nd edn (Oxford, 1974)

PG	*Patrologia Graeca*, ed. by J. P. Migne, 162 volumes (Paris, 1857–66)
PL	*Patrologia Latina*, ed. by J. P. Migne, 217 volumes (Paris, 1844–55)
PsM	*Gospel of Pseudo-Matthew*, in *Evangelia Apocrypha*, 2nd edn, ed. by C. Tischendorf (Leipzig, 1876; rpt., Hildesheim, 1966)
STC	A. W. Pollard and G. R. Redgrave, *A Short-Title Catalogue of Books Printed in England, Scotland, and Ireland and of English Books Printed Abroad 1475–1640*, 2nd edn, W. A. Jackson, F. S. Ferguson and K. F. Pantzer, 3 vols (London, 1976–91)
3KCol	*Three Kings of Cologne*

INTRODUCTION

1 Overview

The most comprehensive medieval account of the legend of the biblical Magi is the version attributed to John of Hildesheim (d. 1375), commonly known as the *Historia Trium Regum* (*HTR*),[1] a summary of which is given in Introduction 6. A number of medieval vernacular versions of *HTR* survive, including three translations into English, all known as the *Three Kings of Cologne*. The present text, the Lambeth *Three Kings of Cologne* (*Lambeth 3KCol*), dated ? *c.* 1425, is independent of the other two and has not previously been studied or edited. Though primarily based on *HTR*, it includes initially material from the apocryphal *Gospel of Pseudo-Matthew*. *Lambeth 3KCol* takes its designation from the major witness, Lambeth Palace Library MS 491 (L). However an extract is also found in Huntington Library MS 114 (H). Both are by the same scribe.

In what follows the *scribe* refers to the hand who copied L and H. The *translator* refers to the person (or persons) who executed the translation of which the two manuscripts are witnesses. The *present work* (text etc.) refers to the translation presented in this edition, that is, *Lambeth 3KCol*. The *exemplar* refers to the Latin text from which the translator worked, the attempted reconstruction of which is printed in parallel with the present text. The *author* refers to the author of the Latin original (*HTR*). The *original Latin* refers to the text as the author intended it (as opposed to the corrupt text which the translator had before him).

Page and line numbers refer to the present edition. A letter 'n' before a number designates a footnote, whereas after a line or page number it draws attention to an entry in the Commentary. Other abbreviations are explained as the need arises.

1 The standard edition is in C. Horstmann, *The Three Kings of Cologne* (henceforth Hm.), where the text of *HTR* appears on pp. 206–312. The work has received various titles; see, for example, Hm. ix/n1.

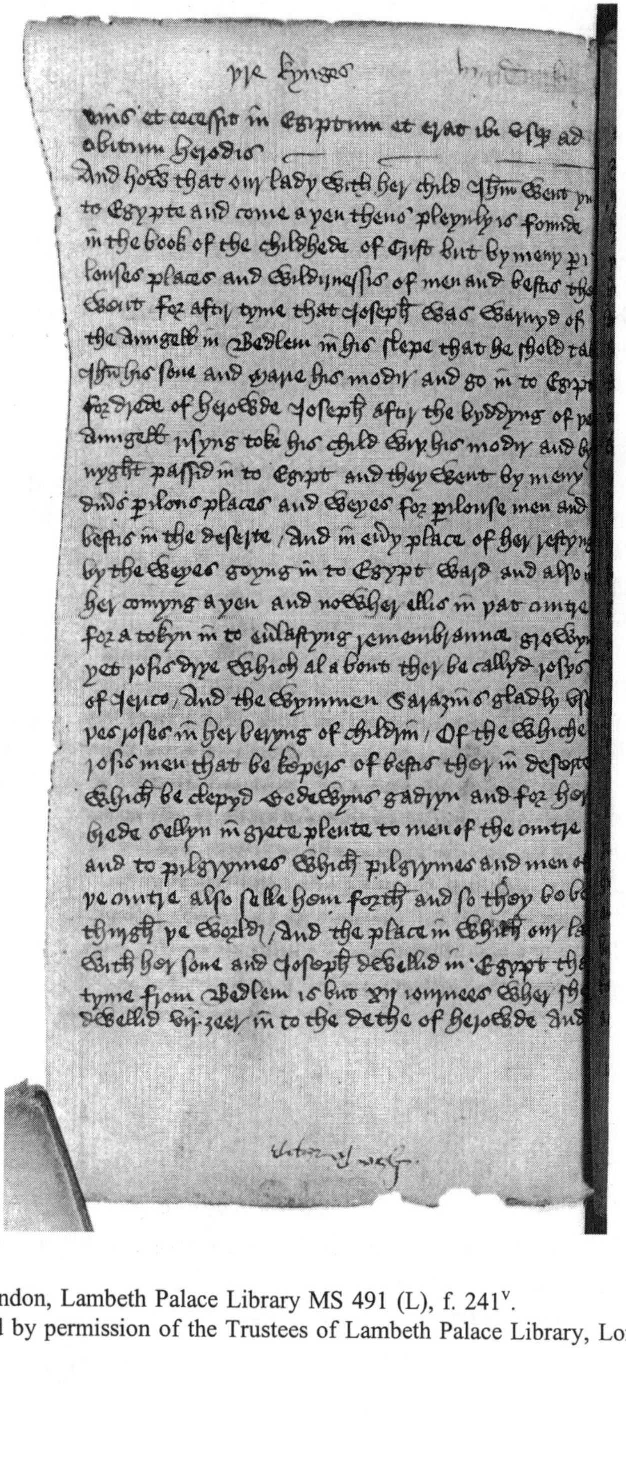

þre kynges

...ctis et secessit in Egiptum et erat ibi vsque ad
obitum Herodis
And how that our lady with her child & hym went in
to Egypte and come ayen thens plenerly is founde
in the book of the childhede of crist but by meny p[er]-
louses places and wildirnessis of men and bestis the[y]
went for after tyme that Ioseph was warnyd of
the aungell in Bedlem in his slepe that he shold ta[ke]
with his sone and mary his modir and go in to Egipt
for drede of Herowde Ioseph after the byddyng of þe
aungell risyng toke his child with his modir and by
nyght passid in to Egipt and they went by meny
dyu[er]s perilous places and weyes for perilouse men and
bestis in the deserte / And in euery place of her restyng
by the weyes goyng in to Egypt ward and also in
her comyng ayen and nowher ellis in þat contre
for a tokyn in to euerlastyng remembraunce growyn
yet roses drye which al a boute they be callyd roses
of Ierico / And the wymmen Sarazins gladly vse
þes roses in her beryng of childryn / Of the whiche
roses men that be kepers of bestis ther in deserte
which be clepyd Bedewyns gadryn and for hem
herde sellyn in grete plente to men of the contre
and to pilgrymes Which pilgrymes and men of
þe contre also sellen hem forth and so they be bo[rn]
thurgh þe world / And the place in which our la[dy]
with her sone and Ioseph dwellid in Egypt th[at]
tyme from Bedlem is but xii iourneys wher sh[e]
dwellid vii yeer in to the dethe of Herowde And

Fig. 1. London, Lambeth Palace Library MS 491 (L), f. 241[v].

2 Description of the manuscripts

L London, Lambeth Palace Library MS 491

Descriptions appear in James and Jenkins 1932: 681–84, Hanna 1989: 130–31. I have followed Hanna's collation and division into booklets.

291 folios (150 repeated in the numeration). Four leaves of modern paper follow, the remainder of the manuscript (ff. 295–329) being a separate codex containing principally a copy of the *Prick of Conscience*.[2] 225 x 147 mm (writing area 170 x 95 mm). Typically single vellum sheets form the outermost and central sheets of each quire, the others being paper. The manuscript comprises three booklets.

Collation:

booklet I, ff. 1–216: [quire 1 lost] 2^{16} (lacks 7, 10) $3–5^{16}$ 6^{16} (lacks 5, 7, 10, 12) 7^{16} (lacks 2, 15) 8^{16} (lacks 4, 5, 6, 7, 10, 11, 12, 13) 9^{16} (lacks 7, 10) 10^{16} (lacks 7, 10, 14) 11^{16} 12^{16} (lacks 7) 13^{16} (lacks 9) $14–16^{16}$

booklet II, ff. 217–74: 1^{16} 2^{16} (lacks 2, 15) 3^{16} 4^{16} (lacks 3, 14, 15, 16)

booklet III, ff. 275–90: 1^{16}, with the remainder lost.

Contents:

ff. 1–205^{v}, the Middle English prose *Brut*, *IPMEP* 374; printed in Brie 1906–1908.

ff. 206–27^{v}, the alliterative *Siege of Jerusalem*, *IMEV(S)* 1583; Wells 1916: 155–6; *Manual* 160–62; Lawton 1982; Rice 1987: 395–96. An edition by Ralph Hanna and David Lawton is forthcoming.

ff. 228–74^{v}, *Lambeth 3KCol.*

ff. 275–86^{v}, the alliterative poem, the *Awntyrs off Arthure*, *IMEV(S)* 1566; Wells 1916: 61–2; *Manual* 61–2; Rice 1987: 221–26; Allen 1987.

ff. 287–90^{v}, the verse *Book of Hunting*, *IMEV(S)* 4064. The work is extant in one other manuscript, Bodleian Library MS Rawlinson Poet. 143, ff. 1^{r}–11^{av}, dated *c.*1475, perhaps originally part of a manuscript which included the *Awntyrs off Arthure* (see Hanna, 1974: 5, 8), and is the second treatise on hunting in the *Boke of St Albans*, printed in 1486 (*STC* 3308). On this text see Hands 1975: xxxii–xxxvi; the text of the work is reproduced on pp. 57–79 and 168–86. See also Rooney 1993: 9–10.

2 See Lewis and McIntosh's guide to the manuscripts of the *Prick of Conscience* (Lewis and McIntosh 1982: 80–81).

Items 2 and 4 are again associated with the *Three Kings of Cologne* in the oeuvre of Robert Thornton, who copied the *Awntyrs off Arthure* in Lincoln Cathedral Library MS 91, and the verse *Three Kings of Cologne* and the *Siege of Jerusalem* in BL Additional MS 31042.[3]

H San Marino, Huntington Library MS 114

Descriptions, with details of editions of items, appear in Dutschke 1989: 150–52 and Hanna 1989: 129–30.

295 x 140 mm (writing area 165 x 100 mm). Mixed vellum and paper as in L. Items 3 and 4 written more cursively. The manuscript comprises three booklets.

Collation:

booklet I, ff. 1–130: 1-6^{16} 7^{18} 8^{16}

booklet II, ff. 131–92: 9^{16} (lacks 7, 10) 10–12^{16}

booklet III, ff. 193–325: 13–16^{16} 17^{16} (+5) 18^{16} (+5, 6) 19^{16} 20^{16} (+10, 17).

Contents:

ff. 1–130^{v}, *Piers Plowman*, a unique conflation of the A, B, and C versions.

ff. 131–84, *Mandeville's Travels*, defective version, subgroup B, the commonly encountered form of the English text (Seymour 1974: 139).

ff. 184^{v}–90^{v}, the alliterative poem *Susannah*, *IMEV(S)* 3553.

ff. 190^{v}–92^{v}, an excerpt from *Lambeth 3KCol*, under the running title *Ioseph*.

ff. 193–318^{v}, *Troilus and Criseyde*, the so-called α text.

ff. 319–25^{v}, a translation, unique to this manuscript, of Peter Ceffons's satirical *Epistola Luciferi ad cleros*, an attack on clerical abuses and particularly *the four beggyng ordres*.

Both witnesses are in the same anglicana hand which is also 'Hand 1' of BL, Harley MS 3943, another manuscript of *Troilus and Criseyde*.[4] The scribe was probably a person from south-eastern Essex, working on these manuscripts in the later 1420s or early 1430s.[5] He inserted the Latin rubrics himself (apparently somewhat later, as sometimes too little space was left,

[3] See below, pp. 27–8.
[4] On Harley 3943 see Windeatt 1984: 71, and Hanna 1989: 122, 126–28, 129.
[5] Hanna 1989: 122.

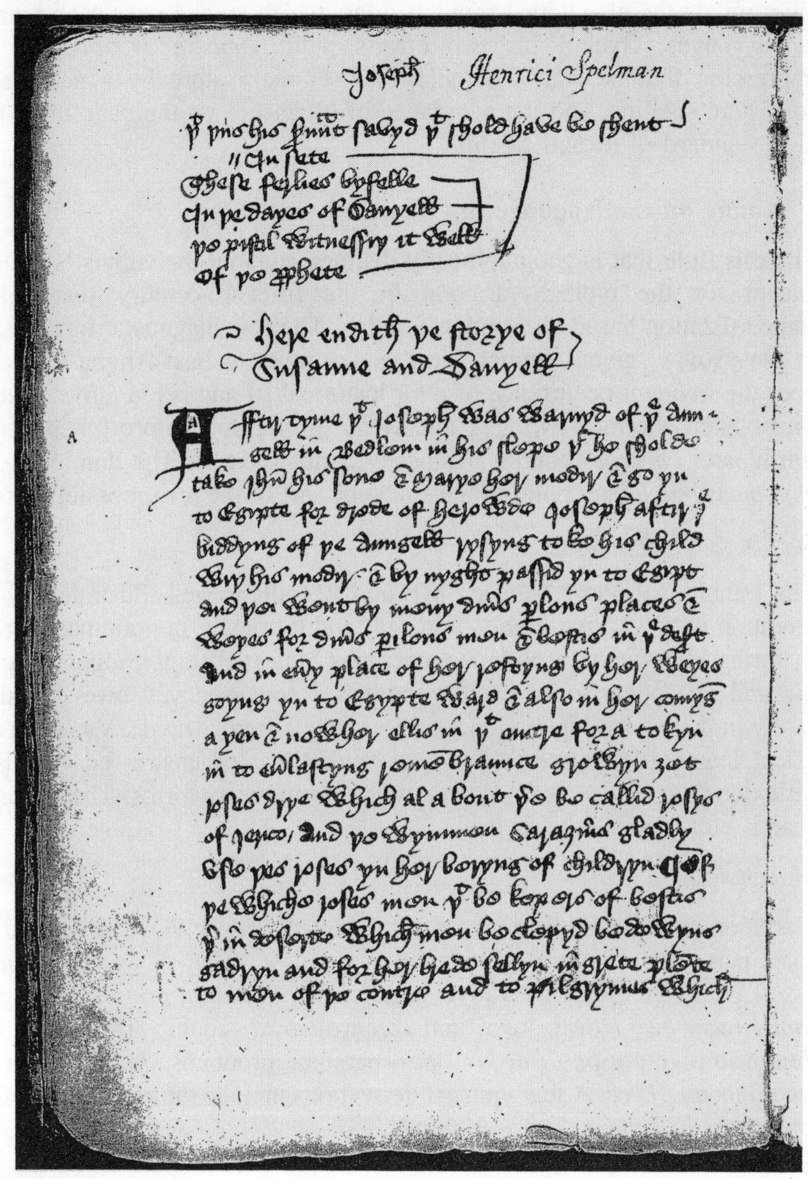
Joseph Henrici Spelman

þt pris his firme saiyd þt shold have be shent
// In sete
These feghtes byfelle
In ye dayes of Danyell
ye pistel witnessith it well
of ye prophete

Here endith ye storye of
Susanne and Danyell

A Aftir tyme þt Joseph was warnyd of þe aungell in Bedlem in his slepe þt he shold
take with his sone & marye her modir & go yn
to Egypte for drede of Herowde Joseph aftir þe
biddyng of ye aungell rysyng toke his child
with his modir & by nyghte passid yn to Egypte
and yei wente by mony dyvers playne places &
weyes for dyvers perilous men & bestes in þe deserte
And in euery place of her restyng by her weyes
goyng yn to Egypte was & also in her comyng
a yen & now her ellis in þe cuntre for a tokyn
in to everlastyng remembraunce growyn zet
roses dyuers which al a bout ys be called roses
of Jerico, And ye wymmen of yat cuntre gladly
use yes roses yn her beryng of childryn. Of
ye which roses men þt be keperis of bestis
þt in deserte which men be clepyd bedowynes
gadryn and for her had fallyn in grete plente
to men of ye contre and to pilgrymes which

Fig. 2. San Marino, Huntington Library MS 114 (H), f. 190v; the corresponding text begins at the seventh line of L, f. 241v (*Fig.* 1).
Reproduced by permission of The Huntington Library, San Marino, California.

sometimes too much), and was presumably also responsible for the red and blue initials; he also added running titles, which spread over each pair of facing pages. Overall his two efforts with *Lambeth 3KCol* give the impression that he was a copyist who set more store by a neat hand, consistent spelling, and the avoidance of blemishes on the page than on a high standard of textual fidelity.[6]

3 A note on the language (by Manfred Görlach)

There is little that is geographically distinctive about the copyist's dialect, except for the typical variation of the fifteenth-century just before standardization based on London English. The few diagnostic forms, such as *yove/yovyn* 'given' (minor form *yevyn*) point to East Anglia/Essex, as does the frequent occurrence of *e* for historical [i] and [y] in *leftyd* 'lifted', *shette* 'shut', *wenges* 'wings', and *yeftis* 'gifts', and before [r] in *berthe* 'birth' and *cherche* 'church' (minority forms have *i*). The dominance of *eny*, *meny*, *such* may point to the southern part of the area, possibly Essex.

Spelling and Phonology:

The transitional phase between ME and EModE is well illustrated by the retention of ȝ (varying with *y-* and *-gh*) and *þ* (mainly in grammar words). In forms like *taught*, a glide is sometimes indicated (*taght*, *toght*, *taught*), *u/v* and *i/y* appear to be used without any consistency. Vowel length is rarely indicated by duplication (*goodes*, *citee*); there is no *ea*. Variation can affect loanwords (*supperflue* / *super-fleu*). Checked unstressed vowels in inflexions are *i/y* (*-is*, *-id*, *-in*, *-ir*), with *e* in minority forms. The vowel in 'hand' etc. is regularly spelt *o*.

Morphology:

Variation is frequently in forms of *be* (pres. pl. *are*, *be*, *beth*, *bene*) and *get* (past part. *yeten*, *goten*), give (past part. *yovyn* / *yevyn*), go (pa.t. *yede* / *went*) etc. Note the conservative superlatives, *breddest*, *grettest*, *strengest*, *tool* / *two* / *twy* / *twey* 'two' and *couth*(*e*)/*cowd* 'could'. The article and demonstrative are *þe* / *þo*, *þis* / *þes*; personal pronouns *she* / *her* and *þei* (*they*) / *hem* / *here*. A few unusual derivations include the zero forms *gladd*

[6] Orthographic slips represent a minority of errors (see footnote 57). The scribe normally corrects his copies of *3KCol* by erasure and not by underdotting. On the assumption that the scribe avoided making corrections, I have deleted a number of apparent false starts (e.g., 147/11 *was of old tyme into now is left from þat tyme*; 150/1 *newe trewe feith*). Certain peculiarities of usage may be due to the same unwillingness to correct slips (e.g., 91/13n *þat landis*).

'were glad', *richid* 'made rich', and *wratthith* 'is wroth', and agent nouns *goers* and *stonders* – the latter probably indications of an incompetent translator, as are peculiarities in word order, such as sentence-final verbs copied from the Latin source. It appears impossible to say how much of the existing variation may be due to copyists introducing their own dialect forms; the mixture found here is frequent in fifteenth-century texts, but would seem to be quite rare after 1500.

4 Authorship and date of the *Historia Trium Regum*

The Latin original of the present translation is usually anonymous in the manuscripts; however, it is attributed on the authority of later authors like Trithemius (1462–1512) to John of Hildesheim (d. 1375), a Carmelite who held a succession of ecclesiastical posts and seems to have enjoyed contemporary renown as a theologian, scholar, philosopher, poet, and preacher.[7] Aside from *HTR*, all that survives of the output attributed to him is a defence of his order, a philosophical work *Fons Vite*, the titles alone of a number of works of an evidently polemical nature, and a corpus of correspondence (the latter unquestionably genuine). The attribution to him of *HTR* has been questioned on stylistic grounds; certainly the rather distinctive style of the letters, not to mention their humanist content, finds little echo in the work on the Three Kings. The fact is that there is little internal evidence to link *HTR* to him or any individual (*cf.*, 95/4–5n).[8]

Internal allusions suggest a *terminus post quem* of 1351 (or 1364, if the dedication to Florencius of Wevelinghoven, bishop of Münster, is original) and a general connection with Cologne.[9] The *terminus ante quem* is provided by the earliest German translation, dedicated to Elisabeth of Katzenelnbogen, of 1389 (or by John of Hildesheim's death in 1375, on the traditional authorship).

Whoever the author was, *HTR* was clearly a great success; over a 100 manuscripts have been identified, mostly of the fifteenth century, and a

7 'Vir in diuinis scripturis studiosus et eruditus, et in secularibus literis omnium opinione suo tempore doctissimus, theologus, rhetor, philosophus, poetaque celeberrimus, in declamandis homiliis ad populum excellentis ingenii fuit' (Trithemius 1601: 146–47). The attribution *Johannes Hildesiensis carmelitae historia trium regum* appears exceptionally in Munich, SB clm MS 14186 (undated).

8 For biographical and literary details concerning John of Hildesheim see Hm. ix–xvii, and more recently Worstbrock and Harris 1982. Scepticism concerning the traditional authorship is voiced in Hendricks 1957: 116 and Christern 1959/60: 43– 44, while Worstbrock and Harris favour the witness of the tradition.

9 The dedication appears in the text at Hm. 211/3–5. For the dating see Hm. xiii (but the figure 1361 among the internal dates is untrustworthy).

number of prints.[10] Versions in Dutch, Flemish, and French survive, as well as three independent English versions (two in prose and one in verse, all known by the title *Three Kings of Cologne*) and no less than six independent German translations.[11] Thereafter the work declined in popularity, and was only rescued from obscurity when a manuscript was discovered in 1818 by the poet J.W. Goethe.[12] However, several decades were to pass before the publication of a sound modern edition, that of C. Horstmann.

5 Horstmann's edition

Horstmann's edition prints three versions of an abridged English prose translation – henceforth the 'standard' *3KCol*, to distinguish it from the independent Lambeth translation – and two of the Latin original, and it remains the standard edition of all these texts. However, subsequent research has modified some of Horstmann's conclusions. In particular it is now known that the fuller version of the Latin text in Hm., with the passages in footnotes reinstated, better represents the usual version of the text. Moreover, a fourth unabridged version of the standard *3KCol* has now been identified, uniquely preserved in Durham Cathedral Library MS Hunter 15, pt. 2.[13]

The English traditions will be examined in more detail later. First, a summary of the Latin original is presented, then an examination of the place of the work in the development of the legend, with a review of the author's sources.

[10] For partial listings see Hm. x–xi, BC 6–7, MV 182–83.

[11] For the translations see Hm. x/n3. The French translation is edited in Elissagaray 1965. Seven German translations are identified in Harris 1958: 366, but the later analysis in Worstbrock and Harris 1982: 644–45/4 appears to identify six groups. In all, over forty witnesses survive, with editions in Harris 1954 and Behland 1968.

[12] Goethe's interest in the work can be followed in his correspondence with Sulpiz Boisserée; see Christern 1958. The manuscript found by Goethe has not been identified.

[13] Arguments for the secondary nature of the shorter Latin text (the main text in Hm.) are presented in Harris 1959: 27. The shorter text is one of a number of anomalous abridged versions found in the Latin tradition, none of which have any relevance to the abridged English versions. An edition of the Hunter version of *3KCol* forms the basis of my doctoral study (Schaer 1992); this version proves to be a secondary form of the text, in which a later translator-redactor, by reference to the Latin, restored in full the passages omitted or condensed in the original (abridged) translation.

6 Summary of the *Historia Trium Regum*

Table of contents. Dedication to Florentius of Wevelinghoven, bishop of Münster. Chapter 1 relates how the fame of the Three Kings (or Magi) has spread from East to West, and their story is compiled at your bidding. Chapter 2 tells of the prophecy of Balaam, 'A star shall arise of Jacob ...' (Numbers xxiv.17). (Chapter 3) A watch was kept for the star upon the highest mountain in the East, Mt Vaus (the Mount of Victory). (Chapter 4) In later times princes of the family of Vaus, descendants of King Melchior, came to the city of Acre, bringing with them books on which the present account is based. (Chapter 5) The prophecies in the Jewish books of scripture became known to the Persians and Chaldeans, and twelve astronomers were set to watch for the star on Mt Vaus. (Chapters 6–7) In the fullness of time, as the gospel tells, Christ was born of Mary in Bethlehem, in the reign of King Herod. At the same hour, the star arose over Mt Vaus, and a voice in the star issued a command to seek the new born King of the Jews. (Chapters 9–13) Having seen the star in their separate kingdoms, each the source of one of the three gifts, the Kings set forth with their retinues, completing their journey miraculously in thirteen days without need of food, drink, or rest. (Chapters 14–15) As the Kings approached Jerusalem, a thick mist delayed Melchior until the other two Kings arrived, whereupon after a joyous meeting the three rode together into the city. (Chapters 16–18) The Kings learnt from Herod and the scribes of the birthplace of the child, and set out for Bethlehem with the star as guide, on their way meeting the shepherds, who told them of the visitation of the angelic host. (Chapter 19) The Kings rode into Bethlehem to the manger, where, by the dazzling light of the star, they offered the child the first gifts that came to hand – gold, incense, and myrrh. Chapters 20–23 describe the significance of the three gifts, and give an account of the apple of gold.

(Chapter 24) The Kings rested in Bethlehem and related the story of their journey. Then, warned of Herod in a dream, they set off home by a different way. But Herod pursued them, burning the ships of the people of Tarshish as a punishment for ferrying the Kings over the sea. (Chapters 25–26) After a journey of two years the Kings returned to Mt Vaus, consecrating a chapel there in honour of the child. (Chapters 27–29) Meanwhile, the Holy Family fled to Egypt. The place where they lived for seven years is now a garden of balm. On the way Mary lost Melchior's gift of thirty golden pennies, and the text relates the history of the thirty pennies.

(Chapter 30) Our Lord sent St Thomas to convert the East. (Chapter 31) On his mission Thomas saw replicas of the child and the star, learnt of the Kings, met them in their old age, and consecrated them as the first archbishops of their lands. Having no children, the Kings made provision that their temporal power should pass to one of their kin with the hereditary title of Prester John, while spiritual power was to rest with an elected Patriarch Thomas. (Chapter 32) Two years after retiring from the world to their new city of Seuwa [Sculla, Suwella] at the foot of Mt Vaus, the present residence of Prester John and the Patriarch Thomas, (chapters 33–34) having transferred their lands to the Princes of Vaus, (chapter 35) the Kings passed away, their bodies being laid to rest in the chapel at Mt Vaus.

(Chapter 36) Their remains long rested uncorrupted, until the Devil spread heresy among their subjects. Then the dissenting parties removed the bones of each King to their separate lands, where they remained until the coming of St Helena, discoverer of the true Cross and other relics. (Chapters 37–39) After building many churches in the Holy Land, (chapter 40) St Helena turned her attention to the relics of the Three Kings. Obtaining the relics of Melchior and Balthazar, she surrendered the relics of St Thomas to the heretical Nestorians in return for the third King, Jaspar. (Chapter 41) St Helena transported the relics to Constantinople, where they remained until the time of the Emperor Maurice (alternatively, Manuel), when they were given to Milan. Finally the relics came into the hands of Rainald, Archbishop of Cologne, in the course of the Emperor Frederick's siege of Milan, whereupon they were translated to Cologne cathedral.

The Kings are held in the highest honour by all peoples of the East, not only by the various schismatic and heretical sects of Christians, namely Nubians, Soldini, Nestorians, Latins, Indi, Armenians, Greeks, Syrians, Georgians, Nicholaites, Jacobites, Copts, Ysini, Maronini, and Mandopolos, (chapters 42–43) who hold special ceremonies in honour of the Epiphany, but even by the Saracens, Jews, and Persians. (Chapters 44–45) In A.D. 1268, the Tartars subjugated the heretical Nestorians and defeated Prester John, but the Nestorians still possess the relics of St Thomas, which according to prophecy are one day to be transferred to Cologne from the East, where his festival is celebrated with great honour. The people of Inde[14] show great devotion to the Three Kings, and would come to visit the relics if only they could bear the cold in this part of the world.

The Three Kings may be likened to the Labourers in the Vineyard. Cologne is especially privileged to have custody of the relics of the Kings, (chapter 46) whose praises are sung in the East and West.

[14] I retain the Middle English term *Inde* (Latin *India*) for this vaguely defined area of the distant East.

Some texts (including the one the present translation is based on) have an alternative ending, a passage by a later annotator on the names of the Magi, their journey, and the three miracles that occurred on the night of the Nativity.

7 The legend of the Three Kings

The basis of the legend is the gospel account of the visit of the Magi to Bethlehem (Matthew ii).[15] However, centuries of speculation and elaboration introduced into the story elements from non-Christian religions, and much variation appears in the development of individual motifs. For example, in some eastern traditions the number of Magi is set at twelve, a tradition echoed in *HTR* by the twelve astronomers on Mt Vaus. Apocryphal gospels (e.g., the *Book of James*, or *Protevangelium*, *Pseudo-Matthew*, the *Evangelium Infanciae*, the *Acts of Thomas*) are the ultimate source of many of these accretions.

The identification of the Magi as kings was a Western development, probably based on Old Testament passages such as Isaiah lv.3 or Psalm lxxi (lxxii).9–10, 'The kings of Tarshish and of the isles shall bring presents, the kings of Sheba and Seba shall offer gifts'. Tertullian comments that 'the East regarded the Magi almost as kings' (or 'generally as kings').[16] In artistic representation as early as the second century and in written sources from St Jerome their number is fixed at three, a figure presumably deriving from the three gifts and reinforced by the symbolism of the Trinity. However, only much later do we encounter the names Melchior, Balthazar, and Caspar (or Jaspar), or, apparently first in *HTR*, an explicit statement that one of the Kings was black.[17]

A significant new development was introduced in the West by the so-called *Opus Imperfectum in Mattheum*, a gospel commentary attributed to John Chrysostom (*c.* 347–407) and perhaps composed in the fourth or fifth century, though apparently not widely known till the thirteenth

[15] Secondary sources which treat the legend include MV, Kehrer 1976, Kaplan 1985: 20 ff., Elissagaray 1965: 11 ff., Harris 1954: i–x, Harris 1959, and Christern 1959/60: 46–48; see also Hm. xviii/n5. Much further information is found in: *Die Heiligen Drie Könige: Darstellung und Verehrung*, Austellungs-Katalog des Wallraf-Richartz-Museums (Köln, 1982); *Lexikon für Theologie und Kirche*, 3, Aufl., Bd. III (Freiburg, 1995), 364–67.

[16] 'Reges Arabum et Saba munera offerent illi. Nam et Magos reges habuit fere Oriens' (*Adversus Marcionem* 3.13).

[17] The names appear in the ninth century *Excerpta Latina Barbari* (Hm. xv/n1); twelfth-century Pseudo-Bede *Collectanea*; Peter Comestor's *Historia Scholastica*. The motif of the black Magus is fully explored in Kaplan 1985; see 69/17–18n.

century.[18] Here the Magi figure as twelve star gazers who keep an annual watch on the Mount of Victory for a star prophesied in the Book of Seth. The star duly appears, 'having in it the form of a child and above the likeness of a cross', and commands the Magi to set out for Judea, a journey which they complete in two years without need for food or drink, after which they return to their kingdoms, are visited by St Thomas, receive baptism at his hands, and become associates in his preaching. The influence of this tradition on *HTR* is clear. In particular it introduces a link between the Kings and St Thomas, whose missionary activities in the East figure prominently in various apocryphal gospels. Another figure who was to play an important role in the European concept of the Orient, Prester John, makes his appearance in documentary sources in the twelfth century, and from the start his name was linked with the biblical Magi.[19]

Western interest in the Three Kings increased markedly after their supposed relics, discovered in Milan in the course of Emperor Frederick the Great's Italian campaigns, were translated to Cologne in 1164 by Rainald of Dassel, Archbishop of Cologne.[20] Whereas this much of the story of the relics is historical, the accounts of the earlier translations are contradictory and generally held to be an elaboration after the event; the story of the original discovery of the relics by St Helena is no doubt a pious fiction attached to the name of this celebrated relic hunter.[21]

Harris has shown how the efforts of various Western authors to complete the story can be traced through thirteenth- and fourteenth-century German sources, with the inclusion of motifs such as Balaam's prophecy, the escape from Tarsus and Herod's revenge, the death and burial of the Kings, and the earlier translations of the relics, all of which reappear in *HTR*.[22]

8 Sources of the *Historia Trium Regum*

From Harris's researches it would seem that the basic elements of the legend were already fixed when our author came to write his account, though traditions varied and were in some cases contradictory.[23] The homiletic and exegetic digressions which the author adds to the narrative

[18] *PG* 56; see especially cols 637–38. See MV 20 ff., 236.

[19] Otto of Freising's *Chronicle* for the year 1145 (cited, for example, in *ERE* 'Prester John'). See also the references under 'Prester John' in *ODCC*.

[20] Harris 1954: iii–iv, MV 223 ff.

[21] Hm. xviii–xxi; Freeman 1955: 68b–70a.

[22] Harris 1954: iv–x and xiv–xvii; for comparable developments in French sources see Elissagaray 1965: 38–57.

[23] *Cf.*, Hm. xiv–v.

framework are usually from named or identifiable sources,[24] while the extensive additions of descriptive material have close links with two near contemporary works dealing with conditions in the East, Ludolf of Sudheim and the *Book of Cologne*, though neither is named in *HTR*.

Ludolf of Sudheim's description of the Holy Land – henceforth 'Ludolf' – was compiled *c.* 1350 (certainly before 1361) on the basis of his experiences in the East in 1336–41 while in the service of the kings of Armenia. However, the account is supplemented from written sources, particularly William of Boldensele (composed 1336), though apparently also from sources common to the *Book of Cologne*.[25] There are many unresolved problems regarding Ludolf, which survives in at least two Latin versions and one low German version.[26] Nevertheless, it is commonly held to be one of the immediate sources of *HTR*, particularly for many of the descriptions of places of interest in the Holy Land, as well as the story of the roses of Jericho, the garden of balm, and the thirty pennies.

As it survives, the anonymous travel account generally known as the *Book of Cologne* (*BC*) is defective in its beginning, middle, and end, and is composed in a Low German dialect; this dialect, and the interest the author shows in the Three Kings, is taken as evidence that he was a native of Cologne.[27] *BC* may or may not be earlier than Ludolf; the first manuscript dates to 1408 and the second to *c.* 1412, but the work was undoubtedly composed earlier, since the author had been in Egypt in 1338 and in Armenia in 1348. The first part of the work is a description of the

[24] For example, Fulgentius (68/13–17n in the present work, without acknowledgement, *cf.*, Hm. 236/17–n16; also Hm. 235/n10–n13, omitted in the present work, *cf.*, 67/13n); Gregory (Hm. 234/n7–n10, abridged and unacknowledged in the present work, *cf.*, 66/2n); Rabanus Maurus (Hm. 276/n.22, without acknowledgement, and omitted in the present work, *cf.*, 116/11n).

[25] For example, the story of the fall of Baghdad in Ludolf 73–6 also appears in *BC* 58–9; Ludolf here cites as source 'the chronicles and histories of the kings of Armenia'.

[26] The edition of the standard Latin version is by F. Deycks, but reference here will be to the English translation of Deycks's text by Aubrey Stewart. The other Latin version is edited in Neumann 1883, the German in Stapelmohr 1937. The text edited by Neumann is particularly problematic; see the editor's introduction and Schaer 1992: 55–6. For details about Ludolf and his work see Bulst-Thiele 1985, Stapelmohr 1937: 1–18, MV 196–8, and Harris 1954: xviii.

[27] Ed. by Röhricht and Meisner 1887 from Cologne, Historisches Archiv MS W 261 A (formerly Stadtarchiv M. G. nr. 1). However, the text is also preserved, as Harris (1954: xvii) notes, in MS W* 3 of the same collection, the latter witness probably a copy of the former. For details see the editors' introduction, MV 198–9, Harris 1954: xvii–xviii, and Kaplan 1985: 65 ff.

peoples of the East, to which the last chapters of *HTR* on Christian sects and other Eastern religious groups show extensive parallels, while the second deals with oriental flora and fauna and makes a lesser contribution to our work. *BC* could be described as an account of the contemporary East with particular emphasis on ethnography, political and sectarian relations, and natural history, whereas Ludolf is more of a conventional *itinerarium* or pilgrims' guide.

A different perspective is provided by the author's own statement on his sources. The fourth chapter of *HTR* tells of the arrival of the Princes of Vaus in the crusader city of Acre (Akkon) in A.D. 1200, describing the treasures which they brought with them from their homeland in Inde, and in particular certain books:

> Ceterum ijdem principes de Vaus portauerunt et detulerunt secum de India libros hebrayce et caldayce scriptos de vita et gestis et omnibus materijs trium Regum beatorum: qui in Acre in gallicum fuerunt translati et transcripti et in ipsis partibus apud quosdam principes et nobiles ijdem libri translati in alijs partibus adhuc permanserunt. Et ex ipsis libris transcriptis, et ex auditu et visu et aliorum relatu, hec sunt conscripta, et quedam ex alijs diuersis libris et sermonibus et omelijs sunt extracta et hijs addita et presentibus sunt inserta, et in hoc libello in vnum conscripta et redacta. (Hm. 215/n9–n19)

In other words, our author claims to base his story of the Kings on books in Hebrew and 'Chaldean' brought by the Princes of Vaus to Acre and there translated into French, as well as on what he has seen and heard from others, and material extracted from other books, sermons and homilies.

These claims have met with general scepticism.[28] The main problem is that outside *HTR* the existence of the Princes of Vaus is shadowy and evidence for their alleged books non-existent.[29] Nevertheless purely on internal grounds these claims have a degree of plausibility.[30] The issues

[28] Horstmann – even without knowledge of Ludolf and *BC* – dismisses this passage summarily: 'These Hebrew and Chaldaic books are, no doubt, a mere fiction, or perhaps mention was made of them in his real sources' (Hm. xiv). Harris gives rather more consideration to the possibility that such translations existed, but concludes in much the same vein: 'That Johannes, however, actually made use of such sources from the East is doubtful. ... The mention of books brought from the East was no doubt intended to increase the credibility of his tale' (1959: 30); similarly MV 205.

[29] MV 195 ff.

[30] We can identify the three strands noted in the introductory paragraph of this section: the narrative framework in the *vita et gestis* of the Kings, the homiletic component in the 'sermons and homilies', while the descriptive material could be taken to be covered by the reference to 'diverse other books', together with the *auditu et visu et aliorum relatu* which presumably lie behind the author's personal observations.

associated with the author's intriguing assertions are probably incapable of final resolution, but conditional acceptance of his claims at least allows the question to be explored a little more fully.

The relationship between Ludolf, *BC*, and *HTR* (not to mention their identified and unidentified sources) is undoubtedly complex. The customary designation of Ludolf and *BC* as the sources of the descriptive matter in *HTR* is clearly an oversimplication: there are discrepancies between the so-called sources and the parallel passages in *HTR*,[31] and an appreciable amount of material in *HTR*, cited by the author with confidence and specificity of detail, has no parallel in either work. No doubt if fuller versions of Ludolf and *BC* survived they would account for a portion of these passages.[32] A different perspective can be obtained by isolating and comparing passages not paralleled in or obviously referable to Ludolf and *BC*. A number imply sources of a different nature, such as 'the books of the men of Inde'.[33] There are also more general references to Eastern sources.[34] It is arguable that these sources are at least to a point one and the same. If so, there is nothing exceptional in identifying them with the books of the Princes of Vaus.[35] Similarly the author's citations of Jewish sources tie in with his references to 'books written in Hebrew'.[36]

[31] An example is the story of the thirty pennies, which appears both in *HTR* and Ludolf, but with many minor variations (Hm. 248/n27–251/n16, 84/14–88/4 in our text, *cf.*, Ludolf 110–12; *cf.*, MV 214–15). Similarly the account of the garden of balm in *HTR* (Hm. 247/2–248/n26, 81/4–83/15 in the present work) supplies details such as the name *serra/zerra*, not found in Ludolf 68–71 and elsewhere unattested. *BC* preserves summary notices of matter more fully recounted in *HTR* – for example, the topography of the East at Hm. 223/n3–15 (*cf.*, 54/8–9n in the present work), *cf.*, *BC* 64; the description of the women's apparel at Hm. 265/n12–n13 (101/12–102/13 in the present work), *cf.*, *BC* 66; and the investiture customs at Hm. 251/n16 (omitted in the present work, *cf.*, 88/4n), perhaps intimated at *BC* 68.

[32] One could tentatively assign to one or other source passages in *HTR* which reflect matters of preoccupation to *BC* (e.g., ethnography, apparel) or to Ludolf (buildings).

[33] 'Item dicunt Indi et in eorum libris legitur ...' (Hm. 304/25, 305/2 etc.).

[34] For example, 'volunt quidam libri in Oriente ...' (Hm. 234/n34, *cf.*, 67/7n).

[35] As indeed MV 215. An important insight is provided by the source references in *HTR* and Ludolf for the story of the thirty pennies. Ludolf in this instance cites a 'history of the Kings from the East who offered gifts to our Lord' ('Legitur in quadam historia regum orientalium qui domino munera optulerunt quod Thare pater Abrahe monetam seu denarios ...'; quoted in Harris 1954: vii); *HTR* on the other hand refers vaguely to 'other books' (Hm. 248/n27, 'prout in alijs libris continetur'; the variant 248/18 'prout in libris Indorum legitur' is less original). To the extent that the respective sources can be equated, Ludolf's reference provides independent confirmation of our author's claims.

[36] See 67/7n and 136/11 ff.; *cf.*, 72/4 ff.n and Hm. 212/2 ff.

I have elsewhere suggested that the author's references to oriental books, while perhaps not of uniform origin, are not inconsistent with the notion of a lost source in the form of an Eastern account of pilgrimage to the Holy Land and beyond, containing special reference to Cologne, the Three Kings, and the connections between the latter and the princely house of Vaus – in other words, a source comparable to numerous other examples in Western pilgrim literature, but with the novel feature of being told from the perspective of an oriental traveller.[37]

At the same time it is important to place the matter in perspective. There is no reason to believe that any putative oriental sources were in reality of great antiquity, since there is no sign in *HTR* of other than late traditions regarding the Magi or anything else. Nevertheless, both Ludolf and *BC*, even in their extant state, have not a little to contribute to the development of the legend of the Three Kings: Ludolf has the story of the thirty pennies, *BC* has references to Prester John, St Thomas, the Nestorians, the kingdoms of the Three Kings, and so on. It is in this context that the question of the relationship between *HTR* and its sources, extant or otherwise, assumes its importance.

9 The English versions

Of the three surviving English translations of *HTR*, all anonymous, the most widely disseminated is the standard prose version, composed *c.* 1400 (Hm. viii) and extant in twenty-one copies (mostly in Midland dialects) in manuscripts of varied contents,[38] as well as at least four prints by Wynkyn

[37] Schaer 1992: 63–7.

[38] *Olim* Astor A2 (sold at Sotheby's in 1988); London, BL, Add. 36983 (*olim* 'MS at Bedford') (#); Oxford, Bodleian Library, Douce 301 (#); Cambridge Mass., Harvard College Library, Eng. 530; Durham, Cathedral Library, Hunter 15, pt. 2; London, BL, Harley 1704 (#); Oxford, Bodleian Library, Laud Misc. 749; Oxford, Bodleian Library, Laud Misc. 658; Cambridge, University Library, Ee IV, 32 (#); Cambridge, University Library, Kk 1,3 section 12 (#); London, Lambeth Palace Library, MS 72; Cambridge, Magdalene College, Pepys 2006; Cambridge, Trinity College, R.5.43; Oxford, Bodleian Library, Eng.th.c.58; Cambridge, University Library, Add. 43 (*olim* Patrik Papers 43) (#); Oxford, Bodleian Library, Ashmole 59 (#); London, BL, Royal 18 A X (#); London, BL, Stowe 951; London, BL, Cotton Titus A XXV (#); London, BL, Cotton Vespasian E.XVI (#); Blackburn, Lancs., Stonyhurst College, B.xxiii. The ten tagged with # were known to Horstmann. I am grateful to Dr A. I. Doyle for originally supplying this list of manuscripts. The list is repeated in *IPMEP* 290; note however (i) the incipit varies in the manuscripts; (ii) Hm. prints the version in the Harley manuscript as marginal additions on the even pages; (iii) Wright's transcription of the same is unsatisfactory; (iv) the Whalley manuscript is untraced; (v) Huntington HM 114 does not belong with this version of the *Three*

de Worde.[39] Apart from the unabridged Hunter version all the witnesses fall into one of the three groups identified in Hm.[40] All three reflect a common underlying abridgement, in which many of the descriptive passages, particularly in the later part of *HTR*, are omitted, thereby considerably shortening the text. The translation is on the whole accurate, the style relatively free and graceful.

A verse version of the Latin was executed independently of either of the English prose versions.[41] The *Manual* describes it as a 'fragment of 123 rime royal stanzas with two lines of [the] first stanza missing', adding that '[Lydgate's] authorship ... is considered at best doubtful' (VI: 1862–63). The fragmentary state is due to the loss of an initial folio which according to the editor contained probably the first hundred lines of the poem. Concerning the authorship, the editor merely asserts that the story is told 'in the style of' the monk of Bury.

The verse account is divided into three *passus*, the first (to line 173) describing the journey to Jerusalem, the second (174–509) the Kings' return and St Thomas's ministry, and the third (510–859) the Kings' death and the translation of the relics. While *HTR* supplies the framework of the story and many incidental details, the poet takes considerable liberty with his material, omitting many of the digressions (e.g., the story of the thirty pennies) but including motifs which do not find a place in *HTR* (e.g., the details of the Nativity, 76–82).[42]

The edition is from the unique witness, BL Additional MS 31042 (the London Thornton manuscript), one of two miscellaneous collections copied in the middle years of the fifteenth century by Robert Thornton of East

Kings.

39 The *STC* numbers of those editions I have examined are: 5572, printed at Westminster and dated '1496?'; 5573, 'another edition', also printed at Westminster and dated 'after July 1499'; 5574, 'another edition', printed according to the colophon in the year 1511 'at London in flete strete at the sygne of the sonne'; and 5575, 'another edition', dated 1526. In each edition the text is virtually identical, a notable peculiarity being the displacement of the chapter on the siege of Milan and the corresponding adjustment of the surrounding text. For details see Schaer 1992: 83–5; *cf*., Hm. v.

40 For the Hunter manuscript see footnote 13 above. The tradition, described in Hm. v–viii, is reassessed in the light of newer witnesses in Schaer 1992: 130 ff.

41 Ed. MacCracken 1912 (under the general heading of 'Lydgatiana'); *IMEV(S)* *31. The independence of this version, noted by the editor, is confirmed by the inclusion of matter from the Latin original which does not survive in either of the English prose versions (Schaer 1992: 74).

42 MacCracken 1912: 50.

Newton in North Yorkshire.[43] However, in spite of the copyist's Yorkshire dialect, the language of the poem shows signs that it may be of Scottish origin.[44] The *MED* assigns the date *c.* 1450 to the verse version, while the editor specifies 'some time in the first half of the fifteenth century, perhaps soon after Lydgate had compiled his Legend of St. Edmund (1433)'; on the other hand, the relatively good Latin text on which this version is based might point to an earlier date.[45] The editor judges the style 'straightforward and efficient' but 'not inspired', but the author's enthusiasm for his subject together with his rhetorical skills sometimes achieves a telling effect.

Neither of the two surviving witnesses of the second prose version, *Lambeth 3KCol*,[46] is a complete translation of *HTR*. L omits the table of contents and the first five chapters of the Latin, beginning the story at the nativity with passages from the sixth chapter of *HTR* interwoven into matter of extraneous origin, namely the story of Mary's vision, the two midwives, and other details making up chapters 13 and 14 of the apocryphal *Gospel of Pseudo-Matthew* (*PsM*);[47] thereafter, apart from omissions by the translator and physical losses in the manuscript, L follows *HTR* to the end. H overlaps L but is much shorter, comprising a self-contained episode, the description of the garden of balm in Egypt from chapter 27 of *HTR* (80/4–83/14 in the present text); the extract makes no direct reference to the Three Kings, and appears in the manuscript under the not particularly apposite title *Ioseph*, evidently taken from the opening words.

[43] Thompson 1987, esp. item 23, p. 16. See also Keiser 1979 on Thornton's life and milieu, including evidence that he was still alive in 1468, which provides a *terminus ad quem* for the collections. Both contain a mixture of secular and religious or moral pieces (though the London Thornton manuscript is less varied and contains only verse), and are the rare or unique witnesses of many works, particularly alliterative poems and romances; the contents, which include substantial Latin works, suggest a compiler of conservative tastes, interested in edifying subject matter, and possibly of clerical connections (Stern 1976: 210 ff.).

[44] MacCracken 1912: 50–51.

[45] Schaer 1992: 74.

[46] First identified in the Lambeth MS in Bülbring 1891, where its independence from the standard prose version is recognised as well as its dependence on a Latin manuscript similar to that used by the translator of the standard version. The independence of the two translations is confirmed by details in the Lambeth version which appear in the Latin but not in the standard version; if the Lambeth translator knew the (evidently) earlier standard version he borrowed only occasional phrases from it.

[47] Ed. by Tischendorf 1876: 51–112, especially 76 ff. *PsM* is the later version, composed in Latin, of matter first found in the apocryphal *Book of James* (James 1924: 38–49).

Textually a different pattern of copying errors distinguishes L and H. In L the degree of divergence from the Latin (and thus from the putative English original) is fairly uniform throughout. The text in H, on the other hand, starts with only minor disagreements with L, some unquestionably erroneous, but gradually becomes more and more divergent, until by the end of the passage whole phrases and sentences are introduced without warrant in the original.[48] If nothing else, these different responses show that the scribe was capable of copying the same text quite differently on different occasions.[49]

That only two witnesses in the same hand survive might imply a limited circulation for the translation. What further we can learn of the context of the work is set out in Hanna's study of the scribe and his oeuvre (1989).[50] The picture that emerges is of a copyist from south-eastern Essex employed in the London booktrade,[51] copying popular texts, in particular alliterative poetry,[52] with varying degrees of accuracy from a collection of exemplars, possibly under the guidance of a director. Our two manuscripts were copied perhaps in the later 1420s or early 1430s (to judge from the hand and the watermarks) and are put together from booklets which may have formed a small in-house bookseller's stock, cheap copies mainly of popular items in heavy demand. The contents provide evidence for the availability of multiple exemplars of such popular items,[53] but include a number of unparalleled items, possibly special commissions (the version of *Piers Plowman*, the *Lambeth 3KCol*, the translation of Peter Ceffon) – all suggesting an organising mind and a literary milieu of considerable sophistication.

It is clear from their errors that neither of the surviving witnesses represents the original version of *Lambeth 3KCol*. However, Hanna's reconstruction of the scribal context suggests that the original does not much antedate the surviving witnesses. The date 1424 of the Latin witness

48 *Cf.*, Hanna 1989: 128.

49 If the scribe was working from different exemplars the variations could have been introduced from intermediate copies which have not survived; but we shall see that there is other evidence to suggest that the scribe's standards of accuracy were erratic.

50 See also Doyle 1982: 94 ff.

51 On the dialect see also Allen 1985: 7, note 18.

52 Doyle's suggestion (1982: 96) that the particular four alliterative poems copied by the scribe have some not entirely random significance as a group is taken up in Lawton 1989: 150 ff.

53 Namely the conflated *Piers Plowman* (assuming this version was an in-house production), as well as the addition on inserted leaves in Huntington (but not Harley) of passages missing from the α version of *Troilus and Criseyde* (from which the scribe's Huntington and Harley copies derive); see Hanna 1989: 122 ff.

T, closely related to the translator's exemplar, fits this general time frame. The date '? *c.* 1425' might therefore be assigned to *Lambeth 3KCol.*

Owing to the scribe's contribution to the textual tradition of a number of well known texts, his output has been examined in various contexts and has won him a certain notoriety. The readings of his *Piers Plowman* (basically a B-text) were excluded from the Kane and Donaldson edition on the grounds that it failed to produce one useful reading, and inclusion of its variants would have more than doubled the size of the apparatus.[54] An editor of *Mandeville* was so perplexed by the aberrations of the Huntington copy that he suggested it might be the product of an innovative technique of textual reproduction.[55] By contrast, the scribe's copies of *Troilus* have been praised for their fidelity to the transmitted text.[56] His two versions of *Lambeth 3KCol* hardly give the *prima facie* impression of being slavishly faithful copies.[57] Nevertheless, in the light of his overall

[54] Kane and Donaldson 1975: 14–15; *cf.*, Skeat 1873: xix–xx/n.1, Chambers 1935: 18, Russell and Nathan 1963: 119 ff., Hanna 1989: 121. My collation of random pages counts from eight to twenty-one peculiar readings per page (defining these as readings without parallel in any of the witnesses cited by Kane and Donaldson).

[55] Seymour 1974: 142–43 ('this mediaeval rapid-copy device'). However, the illustration cited by Seymour is an extreme example of the divergences in this version, which, judging by comparison with East's text (Ashton 1887), typically comprise more modest rearrangement, abbreviation, and elaboration, together with countless minor variations in word order. Moreover, we cannot be certain what proportion of the textual deviance is attributable to the scribe; the very short variant passages cited in Seymour 1964: 204/n1 imply considerable textual variability in the tradition of Mandeville.

[56] Hanna 1989: 126–27. The Huntington and Harley texts are both quite accurate copies of a relatively poor archetype, each containing between 0 and 8 peculiar errors per page (by my collations of random pages, counting as peculiar errors those readings not found in Windeatt's text or the other manuscript at the same point).

[57] The transmitted text is marred by many kinds of copying errors. The misreading of a word for one similarly spelt, but normally the same part of speech (e.g. 53/14 etc. *cherche* for *crecche*, 114/17 *plesyn* for *chesyn*, 138/9 etc. *with* for *without*, 142/5 *his* for *her*, 149/12 *at* for *an*) is the largest single class of error (30% of the emendations introduced into the present edition). The next largest category (25%) is the addition or omission of individual words, the single commonest being *and*; these errors may or may not disturb the syntax. Confusions of inflexion (86/14 *prestis* for *prest*, 86/17 *prince* for *princes*) and tense (107/13 *be bygunne* for *bygunne*, 135/11 *is* for *was*) account for another 7%; losses of more than one word (93/18 *he writith*, the lacuna at 113/4) for 6.9%; errors in copying Latin (64/9 *Fortidudo* for *Fortituto*, 79/17 the loss of *ad ... puerum*) for 6.9%; confusion of single words which are dissimilar (106/13 *chapell* for *est*) for 5.3%. All other categories of errors each account for less than 5% of all emendations – misspellings, mostly of proper names (55/18 *desidyd* for *desiryd*, 97/17 *Gololye* for *Godolye*), transpositions (133/1 *bathid & nakid*),

oeuvre, *Lambeth 3KCol*, or at least the L copy, may perhaps be classed as one of his more conservative efforts.[58]

As a translation *Lambeth 3KCol* cannot be said to shine, even discounting the film of error in the witnesses. It is usually a literal, at times word-for-word version, careful and accurate for the most part, but lacking the stylistic ease and occasional panache of the standard prose translation.[59] The translator is alive to subtleties in the original,[60] rarely guilty of unthinking mechanical conversion from one language to another,[61] and capable of sensible decisions when faced with corruption in his exemplar;[62] while some of his interpretations are questionable, outright mistranslations are rare.[63] But his efforts at rendering his understanding of the original into idiomatic English are marred by a stylistic clumsiness at times bordering on unintelligibility; one wonders what a medieval reader, lacking modern punctuation and reference to the original language, can have made of it.[64]

garbled text (96/17 *ouere þo Kynges*), larger variations (83/9–10 *is vnpercid and vnsene*), loss or addition of letters (87/8 *pilgymes*, 67/4 *hard* for *had*), larger additions of text (147/11 *was of old tyme into now*), addition or omission of the article (59/7), loss of the main verb (87/8). The argument assumes a correlation between scribal error and editorial emendation, broadly justifiable given the style of the translation and our controls over the text, but ignores some classes of error, such as stylistic variation of a non-significant kind. Overall my impression is that the scribe was primarily concerned with the appearance of his copy, and was content, as far as the text was concerned, if the general sense was reproduced with more or less the right word (correctly spelt) in more or less the right place, minor violations of concord, grammar, or syntax being overlooked.

58 Again, the number of emendations introduced in the present edition provides a rough measure of the accuracy of the scribe. Over the whole text these average just over two per page of manuscript. However, as we shall see, the evidence of H suggests that the text of L contains many otherwise undetectable errors, on which basis the real error rate could be between four and ten per page of manuscript. This is ostensibly somewhat more conservative than the 8 to 21 deviations per page of *Piers Plowman*, though less so than the 0 to 8 per page for *Troilus* or the scribe's 9 indisputible errors in over 13 manuscript pages which the editor of *Lucifer's letter* identifies (Raymo 1969: 247–48).

59 Compare, for example, 76/7 ff., 95/7 ff., 115/9 ff., with Hm. 86/7 ff., 118/5 ff., 136/16 ff.

60 E.g., 51/15 *softly loghe*: *subrisit*; 72/13 *the deppest of hell*: *novissima inferni*; 140/7n *defoulid*: *oblita*; 151/7 *to worship ... and to tylie* (two senses of *colere*).

61 *Cf.*, 152/1n *declarid.*

62 E.g. 72/10–13n, 106/10–11n, 127/6n.

63 *Cf.*, 135/18 ff.n, 139/9n etc. A curious feature is the translator's tendency to treat datives as ablatives of comparison, e.g. 77/14n, 123/6–7n, 146/11n.

64 E.g. 54/1–4n, 54/10–55/3n, 69/8–12, 116/2–6. That the scribe did not always understand the text is likely from his copying errors and misdivision of words

The style is Latinate in the retention of Latin word order, the omission of subject pronouns,[65] and the imitation of Latin idiom.[66] The translator also shows a certain fondness for Latinate translation equivalents,[67] and is among the first recorded users of a number of Latin-based words.[68] Another characteristic is the use of clauses governed by present participles in place of coordinate main clauses.[69] However, it is difficult to generalise about the style of the translation as it may have been the work of more than one hand.[70] Moreover, it is possible that some of the stylistic features are a contribution of the scribal tradition.

10 Evolution of the *Lambeth Three Kings of Cologne*

Given our limited knowledge of the scribal context and the textual tradition, it is not surprising that few firm conclusions can be drawn concerning the evolution of *Lambeth 3KCol*. However, the following observations are offered.

10.1 *The relative dating of L and H*

After citing evidence from the watermarks that the paper of the Lambeth manuscript was produced at an earlier date than that of Huntington, Hanna argues from the disposition of contents that the former was copied before the latter:

(56/16n, the paragraph mark in the manuscript before 32/8 *and*; 112/5 *þer for* written *þerfor*, 117/13 *cause* written *can se*).

65 E.g. 99/1–6, 110/13–15, 114/7–8.

66 E.g. 61/11–12n, 142/5n.

67 E.g. 91/17 *virginal deuocion dignyte and chastite*: *virginalis deuocionis dignitatis et castitatis*; 95/20–96/1 *pontificall and also regal vestimentes*: *vestimentis pontificalibus et regalibus*.

68 E.g. 150/10 *extende*, 149/9 *inchoacion*, 75/14 *inexcusable*; 77/16 *laudable*, 153/2 *precellist*, 156/3 *substitute*. First recorded uses include 110/14 *amplificacion* and 98/14 *gentilite* ‘paganism’ (synonymous with 113/16 *mysbyleue* as a translation of *gentilitas*); 72/14 *subleuacion* ‘alleviation’ found no imitators.

69 E.g. 50/11, 55/19–56/1, 121/9–10.

70 See Introduction 10.3; nevertheless, the term ‘the translator’ will continue to be used. His identity is unknown – though we can be virtually certain that he was not the same person as the scribe (no one who had laboured to produce a translation would be likely to make the thoughtless mistakes committed by the scribe; moreover, the translator was a competent Latinist, whereas the scribe is even more careless in copying Latin than English). The passages translated from *PsM* at the beginning of the work may or may not be the work of a separate person. There are some stylistic parallels between *Lambeth 3KCol* and the Huntington translation of the *Epistola Luciferi*, but no compelling reason to think that both are by the same translator.

> Huntington includes a brief excerpt from *The Three Kings*, probably inserted to supplement a copy of *Mandeville's Travels* in that typically defective English form which lacks much of the description of Egypt. For the excerpt to be supplied, the scribe or his director had, first, to know Mandeville and to recognize that parts of the French text were not reflected in the English version at hand. Second, they had to know an English source for some of this omitted material; the logical inference is that the scribe knew *Three Kings* because he had earlier copied it in Lambeth. (1989: 122)

This is a quite plausible explanation of the presence of the excerpt from *3KCol* in the context of the Huntington manuscript.[71] A feature of this argument is the introduction of a director, a plausible, if not positively attested figure. But granted his separate existence and his intellectual role in the planning of these two collections, there seems no reason why the insight regarding the supplementing of the Egypt gap should not have come from him, from previous perusal of the text of *3KCol* (or its Latin original), rather than from the scribe who copied the text. For all we know the scribe may have been put to copy *3KCol*, or extracts from it, on a number of occasions to fill various codicological contexts.[72] Therefore, in spite of its other merits, this is a weak argument for the relative dating of L before H. In fact, we shall see that there are some arguments in support of the reverse hypothesis.

10.2 *The textual interrelation of L and H*

We are here concerned with an evolutionary rather than a chronological question. Put in its simplest terms, it asks whether H descends directly from L (as the waywardness of H's text might suggest) – *fig.* 3, model I – or whether both were copied from an earlier archetype – model II.[73] If we search the common text for evidence from variant readings, we find four passages where it could be argued that H preserves a superior reading:

(*a*) at 81/15–16 where L reads *and euery man kepith his busshe as his owne body and they close hem and pyke hem*, H in place of *close* transmits the more apposite reading *clense* (*cf.*, *ipsum rubum quasi corpus suum custodit irrigat et mundat*); however, against this it could be argued that H's reading is an independent scribal emendation of an evident error in L (see further 81/16n);
(*b*) at 82/8–9 where L reads *And than þe sowdon gothe with the pot of bawme and kepith hym soft in grete specialite*, H reads for *hym soft* the preferable *it*

[71] The evolution of the Egerton version of Mandeville (BL, Egerton MS 1982) affords a parallel; see Seymour 1961.
[72] *Cf.*, 58/2–3n.
[73] Hanna 1989 does not discuss this issue.

hymself (*Et tunc soldanus recipit omnem balsamum solus*); but again, the H reading could be a scribal emendation;
(*c*) at 83/8–10 where L reads *and the place þat hit droppith on ... is vnpercid and vnsene*, H's version of *is vnpercid and vnsene* reads *shall neuere aftir be corrupt ne scabbid*, which seems closer to the original *et ille locus incorruptibilis permanebit in eternum*;
(*d*) at 83/11–12 where L reads *and þat bawme þat is boyllid is callid sodyn bawme*, H after *callid* adds *bawme coct þat is to sey*. Here the H reading could hardly be an independent addition, given the Latin *et alter balsamus bullitus vocatur ibidem balsamus coctus*; there is no evidence of any other Middle English source of information on the nomenclature of this particular variety of balm; see *MED* baume *n.* 1.(a).

In short, we have in H four variant readings closer to the wording of the original than those in L, which might seem to favour the hypothesis of descent from a common archetype.[74] However, the evidence is limited and the significance of each instance of variation debatable, particularly as both witnesses are the work of the same scribe. It is possible to explain the superior readings by model I on the assumption that they are the product of 'memorial contamination': the scribe realised as he copied H from L that he had made errors in his earlier copy, and retained sufficient recall of the original text to allow him to correct these errors in his second copy.[75] The evidence from variant readings regarding the textual evolution is therefore inconclusive. However, the two hypotheses so far proposed do not exhaust the evolutionary possibilities.

10.3 *Another evolutionary hypothesis*

The discussion to this point has implied the existence of an archetypal text at least coterminous in extent with L. However, this view of the pre history of *Lambeth 3KCol* may be an over simplification. If the matter common to the two witnesses is examined in its textual context, a number of anomalies become apparent. Stylistically the passage is unusual. The translation is looser and freer, lacking the Latinate word order characteristic of other parts of the text, and involves an uncharacteristic amount of rearrangement. There are also formal (structural) anomalies. Just before the beginning of the passage a scriptural citation appears, quoted, as elsewhere, in the

[74] This hypothesis accords with Hanna's picture of the scribal context and the availability of exemplars for copying, though the mention of booklets remaining unbound for protracted periods would fit the first model (1989: 123).

[75] The expression 'memorial contamination' is used in Hanna 1985: 89 (defining it as 'contamination of a scribe's actual archetype with readings which he recalls from other versions of the text he has heard or read').

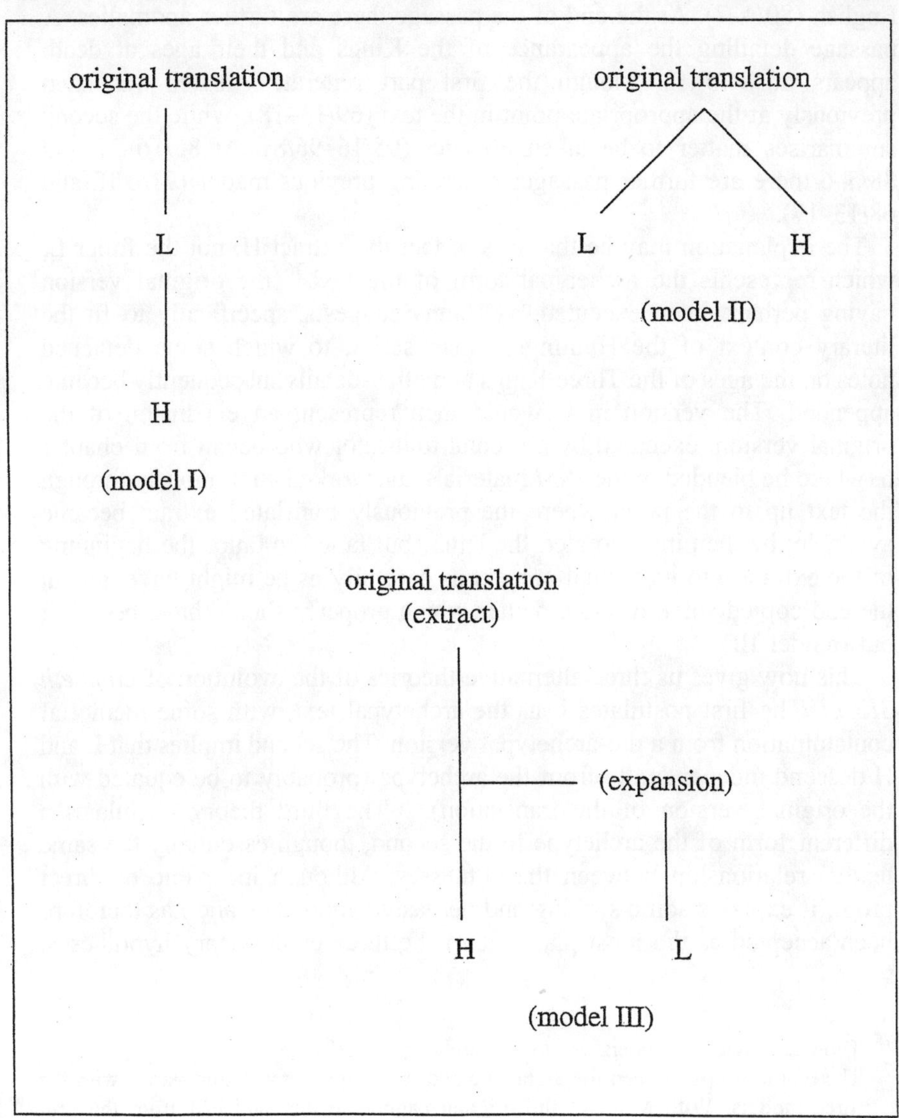

Fig. 3 Evolutionary models of *Lambeth 3KCol*

original language (79/14–19); but at the start of the common text a second version of the citation is found, this time in paraphrased form and in English (80/4–7). At the end of the passage there are further anomalies. A passage detailing the appearance of the Kings and their ages at death appears at 84/5–13, though the first part reiterates matter translated previously at the appropriate point in the text (69/13–18), while the second summarises matter to be taken up later (95/16–96/8). At 85/16–27 and 88/5–6 there are further passages reiterating previous matter (71/6 ff. and 68/13–17).

The explanation may be that it is in fact the extract H, not the fuller L, which represents the archetypal form of the text,[76] the original version having perhaps been executed, as Hanna suggests, specifically to fit the literary context of the Huntington manuscript, to which some detached notes on the ages of the Three Kings and other details subsequently became appended. The version in L would then represent an expansion of the original version, executed by a second translator who began from chapter 6 (where he blended in the *PsM* material) and worked continuously through the text up to the point where the previously translated extract became available; he then incorporated the latter, but failed to tailor the beginning of the extract into its textual context as carefully as he might have, and at the end copied some discrete matter which properly should have been left out (model III).

This now gives us three alternative theories of the evolution of *Lambeth 3KCol.* The first postulates L as the archetypal text, with some memorial contamination from a pre-archetypal version. The second implies that L and H descend independently from the archetype (probably to be equated with the original version of the translation).[77] The third theory postulates a different form of the archetype to the second, though essentially the same textual relationship between the witnesses. Although incapable of direct proof, it explains some striking and pervasive anomalies and has therefore been accepted as the most plausible of the three evolutionary hypotheses.

[76] Though, in view of its errors, not the archetype itself.

[77] The relationship between the archetype and the original translation varies with the three models. With Model I the original cannot be distinguished from the pre-archetypal version (the stage preceding L). With the other two models it is likely that the archetype and the original translation are identical, since no indisputable archetypal errors are to be found in the common text of H and L (the discrepancy at 81/4n could have arisen in the Latin; 81/8 *hym*/*hem* may be a coincident variation). In each case, where H is wanting the text of L effectively becomes the archetypal text, but cannot be equated with the original translation (in view of its demonstrable errors).

The third model adds support to the theory that Huntington was copied before Lambeth. If the extract was translated specifically to fit the context of the Huntington manuscript, then the text was presumably copied in not long after the translation was completed; whereas, it would have required additional time before the expanded translation was available for copying into Lambeth. In fact, all three theories have broadly the same underlying textual implications for the reconstruction of an archetypal text, in that for one part of the work a second set of readings are available as a control over the base text.[78] At the same time, the evidence has some sobering implications for overall editorial policy. Without the witness of H the reading of L in the four passages discussed in 10.2 (except probably the second) would be taken to be a perhaps somewhat free, but not otherwise exceptional, rendering of the original. As it is, if in a passage for which we have a control, a reading like *is vnpercid and vnsene* is rejected in favour of a variant as markedly different as *shall neuere aftir be corrupt ne scabbid*, we are left to wonder just how far at other points the wording of the transmitted text differs from the archetypal or authorial versions.

However, before considering the question of editorial policy we need to discuss certain other features of the translation, and to find out more about the Latin text which lies behind *Lambeth 3KCol.*

10.4 *A possible cross-reference from L to H*

At 113/7 the description of an imperial statue in Constantinople is interrupted by the interpolated comment *of which spekiþ Maundevile &c wherfor no more here*; the remainder of the original description is then omitted, and the text passes on to the next section of the narrative. The implication of the comment is that the passage has been abbreviated because a description of the same subject appears in *Mandeville's Travels*. Indeed, Mandeville's account of Constantinople contains a description of an equestrian statue of Justinian, to which the comment evidently refers.[79]

[78] The implications of Model I are a little different in practice to the other two. If the superior readings in H arose from memorial contamination these readings would presumably still be introduced into the edited text; however more reliance would perhaps be placed on the base text L in regard to non-substantive readings in the extract.

[79] The passage in *Mandeville* (cited from the Huntington MS, ff. 132^{r-v}) runs: 'Byfor þis chirche is an ymage fourmyd vpon an hors & gylte & crownyd. And hit was wont to hold an appill in his hond & now hit holdiþ none. And þerfor men seyn þat hit tokeniþ þat the Emperour haþ lost myche of his lordship ... And the toþer hond holdith vp toward þe west yn tokenyng þat he manaciþ all mydoers [*sic*]. This ymage on þe hors stont formyd on a pyler of marble'. In *HTR* it runs: *Ceterum in hac*

One explanation is that the reference is general; *Mandeville* was such a well known text that it was considered pointless to repeat a description of any subject already treated there. But this is somewhat far-fetched. It is more tempting to see this as a cross-reference from the Lambeth manuscript to the scribe's own copy of *Mandeville* in Huntington. But if so, to whom is the comment directed? It would only have made sense to someone who knew the contents of the other manuscript. A possible explanation is that the same person commissioned both manuscripts, and the scribe knew his client's tastes well enough to feel that the client would not wish to have the same material duplicated in a second manuscript. If so, it is a further argument, albeit a very speculative one, for dating Huntington before Lambeth.

10.5 *Correction of scriptural citations*

There are indications that at an earlier textual stage familiar scriptural citations – regularly cited in Latin in the present text – were revised to conform with the canonical wording of the Vulgate. In the Latin witnesses most closely related to the translator's exemplar such citations sometimes appear in anomalous versions which arose in the course of the transmission of *HTR*. For example, the Vulgate text of Matthew ii.13–15 runs:

> ... angelus domini apparuit in somnis Joseph dicens, 'Surge et accipe puerum et matrem eius ... Futurum est enim ut Herodes querat puerum ad perdendum eum'. Qui consurgens accepit puerum et matrem eius nocte ...

but in the Latin witnesses T and G the text appears as:

> Angelus domini apparuit *Ioseph in sompnis* dicens, Surge accipe puerum *cum matre* eius ... Futurum est (enim) *quod* Herodes querat puerum ad perdendum eum. Qui consurgens accepit puerum et matrem eius nocte ...

The Latin tradition suggests that any reading common to T and G would also have appeared in the translator's exemplar (see Introduction 11 and *Fig.* 4). However the corresponding text in *Lambeth 3KCol* (79/14–19) reads:

ecclesia sancte Sophie magna stat columpna marmorea, supra quam stat ymago imperatoris equestris enea optime deaurata, et habet pomum rotundum more imperiali in sinistra et contra orientem rebellibus Sarracenis quasi minans dextera (Hm. 273/28–274/2; the text continues *et iuxta et subtus hanc columpnam venerabilis Helena trium Regum corpora* ..., as at 113/9 in the present text). The statue, apparently something of a contemporary tourist attraction, is not the only subject which the two works have in common, but is the only one to attract such a comment from the scribe.

Angelus domini comperuit in sompnis Ioseph dicens, Surge, accipe puerum et matrem eius ... Futurum est enim vt Herodes querat puerum et matrem eius ...

At least two of the variants are simply copying errors (*comperuit* for *apparuit*, the loss of *puerum ad ... accepit*, and presumably the final loss of *nocte* as well). But in three places the wording is closer to the canonical version. If this passage were an isolated example these regularisations could be dismissed as chance variants, but comparable instances are to be found at 73/14–15 (which exactly reproduces the canonical wording of Matthew ii.12, whereas the word order of the exemplar is anomalous), 79/8–9 (*cf.*, Luke ii.29 ... *domine secundum verbum tuum in pace*), and 88/8–9 (*cf.*, Matthew ii.19 ... *apparuit in somnis Joseph* ...). I take this as sufficient justification for emending the text in *Lambeth 3KCol* at these and similar points in conformity with the canonical wording. The revision perhaps already appeared in the translator's exemplar, or it may have been carried out by the translator himself (but undoubtedly not by the scribe, whose contribution was evidently limited to the imposition of a further layer of corruption on the transmitted text).

11 The translator's Latin text

One of the interesting aspects of the present translation is that it is possible to reconstruct with a considerable degree of confidence the text of the lost Latin exemplar on which the translation depends (Eng_2) – the parallel Latin text printed in the present work being that reconstruction. Eng_2 (and indeed Eng_1, the reconstruction of the exemplar used by the translator of the standard prose version) belongs to a subgroup of *HTR* manuscripts whose members bear a precise and demonstrable stemmatic relationship to each other (see *Fig.* 4).[80]

As base manuscript for the parallel Latin text the surviving witness most closely related to Eng_2 should in principle have been be selected. However, the closest congener, C, is a contaminated witness; while some of its readings belong here, it generally follows the readings of a quite distant

[80] The evidence is fully presented in Schaer 1992: 86–127; the traditional methods of analysis of error were used in determining the stemmatic relations. The members of this group and their sigils are as follows: C = BL, Cotton Cleopatra D VII; CC = Cambridge, Corpus Christi College, 275; D = BL, Cotton Claudius A XII; Eng_1 = the witness of the standard prose *3KCol*; Eng_2 = the witness of *Lambeth 3KCol*; G = BL, Cotton Galba E VIII; K = Cambridge, Corpus Christi College, 179; M = Munich, Bayer. SB, clm 14547; O = the 'common text' printed in Hm.; T = Copenhagen, Thott 518 4o; V = Rome, Bibl. Apostolica Vaticana, Pal.Lat. 859; Z = Kynžvart, Castle Library, 20 H 24.

group of witnesses. C would thus be a most inappropriate choice as base. The next choice would fall on G. However, G too turns out to be less than suitable. It is a careless copy with many peculiar mistakes, and in addition has suffered physical damage. The final choice therefore lay between T and CC. T is more closely related to Eng_2, and has fewer orthographic peculiarities than CC. T was therefore chosen as base.

The base text was then emended in four stages. First, the peculiar errors of T were eliminated against the consensus of G and CC (and O). In practice this represents the largest category of emendations (76%); more-

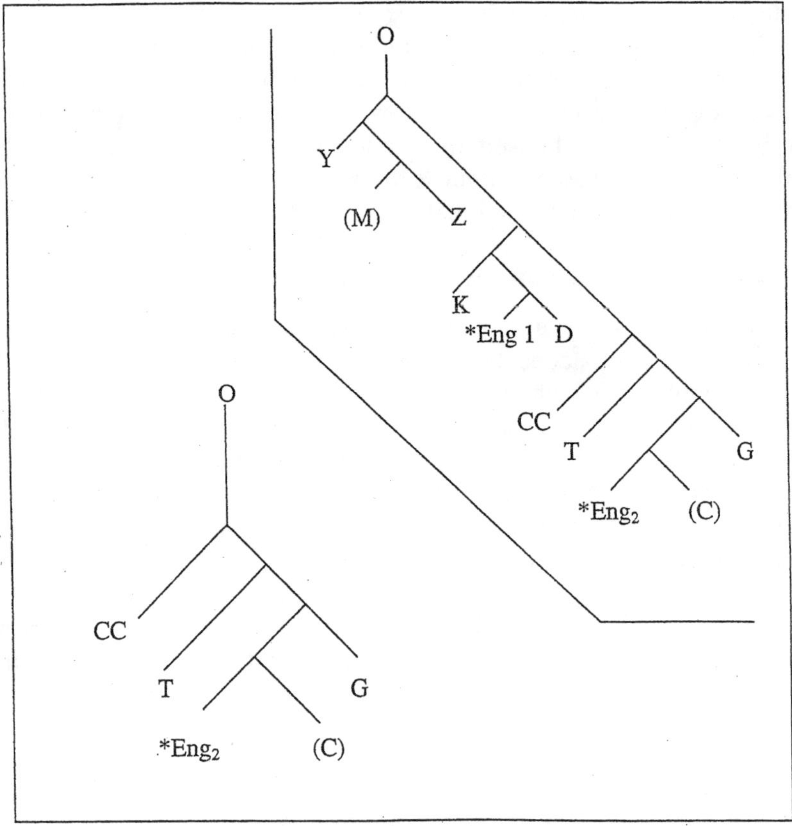

Fig 4. The Latin witnesses most relevant to *Lambeth 3KCol* (inset: a diagram of the complete subgroup). Bracketed sigils refer to contaminated witnesses, asterisks to reconstructed witnesses. The witnesses and their sigils are listed in footnote 80.

over, the validity of these emendations is supported by the stemma.[81] Secondly, a selection of G's readings was introduced into the text (only a portion of G's peculiar readings would have been transmitted to Eng_2 via the common ancestor of G and Eng_2). The selection depends on the evidence of the English text, making this category of emendations less secure than the first.[82] Thirdly, in a handful of instances the reading of C was introduced, where it seems indisputable that the reading is reflected in the English translation.[83] Finally, a small number of emendations were introduced where strong evidence exists that the translator's exemplar had a peculiar reading.[84] These emendations are discussed further under editorial policy.

Manuscript support for emendations to the base text is presented in the Variants to the Latin, at the head of which more details are supplied concerning editorial policy and the conventions regarding emendations (square brackets for additions and alterations, and plus signs indicating omissions). It should be stressed that the term emendation is not used in the sense of bringing the text closer to an original or authorial version. The parallel Latin text printed in this edition is an attempted reconstruction of the text which stood before the translator – a rather corrupt version, in fact, of the original work; it is not an edition of *HTR* as such. Nevertheless, it is

81 Very rarely it appears that G has altered but T has preserved an innovation present in the common ancestor of T and G, and also reflected in Eng_2; e.g. 65/4–5 *And as they ... and be herd ferre* follows the version in the base text, whereas G, CC, and O have other versions; again, 129/1 *or* corresponds more closely to T's unique *seu* than *sed* in the other witnesses.

82 Examples are: p. 61 *subicientur* (*cf.* 61/1n), the loss of text after p. 120 *nos* (*cf.* 120/6n), and the spelling *Sculla* (p. 91 etc.). I have been generous in introducing G's readings (in order to make as much use as possible of the evidence of a manuscript which is potentially a base), though in practice it is not possible to distinguish conjectures arrived at independently by G and Eng_2 from those inherited from their common ancestor (e.g. p. 89 *miracula*, p. 126 *crucem*). Even so the number of imported G readings is still relatively small (on average one per two pages of printed text).

83 E.g. p. 90 *irsutas valde*, p. 121 *vna*, p. 150 *duratas*, p. 154 *Nusquam*; in all, only ten emendations have been introduced from C, most of them in the last pages (where C is linked to the base genetically, and not simply by contamination).

84 E.g. p. 55 loss of *in*, p. 67 loss of *cum*, p. 74 *Indiam* (see 74/1n), p. 146 *mirra* (*cf.* 146/16–17n); in all only 14 such emendations have been introduced. There is no evidence in the Latin tradition to confirm these peculiar errors though we can postulate their existence theoretically. Indeed, it is perhaps surprising that they are not more in evidence (given the comparably large number of peculiar errors demonstrably present in T, CC, and G); this is presumably a reflection of the fidelity of the exemplar, even if the translation process smoothed over some of the evidence.

assumed that the reader will have a general interest in what the author originally had to say. For this reason the readings of the authorial version of *HTR* (as given in the 'common' or fuller text in Hm. – see Introduction 5) have been included under the Latin text (the less original readings of the translator's exemplar being tagged with obeli which direct the reader to the original reading at the foot of the page).

Thus two levels of critical intervention are found in the parallel Latin: the square brackets and omission signs within the text, representing fine tuning of the base text in the direction of the state of the text as it stood before the translator, and the obelised readings beneath the text, which have no direct bearing on the English, but show how far the translator's exemplar had degenerated from the author's original version (and thus indirectly elucidate the translator's method of dealing with unsound text). We can be reasonably confident that the reconstructed text is a close approximation to the text that lay before the translator.[85] This permits the translator's method to be followed unusually closely, and provides one of the more reliable bases for textual emendation.

12.1 Editorial policy

It is difficult to devise a wholly satisfactory editorial policy for a work extant for the most part in one corrupt witness. The transmitted text may retain elements of a number of more or less clearly discernible evolutionary stages – the translator's original draft, the archetype (if different from the original draft), any intermediate stages of copying, plus the extant scribal versions – and our reconstruction of any particular stage depends on varied and unpredictable factors. The accuracy of scribal copying is erratic,[86] the translator's Latin exemplar had a quantity of peculiar errors for which no direct evidence survives, the portion of text for which we have another witness as control is limited (and the evidence of the control is somewhat ambiguous), and the translation is of varying degrees of literalness and may

[85] 388 emendations have been introduced into the Latin text over 102 pages – the matter from *PsM* not being comparable – but the majority of these are corrections of peculiar errors in the base. The less certain emendments (the readings introduced from G and C, and the putative peculiar readings of the exemplar) are introduced at an average of less than one a page. As previously noted, there seems to be no evidence that there were a large number of peculiar readings of a substantive nature in the translator's exemplar.

[86] This would be predictable from the rest of the scribe's output, and is confirmed by the fluctuating error rate (estimated on the basis of emendations) for *3KCol*, which varies between 0 and 6 errors per page on different pages of the Lambeth manuscript.

not even be a literary unity. In the circumstances it might seem most prudent to print the 'best text'. Nevertheless, I have attempted to bring the transmitted text somewhat closer to the translator's intention on the basis of an eclectic set of editorial principles.

In spite of a degree of unpredictability in its reconstruction, the text of the translator's Latin exemplar is probably the most precise control we have over the English. It seems clear that for all his stylistic infelicities the translator generally understood his original and intended to produce an accurate English version.[87] Moreover, for the most part the translation is demonstrably literal, and at times very literal.[88] This makes the evidence of the Latin the most important and far-reaching criterion for establishing and confirming emendations in the English version.[89]

The other major criterion is linguistic validity. If the translator intended to produce an accurate and intelligible version, at least in his own terms, then any passage which fails to meet a minimum standard of intelligibility as written Middle English is *prima facie* suspect. On this basis I have supplied missing text, corrected harsh collocations, restored more appropriate connectives, altered commonly confused words (such as *his*, *her*, *the*, *tho*, and *this*, *aftir* and *afore*), postulated lacunas, and obelised the more intractable corruptions.[90] However, these are probably the more obvious types of errors. The transmitted text usually shows basic grammatical coherence; a more pervasive and subtle problem are the apparent irregular-

[87] These two factors, the competence of the translator and the reliability of the reconstruction of his exemplar, answer reservations expressed by Greetham in the context of the edition of Trevisa's translation of Bartholomaeus Anglicus's *De proprietatibus rerum* concerning the use of non-vernacular controls (in that case, two witnesses of the Latin text) in the reconstruction of a Middle English archetype, when he remarks that their evidence 'rested on two dubious assumptions – one, that Trevisa had worked from a Latin source textually very close to either or both of the cited Latin witnesses, and two, that he had both the competence and the desire to transmit the exact content of this Latin text into English' (1985: 71).

[88] E.g. 112/1 ff., 122/11–13, 151/9 ff. (which virtually guarantees emendations such as those at 151/15 and 153/5–6). Such passages where the correspondence between the versions is so close that there can be no question of any substantial scribal alteration to the English tend to confirm the validity of the Latin as a guide to emendation elsewhere; where the translation is freer (e.g. 80/1–83/15, 101/12–102/13) the Latin loses some, but not all, of its value as a control.

[89] An estimated 38% of emendations have been introduced wholly or principally on the evidence of the Latin, of which perhaps half would probably not have been made without this evidence (e.g. 123/17, 140/16, 148/2, 148/7, 149/1).

[90] E.g. (missing text) 85/1, 119/2, 132/8; (collocations) 112/9, 133/17, 136/4, 147/2; (connectives) 56/9, 108/19, 115/18; (confused words) 86/17, 100/8, 105/11, 127/1, 155/2; (lacunas) 89/3n, 113/4n; (obelised text) 96/17n, 113/14n.

ities in syntax caused, for example, by the insertion or omission of conjunctions or prepositions. I have corrected many of these, but often with some hesitation, given the relative fluidity of Middle English usage.[91]

It is almost certain that other scribal alterations of a non-substantive nature have had an effect on the wording, if not the essential content, of the transmitted text, but as these are not readily detected by the criteria discussed above, the exact extent of the problem is impossible to determine.[92] This means that apart from the general literalness of the translation, there are few stylistic criteria that can be reliably referred to. However, on the basis of sentence patterns commonly encountered in the text, I have made one or two alterations,[93] and also restored the translator's habitual forms of proper names.[94]

Where only one witness is extant, the principle of *lectio difficilior* can only be obliquely applied (i.e., as between a reading and its emendation). Nevertheless, in deference to this established principle I have retained a few otherwise suspect readings.[95] There is only a short passage for which we have another witness as control over L. Here L and H are taken as representing two branches of a divided tradition. All else being equal, I have retained the base reading, since overall L is less aberrant than H. However, in any particular instance H's reading deserves serious consideration, and quite minor emendations have been adopted if supported by stylistic parallels in the passage or by the Latin. If there is a discrepancy between the English and the Latin, I have emended whichever version in

[91] Thus the emendations at e.g. 54/5, 54/16 may be overscrupulous; conversely the text at e.g. 54/1–4n, 62/5–6, 124/10 may be unsound.

[92] Hints of scribal reworking have already been noted in the variant readings of H (10.2–10.3). Other instances are the suspected elaborations 103/12 *noyse and* (*cf.*, *horribili visione perteriti*), 132/5 *or gold* (*cf.*, *crucibus argenteis*), 132/7 *grete ioy &* (*cf.*, *silencio*), 136/5 *of Epiphany* (*cf.*, *festiuitatibus*), 156/7 *all store of vitaille and* (*cf.*, *cum copia omnium rerum necessariarum ad victum*); there are also signs of word order displacement, e.g. 126/6 *her bisshopis*. I have not attempted to emend such putative scribal alterations, as it is impossible to formulate a consistent policy for identifying them.

[93] E.g. 90/11n, 106/7.

[94] E.g. 59/7, 121/11, 142/19. We may also note 114/7 *chese*, an attested alternative form for the translator of the past tense (*cf.*, 90/3), for which the manuscript reading *chesith* may represent a scribal correction.

[95] E.g. 56/16n *housholdis beddyng*; 78/8 *hit* (rather than *þer*) *is sene ȝet a stone* (I am grateful to Elly van Gelderen for her advice in this instance); 106/5 *of*; 138/8 *chose into* (rather than *chosyn to* – *into* being a rare variant, one example in *MED* chosen *v.* 2.(b), *chosen in to office*). However just because a reading is difficult does not mean it is right, e.g. the manuscript readings 140/5 *of*, 145/4 *hit to*.

which the discrepancy seems more likely to have arisen.[96] If it is unclear whether the Latin or the English is at fault, or whether the translation is simply inaccurate or infelicitous, I have left the discrepancy to stand.[97] Many problems remain, and it is often uncertain how closely the printed text approximates the authorial intention. I suspect that among the factors distorting our understanding, the arbitrary and superficial alterations introduced by the scribal tradition have played a greater role than any infidelities in the translation or discrepancies between the translator's exemplar and the reconstructed Latin text. At any rate, there may at least be one advantage in the fact that the text survives largely in a unique witness: the reader who feels unhappy with the nature or degree of editorial intervention can with little difficulty reverse the process and reinstate the transmitted reading from the apparatus below the text.[98]

12.2 Editorial conventions

The English text

Capitalisation, word division, and punctuation are modern.[99] Initial double -f is treated as a single letter. Yogh and z are distinguished in transcription though they are not distinguished in the scribal hand. Otiose strokes, written commonly through final and medial h and final double-l, and rarely over final p (*shap*, *erchebisshop*, *wurship*, *lordship*) and q (*reliqs*), are ignored, but exceptionally in *hertis* (her*t*is) and *cherche* (cher*che*) the stroke through h is taken to represent *er*. Abbreviations, sparingly employed in English by the scribe, are expanded according to his usual full spelling; the standard ones appear for *per-/par-*, *pro-*, *-ro-*, *sub-*, *ser-*, and

[96] E.g. the lacuna at 107/11n probably arose in the English, whereas 146/16n *mirre* must go back to a peculiar reading in the Latin. I have also favoured emending the Latin where there is manuscript support. For example, after the reference to the three Maries at 99/9–10 the original Latin includes a sentence 'and the place where Jesus entrusted his mother to his disciple' which is not represented in the English; the loss could have arisen by eyeskip in either language, but as the passage is missing in G, I have omitted the sentence from the parallel Latin text (*cf.*, p. 87 *peregrinorum*, 120/6n).

[97] E.g. 81/4n, 95/4–5n, 103/1–2n, and the date at 115/9n. Nevertheless, I have on occasion emended the English where the emended reading has contextual support, e.g. 141/13.

[98] My subjective analysis of the emendations puts them in three classes, virtually certain (40%), probable (47%), and marginally probable (13%) – 'probable' including the category where 'this emendation or something similar' is called for.

[99] Apart from initials and so on, scribal punctuation is limited to the oblique slash.

for the words *þou* (þ^{u}), *þat* (þ^{t}), *with* (w^{t}), *aftir* (aft*ir*), *Ierusalem*, *Israel*, *Christe* (xpe), *Ihesus* (Ihc), *Ihesu* (Ihu), *patriarke* (pa*t*riarke). The macron stands for medial and final m or n (who*m*, he*m* 'them', he*m*me 'hem', so*n*ne 'sun'), but the flourish over final n or m in words like *born*, *kyngdom*, and the ending *-cion* is otiose.[100] The backward loop normally represents *er* or *re*, as for example in *þer*, *neuer*, *preve*, but is transcribed *ir* in *(an)oþir* and *ar* in *marchaundise* according to the usual full spelling. Partially legible letters are enclosed in <angle brackets>, with a lowered stop (.) replacing a completely illegible or lost letter. Words written marginally or between lines are enclosed in `accent marks´. Numerals are invariably marked off with .stops. (scribal practice is inconsistent). Latin citations and words evidently intended as Latin are italicised.[101]

Alterations to the base text L are enclosed in square brackets, whole word omissions are indicated by a raised plus sign ($^{+}$), letters omitted internally by square brackets around the letters on either side (e.g., 49/4 [*To*] *whom* for base reading *Tho whom*). Emendations are made to conform to the scribe's orthography as evidenced elsewhere in L, as far as this can be ascertained. Extended physical lacunas (due to loss of leaves or damage in the manuscript) are indicated by three stops on either side of the gap, postulated textual lacunas (arising from scribal oversight) by three stops in square brackets within the body of the text.[102] Text so corrupt that no obvious emendation suggests itself has been obelised (with a † attached to the front of a single word, or at both ends of a phrase).[103] In the apparatus below the English text *om.* means that the text in the lemma is omitted in the manuscript(s); *trs.* that the two words in the lemma (or two words separated by *and* or &) are transposed.

The Latin text:

The same policy and conventions are used as in the English for signalling alterations and omissions in the base text; however, punctuation and obelisation follow conventions more appropriate to the original language. For the matter from *PsM*, Tischendorf's text has been printed unaltered, the Commentary indicating where the translator's exemplar seems (as often) to have followed a variant reading. The text of *HTR* has been printed from the

[100] Graphically the macron is an extension of the flourish, and it is not clear whether the scribe always distinguished the two clearly, but his usual spellings are taken as guide in cases of doubt.

[101] E.g. 49/2 *Exijt edictum a Cesare Augusto &c*, 59/11 *monte*, 60/2 *aromata*.

[102] E.g. 50/3–4, 128/10n.

[103] E.g. 113/14n, 155/13n.

base T, emended to bring it as near as possible to the translator's putative exemplar, with the rejected readings recorded in the Variants to the Latin. A band of readings at the foot of the page (tagged by obeli) supply the more original readings of O, the archetypal text of *HTR* (as given in Hm.); only substantive variants of O are reported, including short losses in the translator's exemplar,[104] or readings which clarify irregularities of grammar, syntax, and idiom.[105] Matter corresponding to extended physical lacunas and omissions in the English is not supplied in the Latin text or the Variants but is summarised in the Commentary. Passages which appear to be corrupt even in O are designated as *archetypal corruption*.

[104] E.g. p. 72 *subleuandam*, p. 107 *Maria*; *cf.*, p. 107 *intende*.

[105] E.g. p. 54 *vel*, p. 57 *villis*, p. 66 *et extunc*.

[f. 228r]

A TRETYS OF ÞE THRE KYNG<ES> OF COLOYNE

Whan al the world was discrevid of Cesar August (as is seyd in þe gospell *Exijt edictum a Cesare Augusto &c*), as Ioseph and our Lady went þat tyme by þe wey that ledith to Bedlem, our Lady seyd to Ioseph, 'Two peple Y se, on weping, anoþir ioying'. [To] whom þan seyd Ioseph, 'Syt still, Marie, on thi best, and will not to speke such supperflue wordis'. Than apperid byfor hem þer a wondur fair child clothid in white and seyd to Ioseph, 'Why seidist þou they were superfleu wordis? Of two peplis of which Marie spak the peple of Iewis she sawe wepyng and þe peple of gentils she saw ioying. The tyme is neighid of our Lord of which he behight to our fadris Abraham, Isak, and Iacob. Tyme is now comyn þat of þe sede of Abraham blessyng of hym be yove in heritage to all peplis'.

And <w ..> þe aungel had seyd þus, he bad our Lady < ..... > her beste þat bere her stond still <f ....> of her birthe was come. And <............

4 To] Tho L.

[*PsM* p.76] Factum est autem post aliquantum tempus ut fieret professio ex edicto Caesaris Augusti, ut profiteretur unusquisque in patria sua. Haec professio facta est a praeside Syriae Cyrino. Necesse autem fuerat ut Ioseph cum Maria proficisceretur in Bethleem, quia exinde erat, et Maria de tribu Iuda et de domo ac patria David. Cum ergo Ioseph et Maria irent per viam quae ducit Bethleem, dixit Maria ad Ioseph: Duos populos video ante me, unum flentem et alium gaudentem. Cui respondit Ioseph: Sede et tene te in iumento tuo et noli superflua verba loqui. Tunc apparuit puer speciosus ante eos, indutus veste splendida, et dixit ad Ioseph: Quare dixisti verba superflua esse de duobus populis de quibus locuta est Maria? Populum enim Iudaeorum flentem vidit, quia recessit a deo suo, et populum gentium gaudentem, quia accessit et prope factus est ad dominum, secundum quod promisit patribus nostris Abraham, Isaac, et Iacob; tempus enim advenit ut in semine Abrahae benedictio omnibus gentibus tribuatur.

Et cum haec dixisset, iussit angelus stare iumentum, quia tempus advenerat pariendi;

...> our Lady shold descende a<nd .... > into a cave vndur erth<e.. ....> enhabitid for it wa<s .... > whan our Lady wa<... ....

... [f. 228[v]] and straungers, and for they were pore, they sog<ht> her herburgh about all the cite and no man wold herburgh hem. And specialy for they sawe Marie a yung maydekyn syttyng on þe asse, wery of traveillyng and grete with child and ny her tyme of birthe, in all the cite non wold take her yn to herborow. And þerfor Ioseph Marie in that cave led than.

And vndirstondith þat Bedleem was no toun of grete reputacion ne of grete quantite, stondyng from Ierusalem but two myle of that cuntre. And hit is callid Dauidis cite for kyng Dauid þerin was born and also by Samuell anoyntid kyng. And above þat cave sometyme byfor the tyme of þe natiuite hit was housyd. But at þe tyme of the natyuite of Crist the

3 *The lower part of f. 228 in* L *is torn away, the tear (viewed from the recto) running (a) diagonally downwards from right to left (49/12-50/3, where the letters and stops in angle brackets represent possible values of partially preserved letters and an estimate of the number of letters lost); (b) then vertically to the bottom of the folio, preserving only the initial letters of each line, namely* byg; at; ing *(or* nig *or* uig); wa; <w . >; and; ces. 4 *At the top of f. 228[v] and all versos appears (with spelling variants) the first part of the running title*: (þe) thre kynges.

et praecepit descendere de [p. 77] animali Mariam et ingredi in speluncam subterraneam ...

[*HTR* f. 11[v]] ... Et quia tarde erat, et omnia loca et hospicia essent occupata et hominibus extraneis et hospitibus essent plena, et quia pauperes erant, [f. 12[r]] totam ciuitatem circuibant et nullus hospitari eos volebat. Et specialiter cum homines vidissent Mariam iuuenculam super asinum sedentem, itinere lassam ac grauidam partuique vicinam, in tota ciuitate [nullus] eam in tectum vel hospicium vel domum recipere voleb[at]. Vnde Ioseph Mariam in illud tugurrium et speluncam duxit de quibus tunc nullus homo curauit. ... [f. 10[v]] ... Et sciendum [est] quod Bethleem vnquam non videtur fuisse magne reputacionis vel quantitatis; et habet †preciosum fundamentum eo quod ibi sunt multe ca[uern]e et spelunce subterranee, et distat ab Iherusalem ad duo parua miliaria illius patrie. Est eciam oppidum non magnum, sed dicitur ciuitas Dauid pro eo quod Dauid rex ex ea fuit natus. Et in ipso loco quo quondam stetit et fuit domus †Ysaye patris Dauid, et in quo eciam natus fuit Dauid et in regem Israel per Samuelem vnctus, in eodem eciam loco deus de Maria virgine homo fuit natus. ... [f. 11[v]] ... Et huiusmodi domus quondam ante natiuitatem domini in eo loco fuit quo deus homo fuit natus. Sed temporibus natiuitatis domini

† preciosum] petrosum. † Ysaye] Ysay.

how<s . n>g was distroyed, so that ther left no þing < ..... > lytil sory cote afor that cave. But the < ....s . ng> left yet þat tyme. And ther þat < .... de> ground byfor that cave was <................ g> place of brede. And yn þe <.................... >f Ierusalem and of þe cuntre <.......................þ>at hous but hit <......................... >þat cave in <th>at ...

... [f. 229^{r}] tyed his asse; in which cave Marie þat night as aftre mydnyght byfor dawnyng as yn an oryson lying without peyne bare her child, wham aungelis stodyn about and in his birthe worshipid hym seying, '*Gloria in excelsis deo &c*'.

And than Ioseph, seyng þe tyme of her berthe comyn, went to seke mydwyves. And whan he had found, he come to Marie into þe cave ayen, and by that tyme fond with her þe child which she had born. Than seyd Ioseph to Marie, 'Y have broght þe mydwyves, Zelony and Salone, which stond without for þe grete light that is wiþ the herwiþin'. Marie, heryng þat, softly loghe. To whom seyd Ioseph, 'Marie, laghe not so, but pray pray hem to come visite the, in auenture if þow nede her help or medicine'. Than Marie bad they shold come yn to here. And whan Zelony was entrid to Marie, & Salo<m>e left stondyng without, Zelony than seyd to Marie,

1-5 *Due to the tear in the folio only the right hand side of the corresponding lines in the MS is preserved, and the final letters of the subsequent lines, namely* if; he; cave; whom; ong; also. 6 *At the top of f. 229^{r} and all subsequent recto pages appears the second half of the running title*: of Coloyne.

ipsa domus fuit totaliter destructa, ita quod in ipso loco penitus nil remanserat nisi paruum et [v]ile tugurrium ante ipsam speluncam. Sed parietes fictiles et muri lapidei dir[u]ti adhuc ibidem steterunt, et super aream illius loci ante ipsum tugurrium panes vendebantur. ... [f. 12^{r}]

Et in ipso tugurrio ante speluncam adhuc paruum presepe lapideum circa vnius vlne longitudinem longo autem muro muratum adhuc ibidem ab antiquo remansit, ad quod eciam bos pauperis, quem eciam nusquam hospitari potuit, fuit alligatus, iuxta quem eciam Ioseph asinum suum alligauit. ...

[p. 77] Et ibi peperit masculum, quem circumdederunt angeli nascentem et natum adoraverunt dicentes: Gloria in excelsis deo et in terra pax hominibus bonae voluntatis. Iam enim dudum Ioseph perrexerat ad quaerendas obstetrices. Qui cum reversus esset ad speluncam, Maria iam infantem genuerat. Et dixit Ioseph ad Mariam: Ego tibi Zelomi et Salomen obstetrices adduxi, quae foris ante speluncam stant et prae splendore nimio huc introire non audent. Audiens autem haec Maria subrisit. Cui Ioseph dixit: Noli subridere, [p. 78] sed cauta esto, ne forte indigeas medicina. Tunc iussit unam ex eis intrare ad se. Cumque ingressa esset Zelomi, ad Mariam dixit:

‘Suffre me to touche the’. And whan she had touchid Ma<ri>e, Zelony seid with a grete vois crying, ‘O Lord, Lord myghty, have mercy on me! Neuer yet hidirto was it herd ne supposid that the woman brestis shold be ful of mylk and a knave child borne shold shew the modur mayde, ne in the child no pollucion or defoulyng of blood, ne in the modir berer anguisshe, peyne, or sorowe. *Virgo verbo concepit, virgo peperit, atque post partum virgo permansit.*’ And than seyd Salome stondyng without, ‘That Y now here Y shall [f. 229^{v}] noght byleve but if Y preve hit’. And whan she was entrid to Marye, she seyd, ‘Suffre me to touche the’. And whan Marie had suffrid Salome touche her and Salome withdrow her honde from Marie, anone her hondis bothe were drye and dede, and for sorow crying and wepyng seyde, ‘O Lord, þou wost that Y have euere dred þe, and all women to whom Y have come Y have curyd. And lo now how wrecchid Y am bycomyn for myn vnbyleve, for Y was so hardy to taste and fele thy mayde’. And whan she had seyd so, a wondur fayr child appering to her seyd, ‘Go, woman, to þe child, and byseche hym praying and touche hym, & of thin hondis he shal hele the. He forsothe is þe saviour of the world’. Which Salome goyng hastily to the child wurshipid hym and touchid the hemme of his clothis yn which he was wrappid and anone her hondis were helid. And she than

11 seyde] s *perhaps corrected from* a.

Dimitte me ut tangam te. Cumque permisisset se Maria tangi, exclamavit voce magna obstetrix et dixit: Domine domine magne, miserere. Numquam hoc auditum est nec in suspicione habitum, ut mamillae plenae sint lacte et natus masculus matrem suam virginem ostendat. Nulla pollutio sanguinis facta est in nascente, nullus dolor in parturiente. Virgo concepit, virgo peperit, virgo permansit. Audiens hanc vocem alia obstetrix nomine Salome dixit: Quod ego audio non credam nisi forte ipsa probavero. Et ingressa Salome ad Mariam dixit: Permitte me ut palpem te et probem utrum verum dixerit Zelomi. Cumque permisisset Maria ut eam palparet, misit manum suam Salome. Et cum misisset et tangeret, statim aruit manus eius, et prae dolore coepit flere vehementissime et angustari et clamando dicere: Domine, tu nosti quia semper te timui, et omnes pauperes sine retributione acceptionis curavi, de vidua et orphano nihil accepi, et inopem vacuum a me ire numquam dimisi. Et ecce misera facta sum propter incredulitatem meam, quia ausa fui temptare virginem tuam. Cumque haec diceret, apparuit iuxta illam iuvenis quidam valde splendidus dicens ei: Accede ad infantem et adora eum et continge de manu tua, et ipse salvabit te, quia ipse est salvator seculi et omnium speratium in se. Quae confestim ad infantem accessit, et adorans eum tetigit fimbrias pannorum, in quibus infans erat involutus, et statim sanata est manus eius. Et

goyng out bygan for to crie lowd the merveilles which she had seyn and what she had suffrid and how she was helyd, so that by her prechyng mych peple turnyd to the byleve herof. For the shepherdis which kept her shepe by night than comyn to Bedlem affermyng that they had seyn aunglis of God at mydnyght, which aungels songe to hem a song *Quia natus est Ihesus Christus deus saluator seculi per quem restituetur salus Israel.* But an houge sterre from þat evenyng into the mornyng above þat cave shone, which gretnesse [f. 230r] of sterre was neuere arst seyn fro the bygynnyng of the world. And the prophetis which were þat tyme in Ierusalem seyd that þis sterre shold bytokene the natyvite of Crist that shold restore the helthe not only of Israel but also of al þe peple. And the thrid day aftir the natiuite of our Lord Marie went out of þat cave to a stable without þe cite of Bedleme in which pore folk and pilgrymes haddyn oft her nightis herborow, wher þe oxe & the asse stood tyed to the c[rec]che; which oxe and asse, seyng her lord, wurshipid hym whan he was leyd in the cracche. Than was hit fulfillid þat was seid by Abacuk þe prophete, *Cognouit bos possessorem suum et asinus presepe domini sui,* and by Isaye, *In medio duum animalium cognoscetur*. And in þat place dwellid Marie and Ioseph and her child thre dayes.

14 crecche] cherche L.

exiens foras clamare coepit et dicere magnalia virtutum quae viderat et quae passa fuerat, et quemadmodum curata fuerat, ita ut ad praedicationem eius multi crederent. Nam et pastores ovium asserebant se angelos vidisse in medio noctis hymnum dicentes, deum caeli laudantes et benedicentes, et dicentes quia natus est salvator omnium, qui est Christus dominus, in quo restituetur salus Israel. Sed et stella ingens a vespere usque ad matutinum splendebat super speluncam, cuius magnitudo numquam visa fuerat ab origine mundi. Et prophetae qui fuerant in Ierusalem dicebant hanc stellam indicare nativitatem Christi, qui restauraret promissionem non solum Israel sed et omnium gentium. Tertia autem die nativitatis domini egressa est Maria de spelunca, et ingressa est stabulum et posuit puerum in praesepio, et bos et asinus adoraverunt eum. Tunc adimpletum est quod dictum est per Isaiam prophetam dicentem: Cognovit bos possessorem suum et asinus praesepe domini sui. Ipsa autem animalia in medio eum habentes incessanter adorabant eum. Tunc adimpletum est quod dictum est per Abacuc prophetam dicentem: In medio duorum animalium innotesceris. In eodem autem loco moratus est Ioseph et Maria cum infante tribus diebus.

And that chrecche in which Marie her child with feble pore clothis wrappid byfor the oxe and asse layd and couchid as in that cuntre is the maner to have in euery stable many cracchis of erthe or of stone of lengthe eche of thre feet as a best may have his stondyng alone þerto. And this place wher þe aungel wiþ so mich clernesse and light shewyd hym + seyng God þan to be born is from Bedlem but half a myle of þat cuntre. And in that same place Dauid kept his flokkis of shepe and from the beris & lyons ther re[f]te. And in meny places in þat cuntre vnnethe wyntir from somyr may wele be discrevyd and knowyn. [f. 230v]

And whan in þat cave in Bedlem þat same almighty God was man borne *qui prope est semper omnibus inuocantibus eum in veritate,* that sterre by Balaham þe prophete by long tymes passid byfor and by the .xij. astronomers of Inde, Perse, and Caldee aboue the hille of Vaus sete longe tyme abydyn in that night that Crist was born on þ<e> same hill of Vaus in manere of a sonne shynyng bygan to rise in manere of an egle, vpon þat hill assendyng, [and] by al þat day in o certayn place stode wiþout mevyng,

5 hym] hym and L. 8 refte] reste L. 16 and] *om.* L.

[f. 12r] ... Et in illud presepe beata virgo Maria paruulum suum vagientem pannis vilibus inuolutum ante asinum et bouem prout melius potuit in fenum posuit et reclinauit. Vnde est sciendum quod in omnibus partibus orientis est consuetudinis quod in omnibus stabulis sunt quamplurima presepia lutea vel lapidea, †vel vnumquodque presepe est circa trium pedum longitudinem, ita quod semper equus vel animal habet per se presepe suum speciale. ... Iterum locus vbi angelus pastoribus tunc cum luce et magna claritate deum hominem [natum] nunciauit distat a Bethleem [f. 12v] ad dimidium miliare illius patrie. Et in eodem loco Dauid eciam greges pascebat et a faucibus vrsi et leonis e[o]s ibi eripiebat. ... De quibus est sciendum quod terra circa Bethleem et terra promissionis et tota terra orientis mirabiliter [est] disposita et pro maiori parte in montanis sita, et in aliquibus locis yem[p]s vix ab estate discernitur et distinguitur. ... [f. 13v]

Cum itaque, vt supradictum est, in Bethleem in spelunca deus homo esset natus, extunc [id]em omnipotens deus, qui semper est prope omnibus inuocantibus eum in veritate, ipsam stellam per Balaam †proph[et]am et per longissima retroacta tempora per xij astrologos ab Indis Persis et Caldeis super montem Vaus (vt dictum est) constitutos remote atque anxie expectatam et obseruatam eadem nocte et hora qua ipse deus homo fuit natus tunc super eundem montem Vaus in modum solis radiantis oriri †in modum aquile fecit†. Super ipsum montem ascendit, et per totum illum diem in vno loco super eundem montem in primo intersticio aeris immobilis permansit,

† vel] et. † prophetam] prophetatam. † in modum aquile fecit] fecit et illuminauit universum celi firmamentum et paulatim in modum aquile.

so that bytwene þe sonne at mydday and þat sterre in clerenesse and brightnesse semyd no difference; so þat, as some bokys seyn, in þat day of þe natiuite of our Lord was seyn meny sonnys. And aftir þe passyng of þat day of natiuite hit assendid vp to þe firmament of hevyn. And that sterre as it is in that contre fourmyd and shapyn was not fourmyd as othir sterris, but it had meny long strakis more brennyngly þan fire brondis, and as an egle fleyng, the wynd wiþ þe wenges betyng, so were the stremys and strakis of that sterre styring about. And <þ>at sterre had in hymself the fourme of a yung child and aboue hym a crosse tokyn, and þer was herd in that sterre a voys seying, '*Natus est hodie rex Iudeorum qui est <e>xpectacio gencium et dominator. Ite ad inquirendum eum et adorandum.*' Wherfor all manere peple of all þe parties and lond<i>s and regions of the Este, in þe sight of that so seld sayn, wondirful, and vncouthe sterre of which [f. 231^{r}] was in þe Old Testament yovyn to Balam the prophete to prophecie in figuracion also to the Newe Testament, heryng also such a voys of þat sterre, wondirly they were awondrid and adred, and þei fully bylevid þis sterre þe same which of so long tyme byfor by Balaam was prophecied, so long desi[r]yd and abydyn.

And þan the thre Kyngis in þe londis and parties of Ynde, Caldee, and

18 desiryd] desidyd L.

ita quod, cum sol in meridie transiuit, quasi nulla erat distancia in claritate inter ipsam stellam et solem. Vnde quidam libri continent quod ipso die natiuitatis [f. 14^{r}] domini plures soles sunt visi. Et $^{+}$ ipso die natiuitatis domini elapso hec stella ascendit sursum ad celi firmamentum. Sed ipsa stella prout in partibus istis in ecclesiis depingitur non fuit formata †[sicut alie stelle]†, sed habuit radios quamplurimos et longissimos faculis ardenciores; et quasi aquila volitans et aerem alis verberans, sic radij stelle circummouebantur. Et ipsa stella habuit in se formam infantuli et desuper signum crucis, et audita est vox in stella dicens, 'Natus est hodie rex Iudeorum qui est expectacio gencium et dominator $^{+}$; ite ad inquirendum eum et a[do]randum'.

Ad roborandum ergo fidem gencium et confirmandam materiam et rem gestam, omnipotens deus, cuius prouidencia in sua disposicione non fallitur, qui, prout Paulus ait, vocat ea que non sunt tamquam ea que sunt, ex sua prouidencia hoc egit et disposuit vt, qui in veteri testamento vocem dederat ex asina Balaam qui hanc stellam prophetauerat, quod eciam in inchoacione noui testamenti daret vocem ex stella per eundem Balaam prophetam gentilem prophetata. Vnde tunc vniuersi homines vtriusque sexus omnium illarum parcium et terrarum orientis et regionum, visa tam mirabili [rara] et insolita stella et tali voce ex ipsa audita, vltra modum fuerunt perteriti et admirati, et ipsam esse stellam per Balaam prophetam gentilem prophetatam et a longis temporibus desideratam et expectatam esse non dubitauerunt.

Extunc tres Reges qui in terris et partibus Indie Caldee et

† sicut alie stelle] *om.*

Perse þat tyme regnyng, of þat sterre þan enfourmyd and by her astronomers, doctours, and prophetis taught and warnyd, ioyed þan hyly that in her tyme they were worthy to se such a sterre of so long tyme prophecied and of hem so long tyme abydyn and desirid to be seyn. Wherfor these thre Kynges gloriouse, by ferre landis and distaunce of contres disseuerid and departid and echeon of hem of othir vnware and vnknowyn but yet all at o tyme of this sterre enformyd, with riche yeftis, noble ornementis, diuers vestimentis, and kyngly aray on hors, mewlis, camels [with] houge tresours chargid and with houge cumpanyes and hostis of peple and aray as þei myght and couþe best and clennest be ordeynid made hem redy to seche the lord kyng of Iewis that tyme borne and to worship hym, as the voys of the sterre had forsayd and prechid to hem. And þe more nobly and honestly they that tyme arayed hem by as miche as they than knew an hyer kyng aboue hem than borne whom þei purposid so þan to seke. And all her cariage and ordinance of goodis, flokkis, bestis, drovis, housholdis beddyng, [f. 231v] ornementis, oostes of her folkys, and all her necessaries which to hem and to her folk might copiously suffice they made go byfor hem with her cariage. For in that cuntre is the custome

9 with] and L.

Persidis regnabant, de ipsa informati et de [f. 14v] ipsa per astrologos doctores et prophetas instructi, multum sunt gauisi quod ipsorum temporibus stellam tam longe ante prophetatam videre meruerunt quam tam longissimis temporibus omnes populi anxie expectauerunt et videre desiderauerunt. Vnde hij tres Reges gloriosi, per nimiam et maximam earum terrarum et regnorum distanciam sep[a]rati, et quisquis de alio penitus ignarus sed vno tempore de ipsa stella informati, cum ditissimis muneribus veris et misticis ac nobilissimis ornamentis et variis ac diuersis vestimentis ac ornatu regio, cum equis et mulis et camelis et thesauris infinitis et maximo ac ingenti comitatu ac exercitibus et apparatu prout ornacius et nobilius potuerunt ad inquirendum dominum et regem Iudeorum natum et ipsum a[do]randum se preparauerunt, prout vox de stella dixit precepit et predicauit. Et tanto nobilius et honestius se preparauerunt quemadmodum super se regem alciorem natum cognouerunt quem inquirere et adorare proposuerunt. Et omnium eorum expedicionem in †bo[ni]s et gregibus et armentis cum aliis eorum lectisternijs et vtensilibus et ditissimis ac nobilissimis preparamentis et omnibus necessariis que ipsis et ipsorum exercitibus ac comitatui sufficere possent copiose preire fecerunt in multitudine quamplurimorum camelorum et iumentorum. Nam consuetudinis est

† bonis] bubus.

savyng in grete citees in all tounys men may fynd good hostrie for the more partie and good plente of vitaille to selle. But whan lordis or princes with her peple come, for hem in þes tounys be noght to fynde for her astate competent beddyng ne such manere store of housholde conuenient to hem in chaumbir or yn kychyn but as þei trusse such cariage euermore with hem on mewlis, camels, and othir bestis. For comynly peple of that cuntre for passyng and insuffr<i>ble hete in that cuntre of the sonne trauaile, ride, and walk by night.

And of thes thre Kynges gloriouse her kyngdomes and londis ben in thre Yndes, of which londis and regions the moost partie stont by yles ful of watris, grete wildirnessis, serpentis, perilouse bestis, and marices in which growyn grete redis and hye that in that cuntre þei make þerof housis and shippis. An thes londis be ferre atwynne eche from othir, and yn eche londe and yle of hem growyn meny diuers herbis, bestis passyngly perilous, and harde and traueyllous to go from the yles of the o lond ynto the yles of the tothir londis. For it `is´ red that kyng Assweris regnyd ouere .xxv. prouinces from Inde into Ethiope.

7 insuffrible] *perhaps* insuffrable L.

in oriente et in omnibus partibus vltramarinis excepto in magnis ciuitatibus quod in omnibus locis et †villis quamplura delectabilia hospicia et amena, in quibus pro [f. 15[r]] maiori parte omnia commestibilia et pabula et huiusmodi in optimo foro reperiuntur. Sed principibus et dominis cum aliqua multitudine inc[e]dentibus in ips[is] non sunt commoda lectisternia et huiusmodi vtensilia ad cameram et ad coquinam pertinencia necessaria, sed cum principibus et dominis portantur in mulis et iumentis et camelis. Nam communiter ibidem homines propter intolerabilem et inestimabilem solis ardorem semper de nocte equitant ambulant et vagantur. Iterum de regnis [et] de terris istorum trium Regum gloriosorum qui se itaque tam nobiliter ad inquirendum et a[do]randum dominum preparauerunt est sciendum quod tres sunt Indie, quarum omnes terre et regiones pro maiori parte sunt insule. Et omnes hee terre et insule et regiones sunt plene aquis et desertis ac serpentibus maximis et aliis animalibus †periculosissimis et paludibus horribilissimis in quibus crescunt arundines tam grosse †quam alte quod ex hiis in partibus illis domus vel naues construuntur. Et hee sunt †diuerse et abinuicem separate. Et in vnaquaque †terrarum eciam† regionum terris et insulis nascuntur et crescunt herbe et animalia et bestie speciales †et quod vltra modum periculose et laboriose de vna terra regione vel insula ad aliam peruenitur. Vnde legitur quod Asswerus regnauit super centum viginti quinque prouincias ab India vsque ad Ethiopiam.

† villis] villis sunt. † periculosissimis] periculosissimis et venenosissimis. † quam] et. † diuerse] diuise. † terrarum eciam] istarum terrarum et. † et] ita.

In the ferst Inde þat tyme was þe kyngdom of Newbye in whiche at þe natyuite of our Lord regnyd Melchior, which offrid to our Lord gold and an appil of gold; [f. 232r] among whos londis was þe londe of Arabye, in which is *mons Synay* and the Reed See. And fro Surye and Egipt lightly men may sayle into Inde. But marchauntis on þis syde of the Reed See and oþir men be not suffrid þer to have passage ouir þat see, for the soudon on this syde of the Reed See hath strong castels which kepe the passage of þat see, that none bere lettris ne tydynges into Medee to Prestre Iohn, lord of Inde, ne to othir kyngis in the Est. But men born of þat cuntre byȝend þat see be suffrid to passe that se, and they be examynid wele of the cause of her goyng. And Prestre Iohn in the same wise kepiþ the passage from his lond ouir þat Rede See and examinith diligently þe cause of þe goers ovir that see from his lond, and he hath strong castels in his honde. And freris, marchauntis, and oþir men gon by Perce by a long, tediouse, and laborous wey. And pilgrimes and marchauntis goyng þat wey ouere þat see seyn that the ground of that see is so rede that for redenesse þerof the watir al above semith rede as reed wyne. And þogh the watir be of anoþir colour ȝet it is salt, and so clere þat in the grounde may be wele seyn fisshis, stonys, and

17 ȝet] *perhaps altered from* Et L.

In prima ergo India fuit regnum Nubie, in quo temporibus natiuitatis domini regnauit Melchior [f. 15v] qui domino aurum optulit; cuius eciam inter alias terras fuit Arabia, in quo mons Sinay est situs et mare rubrum. †De Siria et Egipto in Indiam faciliter nauigatur. Sed mercatores et alij homines nati in partibus cismarinis transire non permittuntur, quia soldanus ab ista parte maris rubri in insula fortissima habet castra in quibus captiui nobiles detinentur, et ab illis castris cauetur ne aliquis homo de partibus cismarinis natus ad partes et terras †ad Medos† transeat, ne quis presbitero Iohanni domino Indorum vel aliis regibus in India †in oriente aliquas litteras de regibus christianis deferat vel conspiraciones. Sed homines incole de partibus vltramarinis nati transire permittuntur, sed tamen de negociis eorum quare transeant diligenter examinantur. Et econuerso presbiter Iohannes dominus Indorum ab alia parte maris rubri habet castra fortissima de quibus eciam cauetur eodem modo ne aliquis de partibus illis transeat ad dominum soldanum in suum detrimentum. †Cum fratres eciam minores et augustinenses, carmelite et predicatores et mercatores et alij homines de partibus cismarinis nati ad partes Indie volentes ire transeunt et circuiunt per regnum Persarum per viam multum longam tediosam et laboriosam. Sed [peregrini et mercatores] qui per mare rubrum de India transeunt dicunt quod totus fundus maris rubri e[s]t tam rubeus quod pre rubedine fundi desuper existens aqua vt vinum rubeum appareat rubea; †[et] licet [fu]erit alterius aqu[a] coloris [tamen]† est salsa, [f. 16r] et tam clara quod in profundissimo eius loco et fundo lapides et pisces vel

† De] et per illud mare rubrum de. † ad Medos] Indie. † in] et. † Cum] Vnde.
† et licet ... tamen] licet sit vt alterius aque coloris et.

all oþir thingis. And that se is thre cornerid, and hit goth & flowith into þe Occean, and it is about .iiij. or .v. myle brode in the breddest place wher the childrin of Israel went ouir drie foot whan Pharao with his oost folwid hem and was þan dreynt þerin. And out of that s<e>e flowith also anoþir riuer which goth & fallith into Nile, on of þe flodis of Paradis; [f. 232v] which flood passith þurgh Egipt, and by þat flood meny diuers riche marchaundises passe from the Est and + Inde into Egipte, Sirye, Babyloigne, and Alisaundre, which be bore into all the world. And in Arabie in which is Mount Syna + stones, trees, and all þing þat growith for þe moost parte is reed, and in maner of thenne rotis growith there [f]yn gold. And þer also in *monte* be found smaragdis, which with grete trauaill craftily be corvyn out, and be wele kept of þe seruantis of þe sowdon. And þat londe of Arabye was wont perteyne all to Pretre Iohn, but now for the more partie hit perteynith to the sowdon. But for to lete marchaundise passe from Inde pesibely and for othir diuers causes the soudon for the lond of Arabye yeueth tribute to Prestre Iohn into þis day.

Also in the second Ynde was the kyngdom of Godolye in which in the tyme of the natiuite of our Lord regnyd Baltazar, which offrid to our Lord

7 and] and the L.   9 Syna] Syna and ther be L.   10 fyn] thyn L.

alique alie res bene discernantur. Et ipsum mare rubrum est triangulariter formatum, et incidit et influit in terram †et Occeanum†, et est circa quinque vel quatuor miliaria latum in eius loco laciori, vbi filij Israel sicco pede transierunt quando Pharao cum exercitu suo fuit insecutus et ibidem submersus. Et ex ipso mari rubro alius fluuius effluit qui incidit in [Nil]um fluuium paradisi, qui fluuius transit per Egiptum, et per illum fluuium quamplurima ditissima et nobilissima mercimonia de oriente et India transeunt in Egiptum Cyriam Babiloniam et Alexandriam, que deinde per vniuersum mundum deportantur et deferuntur. Iterum tota terra in Arabia in qua mons Synay est situ[s] est multum rubea; et lapides pro maiori parte et quamplurima ligna que ibidem crescunt et quicquid de talibus ibidem nascitur vel crescit et reperitur est multum rubeum. Vnde in modum et formam tenuissimarum radicum †crescit ibidem eciam optimum aurum multum nimis† rubeum reperitur. Et ibidem eciam in monte †bonus smaragdus† reperitur, que nimis laboriose et artificialiter exsciditur, et multum diligenter a ministris soldani custoditur. Et ista terra Arabia quondam presbitero Iohanni totaliter pertinebat, sed nunc pro maiori parte pertinet soldano. Sed ut mercimonia de India transire permittantur pacifice, et propter alias causas, soldanus ex illa terra Arabia dat tributum presbitero Iohanni in presentem diem. Sed vt ad propositum redeatur. [f. 16v]

Item in secunda India fuit regnum Godolie, in quo temporibus natiuitatis domini regnauit Baltasar, qui domino thus optulit;

† et Occeanum] ex occeano.   † crescit ... nimis] ibidem optimum et multum nimis aurum.   † bonus smaragdus] vena smaragdina.

encense; whos also among othir londis was the kyngdom of Saba in which more than in othir londis specialy growyn meny noble *aromat<a>*, and specialy ensence, which droppith of speciall trees in manere of gumme, and in othir londis litil or none is fondyn.

Also in the thrid Ynde was the kyngdom of Tarce in which þe tyme of þe natiuite of our Lord regnyd Iaspar, which offrid to our Lord mirre; whos also among all othir londi<s> was þe famouse londe and yle of Grisailla [f. 233[r]] – and with some it is callyd Egrisculla, or Egrocilla, or Egriscula – in the which the body of Seynt Thomas þe Apostil restith, in which lond more than in eny othir londe growith myrre, and in manere of eris scorchid with fire, in grete quantite. And whil it ripith it is so soft that it clevith on mennys clothis as they go þerby, and it is gadrid in girdlis and bondis with all þe herbe and pressid.

Wherfor of grete forsight of God thes thre Kyngis gloriouse, Melchior, Baltazar, and Iaspar, of tho thre londis in whiche grewyn th<e> yeftis which they shold offre to our Lord were callid kyngis raþer than of [her] othir gret[ter] kyngdomys or londis; wherof seith Dauid, *Reges Tharsis et insule munera offerent, reges Arabum et Saba dona adducent.* And the

7 Grisailla] *catchword* and with L.   16–17 her othir gretter] the othir grete L.

cuius eciam inter alias terras fuit aliud antiquum regnum Saba, in quo plus quam in aliis terris et partibus specialiter crescunt quamplurima nobilissima aromata. Et specialiter plus quam in aliis mundi partibus crescit ibidem thus, quod stillat ex specialibus arboribus in modum gummi, et in aliis terris parum vel nichil reperitur.

Item in tercia India fuit regnum Tharsis, in quo temporibus natiuitatis domini regnauit Iaspar, qui domino mirram optulit; cuius eciam inter alias terras diuersas fuit illa famosissima insula †Grisculla vocata (alibi scribitur Egrisculla vel Egrosilla vel Egriscula)† in qua nunc corpus beati Thome apostoli quiescit. In qua eciam plus quam in alia parte mundi vel terra crescit mirra. Et crescit super herbas in modum spicarum adustarum formatas in maxima quantitate. Et dum in herbis maturescit est tam mollis quod vestimentis pertranseuncium se connectit. Et extunc quamplurime zone et corde per ipsas herbas trahuntur †et compr[imun]tur†. Et eodem modo et forma crescit thymiama.

Quapropter ex magna prouidencia et predestinacione diuina nouimus fore factum quod hij tres Reges gloriosi Melchior Baltasar et Iaspar ex illis tribus terris in quibus munera crescebant que domino offerre debebant in antiquo presagio plus quam de eorum maioribus regnis debebant reges appellari – vnde ait Dauid: Reges Tharsis et insule munera offerent, reges Arabum et Saba dona adducent. Et

† Grisculla ... Egriscula] Egrisoulla vocata.   † et comprimuntur] et illis sicut cera mollis abstrahitur et comprimitur.

namys of the gretter kyngdomys shal be subget to hem. For that tyme þes glorious Kynges on þe name of tho kyngdomys were callyd kyngis; for Melchior kyng of Nubye & Arabum was callid, Baltazar kyng of Godoly and of Saba, and Iaspar kyng of Tharce and of þe yle of Egrisculle; & it is callid þe kyngdom of Thars.

And aftir that thes thre glorious Kyngis with her tresours, ornementis, and peple, as hit is byfor seyd, had made hem nobly redy, goyng and takyng her iourne, eche of hem of the intencion and purpos of othir for the distance of cuntre bytwene hem vnware & vnknowyn, natheles eche Kyng with his ost and cariage the sterre evyn ylich ȝaf light goyng byfor hem. And [f. 233v] the sterre with the goers of eche Kyng yede and wiþ the stonders stode in his ful vertu, and all her weyes lightyd. And in alle citees and tounys, which that tyme for pes thurgh all þe world were not shette but opyn by which þei passid by night, hit semyd hem as hit had be day for lightnesse of þe sterre, wherfor all peple and folk dwellyng in þo citees & tounes by which þei passid be night wondirly were dred and awondrid. For they saw the folk and multitude of bestis with passyng spede iourney by

13 for] f *corrected from* p L.

eorum [f. 17r] †nomina regnorum maiorum† sub[ici]entur. Nam tunc temporis ipsi tres Reges gloriosi ex parte eorum †regnorum rex Nubie et Arabum Melchior vocabatur, Baltasar rex Godolie et Saba,[ac] Iaspar rex Tharsis et insule Egr[i]sculle appellabatur. †Et regnum Tharsis nominatur quia ipsi insule fuit annexum; ad differenciam aliarum ciuitatum et insularum eorum nomina specialiter exprimuntur†. Sed vt ad propositum redeatur.

Postquam, vt dictum est, hij tres Reges gloriosi itaque cum thesauris et ornamentis ac comitatu et diuersa expedicione se nobiliter in omnibus et per omnia preparassent, et exeuntes †et extendentes† fines regnorum suorum, quiuis de proposito et de intencione alterius penitus ignarus propter multam et nimiam ac longam inter eos et terras eorum distanciam, tamen vnumquemque Regem et suum exercitum ac comitatum et expedicionem stella eque bene precedebat. Et stella cum euntibus ibat et cum stantibus [stabat] †in virtute sua omni[a] ipsorum itinera illuminabat. Et in omnibus ciuitatibus et villis que tunc temporis propter pacem die noctuque in vniuerso mundo non claudebantur per quas transierunt de nocte videbatur eis esse dies. Vnde homines et habitatores omnium illarum ciuitatum et locorum per quos et que itaque de nocte transierunt vltra modum fuerunt perteriti et admirati. Nam viderunt reges et maximos exercitus et comitatus cum maxima ambicione et expedicione transire

† nomina regnorum maiorum] maiorum regnorum nomina. † regnorum] regnorum et terrarum fuerunt binomij nam. † Et regnum ... exprimuntur] *archetypal corruption.* † et extendentes] *om.* † in] et de nocte non ut luna vel stella sed ut sol radians in.

hem and þe night was to hem as þe day, noght knowyng whidir they woldyn ne whens þei comyn, and on the morow þei sawe the erthe in diuerses places of her citees and tounes with the steppis of bestis, hors, and of her peple fortrodyn and defoulyd. Wherfor they were sette in grete dowte and drede, and among hem long tyme grete disputison and question þerof. And aftir þat thes thre gloriouse Kyngis out of the marches of her owne kyngdomes were passid, they come into othir regions and londis to hem vnknowyn. And þan without lettyng or dissese þei passid all watris, wildirnes, hillis, playnes, and perilous merches; *sed erant illis omnia plana et indirecta in vias planas*. And neuere toke þei herborow ne restyng in no toun by night ne by day, but they, her peple, and all her bestis without mete or drink abode til they come to Bedlem. And al that iourne to hem all semyd but as for o day ...

... [f. 234r] sins have stoppid wiþ stonys the dores of this chapell, which is corvyn out vndur the mount of Calvarye. And whan þat Melchior, kyng of Newbye and of Arabum, with his ost restyd byside the mount of Caluarye, lastyng the clowd and derknesse, Baltazar, kyng of Saba and of Godolye, with his cumpany come yn his wey byside þe mount of Olyuete

13 *a lacuna of one folio follows.*

quibus per omnem eorum viam de nocte erat dies, nescientes vnde venerunt aut quo tenderunt; et de mane videbant terram in locis eorum vestigiis equorum et iumentorum conculcatam. Vnde omnes homines per quos itaque transierunt facti [f. 17v] sunt in extasi, et de hiis maxima questio fuit in populis vn[i]uersis temporibus longis. Et postquam hij tres Reges gloriosi de finibus regnorum suorum sunt egressi, ad alias terras et regiones [ignotas] peruenerunt. Et extunc per omnes aquas et deserta montes planicies valles et paludes horribilissimas absque aliquo impedimento transierunt, sed erant eis omnia †plana et indirecta† et aspera in vias planas. Et nusquam de nocte vel die quiescebant vel hospicia capiebant, sed tam ipsi quam eorum exercitus et expedicio et equi eorum et omnia eorum animalia et iumenta absque cibo potu et pabulo quousque peruenerunt Bethleem manserunt. Et ipsis omnibus in via nisi vna dies in transitu videbatur. ... [f. 19r]

Et vocatur ibidem Capella trium Regum Nubianorum in presentem diem; sed nunc Saraceni ianuas ipsius capelle lapidibus obstruxerunt. Et illa capella est subtus montem Caluarie exscisa.

Iterum postquam Melchior rex Nubie et Arabum itaque cum suo exercitu iuxta montem Caluarie in nebula et tenebris resedisset, parum extunc in eadem nebula et caligine Baltasar rex Saba et Godolie cum excercitu suo venit ex itinere speciali, et iuxta montem Oliueti

† plana et indirecta] praua in directa.

in a litil towne which is callyd Galilee, and ther restid hym; in which toun our Lord aftir his resureccion ofttymis apperid – wherof seith the scripture, *Precedet vos in Galileam*. But ther is also a londe which is callid Galile, from Ierusalem thre dayes iourne.

And whan the too kyngis Melchior & Baltasar in thes too places restyd in the tyme of the derkenes of that cloude, than a lytil and a litil the cloude and þe derkenesse assendid fro hem. But yet the sterre apperid noght. And whan thei sawe þat they were eche of hem, vnware of othir, with his cumpany ny the cite, they toke þan forthe her way. And whan they were fallyn both into þe threwey byside þe mount of Caluarie, than Iaspar, kyng of Thars and of the yle of Egrisculle, with his cumpany come fallyng on hem. And so the thre glorious Kynges with her cumpanyes and cariages ech from his lond and kyngdom by his speciall wey in this threway thus mette togidir. And thogh none of hem byfor þa tyme neuere had knowleche of oþir, yet eche of hem hyed to kysse othir, and þogh eche of hem were of diuers langage, yet semyd it to eche of hem that oþir spak his langage. And whan eche of hem had shewid to oþir the cause of her comyng and þer in all thingis acordid yn en[f. 234v]tente, than were they miche gladder than byfor, & more feruent and willy in her iourne. And whan the cloud

in villa parua que ibidem Galilea vocabatur resedit in tenebris et remansit. Et de eadem parua villa multum loquntur euangelia et sacra scriptura. Nam in eadem apostoli et discipuli ante resurreccionem domini et post propter metum Iudeorum extra ciuitatem Iherusalem semper secrete conuenire consueuerunt. Et in ipsa parua villa dominus post resurreccionem suam discipulis suis sepius apparuit, vnde dicit scriptura: Precedet vos in Galileam; ibi eum videbitis &c. Et plurima alia de hac parua villa sacra narrat scriptura. Sed alia est terra que est principatus que eciam vocatur Galilea, et distat a Iherusalem ad tres dietas vel circa. Sed vt ad propositum redeatur.

Cum itaque duo Reges Melchior et Balthasar in locis supradictis in nebula caligine et tenebris subsistebant, extunc paulatim nebula et caligo sursum ascendebant; sed [f. 19v] stella non apparuit. Vnde dum se prope ciuitatem vidissent, extunc quiuis Rex, de alio adhuc ignarus, cum excercitu suo viam versus ciuitatem arripuerunt. Et dum venissent ad triuium iuxta montem Caluarie, †vt tunc† Iaspar rex Tharsis et insule Egr[i]sculle cum exercitu suo superuenit. Et itaque hij tres Reges gloriosi cum omnibus exercitibus et expedicionibus quiuis de terris et regnis suis ex via speciali in hoc triuio conuenerunt. Et licet vnus nunquam alterius personam vidisset, tamen in oscula et amplexus insimul gaudio ruebant. Et quamuis diuersorum essent ydiomatum, tamen vnicuique videbatur quod alter loquelam suam loqueretur. Et cum vnusquisque alteri causam sui itineris exposuisset et in hiis [per] omnia concordassent, extunc multum leciores et ardenciores in eorum negociis sunt effecti. Et extunc nebula

† vt tunc] extunc.

and derkenesse was passid, thus sone sodenly vpon the sonne arisyng they were entrid into the citee of Ierusalem. And whan they knew that it was Ierusalem which byfortyme by her predecessours had be bysegid and distroyed, they gladd mych, hopyng to fynd the kyng of Iewys to be bore þerin. But of her sodeyn and vnavisid comyng Herode and al þe cite was gretly troublyd and sorid. For her ostis and peple with her cariage and ordynance was so myche þat þei might noght be comprehendid within the cite but as for the most partie as in manere of a sege herborowid in cumpas about þe citee – wherof seith Isaye, *Forti[t]udo gencium venerit tibi, inundacio camelorum operiet te, dromedarij Madian et Offa. Omnes de Saba venient aurum et thus deferentes et laudem domino annunciantes. Omne pecus Cedar congre[ga]bitur et arietes Nabaoth ministrabunt tibi.*

And vndirstondith that thes thre Kynges made al þe peple and multitude of bestis go byfor hem. And the kynd of the rammys of Nabaoth is, they be grete and houge in the hyndre parties and in the taylle, and in the body byfor as who seith litil or noght. And the brede of her taylis strecchith ouer the brede of the hipis, and the lengthe of the taile to the myddis of the hyndir thies. And some of þo rammys, whan they be hilt, the tayle weieth

9 Fortitudo] Fortidudo L. 12 congregabitur] congrebitur L.

et caligo totaliter se abstulit. Et ita inopinato et inprouiso orto iam sole ciuitatem Iherusalem intrauerunt. Et cum ipsi tres Reges cognouissent quod illa esset ciuitas Iherusalem regalis quam antea olim predecessores eorum et Caldei sepius obsederunt et destruxerunt, multum sunt gauisi, †suspicantes in ea regem Iudeorum natum inuenire. Sed de tam forti valido inopinato et inprouiso ipsorum introitu Herodes et vniuersa ciuitas est turbata et commota. Nam tantus erat eorum exercitus expedicio et comitatus quod eos [intus] ciuitas capere non poterat, sed pro maiori parte extra ciuitatem manserunt et eam quasi obsidione circumuallauerunt et totaliter circumdederunt. Vnde inter alia ait Ysaias: Fortitudo gencium ven[eri]t tibi, inundacio camelorum operiet te, dromedarij Madian et Effa. Et omnes de Saba venient aurum et thus deferentes et laudem domino annunciantes. Omne pecus Cedar †congregabitur et arietes Nabaioth minis[f. 20r]trabunt tibi (Ysaie sexagesimo capitulo).

Vnde [est] sciendum quod, prout est supradictum, ipsi tres Reges omnem expedicionem †vel multitudinem† pecorum diuersorum prout in partibus illis est consuetudinis preire fecerunt. Et de generibus arietum Nab[a]ioth in partibus illis adhuc communiter permanserunt. Et sunt magni arietes †in posterioribus corpus nimis† habent in cauda et quasi nichil vel parum in corpore habent. Et latitudo ipsius caude †extendit iuxta latitudinem coxarum, et longitudo vltra medietatem crur[i]um posteriorum. Et aliquando reperitur talis aries qui, cum est excoriatus, [quod] cauda plus ponderat

† suspicantes] sperantes. † congregabitur] congregabitur tibi. † vel multitudinem] suam in multitudine. † in ... nimis] qui omnem pingwedinem quam alij arietes in posterioribus corporis intus habent hanc pinguedinem ipsi arietes Nabaioth. † extendit] extendit se.

more þan þat oþir partie of the body or half the body at þe leest. And þere be meny of hem, [f. 235r] goyng in flokkis wild in wodys, grete & fatte, havyng grete hornys, and strong, and herid as geete, and they be take with houndis and with lybardis. And as they be huntyd, they renne wiþ þe wynd and be herd ferre. And whan they be take in huntyng, they kun not defend hemself ne stere, althogh they be strong.

And whan thes thre Kyngis with her meyne were entrid Ierusalem, Herode was than ther present, ordeynid of Cesar and the Romayns kyng of Iewys, and he was in age. And the Kyngis in þe cite þan bysily enquerid and askid of þe b[irth]e of this kyng, wherof seith þe euangliste, *Cum natus esset Ihesus in Bedleem*. And wh[y] that þes Kynges come first into Ierusalem rathir than into Bedlem in diuers maners is declarid in bokys. O cause was that Herowde and the cite of her comyng was trowblyd for they sawe the thre Kynges and her cumpanye be of þe Est and of Caldee which of the suffraunce of God þat cite of old tyme had bysegid and distroyed. Also, that thes .iij. Kyngis the kyng of Iewys so newly borne soghtyn of so ferre cuntrees of the Este and Caldee and come to worship hym. And for

10 birthe] blisse L. 11 why] whan L.

quam reliqua pars corporis vel medietas eius. Et ex istorum arietum genere deuenerunt arietes siluestres, qui sunt multum magni et pingues et fortes, habentes magna cornua grossa et pilos vt capriolus, et in maximis turmis insimul incedunt. Et venantur et capiuntur cum canibus et leopardis. Et dum venantur, †currunt per ventum et† per maximum spacium audiuntur. Sed dum a canibus et leopardis t[en]entur, penitus se nil mouent vel defendunt, licet multum sint fortes. Sed vt ad propositum redeatur.

In diebus illis cum itaque hij tres Reges, vt dictum est, cum eorum exercitu Iherusalem intrauerunt, tunc Herodes erat ibidem presens Ierosolimis; et erat ibidem a Cesare et Romanis rex I[ude]e constitutus, et etate annosus. Extunc hij Reges de Iudeorum nuper nato rege ab omnibus in ciuitate querebant et interogabant, vnde ait euangelista: Cum natus esset Ihesus in Bethleem. ... [f. 20v] De hoc quare tres Reges prius in Iherusalem quam in Bethleem venerunt multi libri diuersimode declarant et exponunt; quamplurime cause scripte sunt, de quibus per singula longum esset narrare. Inter ceteras causas erat vna, quod Herodes et ciuitas propter introitum ipsorum trium [Regum] fuit turbata, quia videbant ipsos reges esse et eorum exercitum de [oriente] et Caldea †quia ex permissione diuina ipsam ciuitatem ab antiquo sepius et terram Iudeam obsiderant et destruxerant et †eos reges fuerant persecuti. Item quod hij regem Iudeorum nuper nouiter et breuiter natum ex remotissimis terris et longinquissimis partibus orientis et Caldee ad [ad]orandum peruenerunt; et quia

† currunt per ventum et] et currunt per ventum. † quia] qui. † eos] eius.

Herowd was a myscreaunt, dredyng þerfor Her[owd] & his Iewes hym to be put out of his kyngdom. But moost cause to confusion of þe Iewis, which wer ful of þe spirit of prophecie, for they knew not hym whan he was presently born among hem of whom þei had byfor so mych sayde and prophecied. And þei [f. 235[v]] despisid Christe born whom they prophecied so long tyme byforn, and not only prophecied hym to be born, but shewid þe place also to Herode wher he shold be born – that her forknowyng to hem shold stonde in witnesse of dampnacion, and to vs in help of byleve.

And whan þes Kynges, redily enfourmyd by the doctours and scribis of the Iewys and by Herode, and her peple were partyd out of Ierusalem, than the sterre, as it was wont, into Bedlem went byfor hem, which is of Ierusalem two myle of þat cuntre. And in the same wey they went wher þe shipardis wer<e> to whom the aungels wiþ a multitude of heuynly knyght-

1 Herowd] her L.   10 peple] *first* p *perhaps corrected from* f.

Herodes [f. 21[r]] esset proselitus et alienigena, a Cesare et Romanis rex Iudee constitutus, de eius expulsu Herodes et Iudei timuerunt, de eorum vero rege nouiter nuper nato, quem alij reges adorare venerunt, non curauerunt. Sed maior causa fuit quod ipsi tres Reges amissa stella ex prouidencia diuina Iherusalem ex improuiso coacti moram fecerunt, quia Iherusalem fuit ciuitas regalis, et reges Iude actu semper in ea habitauerunt, et doctores in lege et scribe propheticis scripturis semper specialiter in ea presentes fuerunt; et ipsi Iudei et scribe, natiuitatem domini et eius natiuitatis locum prescientes, nullam deinceps possent pretendere vel habere excusacionem ad eorum perfidiam ab omnibus detestandam et fidem gencium r[obor]andam. Nam Gregorius in omelia sic ait: Iudeos profecto bene Ysaac cum Iacob filium suum benediceret presignauit. Qui, caligans oculis et prophetizans, in presenti filium non vidit, cui tamen imposterum multa preuidit. Quia nimirum Iudei prophecie spiritu erant pleni, †sed quia eum de quo in futuro multa predixerunt tunc in presenti positum non cognouerunt. Nam Christum natum despexerunt quem [longe] ante nasciturum presciuerunt. Et non solum quod nasceretur presciuerunt, sed eciam locum vbi nasceretur Herodi demonstrauerunt, vt ipsis eorum sciencia fieret in testimonium dampnacionis, et nobis in adiutorium credulitatis. Sed vt ad propositum redeatur.

Cvm itaque tres Reges de loco natiuitatis domini regis Iudeorum nuper nati per Herodem et scribas et doctores Iudeorum plenius essent informati, et cum eorum [f. 21[v]] excercitu et expedicione ab Herode et Iherusalem recessissent et ciuitatem essent egressi, †et extunc† more solito et priori iterum eis stella apparuit et eos sicut prius in Bethleem antecessit, que distat a Iherusalem ad duo parua miliaria illius patrie. Et in ipso itinere iuxta eundem locum pastorum quibus angelus domini cum multitudine celestis

† sed] sed ceci.   † et extunc] extunc.

hood apperid, shewyng to hem Cristis natiuyte. And the shippardis, whan þei saw the sterre, come rennyng and seyd that in such a light and brightnes an aungel apperid to hem denouncyng Cristis natiuite, and all þei told there that they h[ad] herd and seyn by the seyng of that aungell. And the thre Kyngis wiþ good hertis herd and toke her wordis, and all her ostis, and miche reioycid hem in the wordis of þe shephardis, noght dowtyng þan of þe light of þe sterre ne of þe voys that was herd þerin. And some bokys wole that the voys herd in þe sterre was the voys of tho aungel which shewid to the shipardis Cristis natiuite and the same aungell also which precedid the childrin of Israel in the fyry clowde aftir her deliueraunce out of Egypt. And þe same sterre so went alwey byfor the thre gloriouse Kynges, and whan the thre Kyngis and þe shepherdis spak thus togidir, euere þe sterre more and more shone in clernes & bright`nes´. [f. 236^{r}]

And whan thes thre glorious Kyngis with all her peple fro the shipherdis were partid and knewe that they were ny the citee of Bethlem, than they arayed hem in regall v<esti>mentis and ornamentis as hem thoght most honest and nobly ordeynid hem to offre to the kyng born of Iewis. And [aye]n the sterre went byfor hem, and þe more they neighid to Bedlem, so

4 had] hard L. 18 ayen] than L

milicie in magna claritate natiuitatem domini annunciabat †et omnino† cum eorum exercitu transierunt. Et ipsi pastores cum vidissent stellam statim accurrerunt et dixerunt quod in tali fulgore et claritate ipsis angelus apparuit et eis natiuitatem domini annunciauit; et omnia que eis ab angelo dicta fuerunt et que secundum dictum eiusdem †angeli viderunt et audierunt et acta fuerunt per omnia narrauerunt. Que ipsi Reges et eorum exercitus libentissime et auide audierunt et verba diligenter considerauerunt; et ex verbis †in testimonio pastorum multum sunt gauisi, et de †illuminacione stelle et voce ex ea audita iam penitus nil hesitabant. Volunt enim quidam libri in oriente quod vox ex stella audita fuit eciam vox angeli qui eciam pastoribus et ipsis Regibus natiuitatem domini nunciauit. Et dicunt eciam †modo in oriente conuersi quod creditur inter Iudeos quod angelus qui filios I[srael] post egressionem de Egipto cum columpna ignis precessit, quod idem angelus cuius vox ex stella audiebatur fuit; et $^{+}$ †stella ipsos tres Reges antecessit, nam cum ipsi tres Reges itaque cum pastoribus loquerentur, stella magis ac magis in sua claritate fulgebat. ... [f. 22^{r}]

Cvm itaque hij tres Reges cum comitatu eorum a pastoribus datis muneribus eis recessissent et iuxta Bethleem se esse cognouissent, extunc regalibus vestimentis [f. 22^{v}] et aliis ornamentis prout nobilius et honestius poterant se diligenter preparabant. Et iterum eos stella precedebat; et quanto magis Bethleem appropinquabant, tanto

† et omnino] iuxta hos pastores ijdem tres Reges. † angeli] in Bethleem. † in] et. † illluminacione] allocucione. † modo] Iudei. † stella] cum stella.

myche þe more þe sterre in his vertu shone. And so thes thre [Kynges] went at the our of prime out of Ierusalem, and at vndryn they come to Bedlem. And they passid by the strete which was clepid *Platea Cooperta*, atte the ende of which strete was a cote in whiche was wont to be sold brede, wher was the cave in which Crist was bore. And anon þan the sterre stood still and vnmevable. And withyn a litil tyme the sterre descendid with so mych light so þat þe cave and all þat were þerin were full of light. And þan þe sterre anon ascendid ayen into his place, stondyng than still, but the light of hym left in the cave; wherof seith the euanglist, *Et intrantes domum inuenerunt puerum cum Maria matre eius, inuenerunt puerum cum Maria matre eius, [et procidentes adorauerunt eum], et apertis thesauris suis optulerunt ei munera – aurum, thus, et mirram.*

And by the offring of the yeftis of thes three Kyngis in o God and Lord is shewyd his diuine mageste, his ryall power, and his humaigne mortalite. The encense perteynith to sacrifise, the gold to tribute, and the mirre to sepulture of dede. And all these the holy faith may not leue to offre whil he byleuith the same o verrey God and verrey man. [f. 236[v]]

1 Kynges] *om.* L. 11 et ... eum] *om.* L.

magis stella in sua virtute fulgebat. Et sic eadem die quando hij tres Reges a Iherusalem hora prima recedebant, extunc in Bethleem hora quasi sexta perueniebant. Et per plateam de qua supradictum est que ibi platea cooperta dicebatur transierunt, in cuius fine erat tugurrium in quo panes vendebantur, †in qua spelunca† Christus fuit natus. Et statim super aream que erat ante tugurrium, in qua panes vendebantur, stella stetit immobilis, et infra muros lapideos et fictiles qui adhuc ibidem ab antiquo permanserunt per modicum interuallum stella cum tali et tanta claritate et fulgore se dimisit vel dimersit quod omnia in tigurrio et spelunca fuerunt illuminata. Et iterum mox in aerem sursum ascendit et supra locum immobilis stetit. Sed splendor eius in spelunca †remansit, prout ait euangelista: Et intrantes domum inuenerunt puerum cum Maria matre eius. Et procidentes adorauerunt eum. Et apertis thesauris suis optulerunt ei munera, aurum thus et mirram. ... [f. 23[r]]

Fulgencius inter alia in suo narrat sermone quod per istorum trium Regum munera in vno eodemque Christo diuina maiestas et regia potestas et humana mortalitas designantur et intimantur. Thus pertinet ad sacrificium, aurum ad tributum, mirra ad sepulcrum et ad sepul[tura]m mortuorum. Et omnia hec sancta fides offerre non desinit dum vnum eundemque verum †deum verumque hominem credit. Et ipse dominus qui sibi in veteri testamento primicias offerri precepit, idem dominus homo natus primicias gencium suo cultui dedicauit.

† in qua spelunca] et spelunca in qua. † remansit] remansit et. † deum] deum verum regem.

And þat day that the .iij. Kyngis in Bedleem soght our Lord to worship & to offre to hym, was Ihesus in manhode a child in the age of .xiij. dayes, and in persone of a man as aftir his age he was sumwhat fatte, and with pore clothis vp to þe armys wrappid, lying in hey in the cracche. And Marie þe modir of hym was of persone sumwhat flesshy and yn a pore mantel of plunket helyd, and she held it closyng with her left honde, and her heed saf the visaige was al lappid with a lynnyn clothe, and she sate on the cracche, holdyng wiþ þe right honde the hede vp of her child. And whan þes .iij. Kyngis þe erþe byfor the cracche and the hondis of the child deuoutly and mekely had kyssid and her yeftis to Ihesu deuoutly had offryd, þo yeftes reuerently they leide byside þe heed of þe child and the knees of the modir deuoutely into þe cracche.

And Melchior, kyng of Arabum and Nubye, which offrid gold wiþ the goldyn appil to our Lord was leste of hem in persone; Balthasar, which offrid to our Lord encence, kyng of Godolye and Saba, was mene yn persone; and Iaspar, kyng of Thars and of the yle of Egrisculle, which offrid to our Lord myrre, was in persone moost of hem, an Ethiope and blak, wherof seith the prophete, *Coram illo procident Ethiopes et inimici eius terram lingent; venient ad te qui detrahebant tibi, et adorabunt vestigia pedum tuorum.* And tho thre Kynges and her peple as in respecte

Ipso die quo ita tres Reges in Bethleem dominum quesierunt et adorauerunt et sibi munera optulerunt, erat Ihesus in humanitate infantulus in etate .xiij. dierum. Et in humana persona secundum suam etatem erat aliquantulum pinguis, et pauperculis pannis vsque ad brachia in presepe et feno iacuit inuolutus. Et Maria mater eius, prout in aliis et pluribus exemplis et libris inuenitur, erat persona carnosa et aliquantulum fusca. Et in conspectu ipsorum Regum palleo †blanco vel albo† et paupercul[o] fuit cooperta, quod clausum ante se tenebat manu sinistra, et eius caput excepta facie panno lineo fuit totaliter circumuolutum. Et supra presepe sedebat, et manu dextera caput infantuli + leuabat. Et postquam ipsi Reges terram ante presepe [f. 23v] et manus infantuli humiliter fuerant osculati et munera sua infantulo Ihesu deuote et reuerenter optulerant, ipsa munera iuxta caput infantuli et genua sue matris in presepe deuote posuerunt. Et quid de ipsis muneribus postmodum factum fuerat inferius audietur.

Erat autem Melchior rex Arabum et Nubie qui domino aurum optulit tunc minor in persona; et Baltasar rex G[o]dolie et Saba qui domino thus optulit erat in persona mediocris; et Iaspar rex Tharsis et insule Egrisculle qui domino mirram optulit erat in persona maior, et Ethiops niger, de quo nullum dubium sit. Nam inter alia eciam ait propheta: Coram illo procident Ethiopes et inimici eius terram lingent. Venient ad te qui detrahebant tibi, et adorabunt vestigia pedum tuorum. Erant autem hij tres Reges et eorum exercitus secundum

† blanco vel albo] blaueo.

of othir peple in stature nere but mene, so that þe peple þan merveillid therof. And that was the more witnesse þat they and her peple come [f. 237^{r}] fr<om f>er<re> of the est cuntre. For the more nerre þe peple be bore toward þe risyng of þe sonne, so myche are they the more feble, tendrer, and lytill. But the herbis in that cuntre be more hotter and beter, and all manere spices and baumes noblere and better, and serpentis of þat cuntre and such wormys more perilous, venimous, and gretter, and all bestis and fowlis bothe wild and tame more in quantite. And pilgrymes goyng into that cuntre seyn that at þe tyme of the sonnerisyng ther in that cuntre of þo .iij. Kyngis the sonne risith with so passyng noyse that, but they were wont þerto and the sowne costoumable to hem, þat they might not suffre it. And beyend tho cuntres the peple be doumbe for the grete noyse of the firmament and they bye, selle, and worke þere by signes for defaute of heryng. And they be ther redy and riche marchauntis, and they come seld on this half into Ynde, Surye, or Egipt.

And vndirstondith that thes .iij. Kynges out of her kyngdomes broght with hem ricchest and noblest iewels, ornementis, and yeftis to offre to our Lord — that is to sey, all the iewels and ornamentis which Alisaundre

3 *The top half of these letters is lost.*

staturam hominum tunc temporis respectu reliquorum in personis et statura multum pusilli, ita quod omnis mirabatur populus. Et hoc testimonium ipsis adhib[ui]t de remotissimis et longinquissimis partibus orientis et finibus terre illuc peruenisse. Nam quanto magis est versus ortum solis propinquum, tanto minores debiliores ac teneriores nascuntur homines, †et multum parui†. Sed herbe sunt calidiores et meliores, et aromata [nobiliora meliora] et rariora, et serpentes et huiusmodi vermes periculosi sunt venenosiores et grossiores, et omnia †animalia volatilia siluestria et domestica sunt maiora. Nam dicunt Indi et alij homines qui de partibus [f. 24^{r}] orientis in Iherusalem et alias circa partes causa peregrinacionis vel mercimoniorum vel delectacionis quotidie et frequenter perueniunt quod in partibus et regnis istorum trium Regum in ortu diei et aurora solis cum tali et tanto strepitu ac †frangore et horribilissimo sonitu sol oriri audiatur quod, nisi sonitus esset consuetus, nullus posset tolerare. Et vltra illas terras et partes homines multum parui nascuntur qui pre sonitu firmamenti surdi effecti sunt, et per signa emunt et vend[unt] ac operantur. Et sunt homines in temporalibus multum astuti et ditissimi mercatores. Et tales homines et quamplures alij homines rari ad partes reg[ni] Indie Sirie et Egipti frequenter perueniunt (de quibus singulariter longum esset narrare). Sed vt ad propositum redeatur.

Et sciendum est (prout omnia sunt supradicta) quod hij tres Reges de regnis eorum quamplurima ditissima et nobilissima munera et ornamenta more regali ad offerendum domino secum sumpserunt, videlicet omnia ornamenta que Alexander

† et multum parui] *om.* † animalia] animalia et. † frangore] fragore.

Macedo Philippi left in Ynde, Caldee, and Perce, & also all the ornamentis which the qwene Saba had in the temple Salamon of vessell and of þe kyngis hous in Ierusalem whan hit was by the Caldees & Perces distroyed, which were than translate and broght into her londe, and meny othir ornamentis of gold, syluer, gemmys, margarites, & precious stonys [f. 237v] which the thre Kyngis broght with hem < ... offre . t>o our Lord. But whan they fond þe child Ihesu lying in the cracche in so pore aray, as the shepherdis had told hem byfor, and þat the sterre abode bytwene þe wallis of þe cave so þat hem þoght they stood as in a fire brennyng for þe grete light of þe sterre, than the kyngis, lightyng of her dromedaries and hors, were smyte wiþ so myche fere and astonyed, of all her riche and noble ornamentis & iewels which þei had broght with hem to offre euery Kyng of his tresour couth not fynd ne take in honde but only that fil ferst to her hond. That is to sey, Melchior, kyng of Nubye and Arabum, toke only wiþ hym to offre .xxx. pens of gold and a litil apple of gold þat was as mych as might be hold esily withyn the hond of þe child, which he deuoutly offrid. Whom folowyng Balthazar, kyng of Godolye and Saba, offrid only encense, as hit come to his hondis. And þan Iaspar with wepyng chere offrid mirre. And in so miche drede were þes thre Kyngis and

6 *The loss corresponds to that on the recto.*

[Macedo Philippi] in I[ndi]a Caldea et Perside reliquit, et omnia ornamenta que regina Saba in templo †Salamonis vasa concupiscibilia de domo regis et de templo domini in Iherusalem que per Caldeos et Persas in destruccione Iherusalem in terram eorum fuerunt portata et translata, et quamplurima alia ornamenta in auro et argento ac gemmis et margaritis preciosis que hij tres Reges de terris et regnis eorum ad offerendum domino secum sumpserunt et magnifice detulerunt. Sed cum infantulum Ihesum in presepe et feno positum [f. 24v] pauperime inuenerunt, prout ipsis pastores in via retulerunt, et, vt dictum est, quod stella itaque inter parietes ante speluncam qua Christus natus fuit se dimisit quod in [tu]gurrio et spelunca pre splendore et fulgore steterunt quasi in camino ignis, extunc hij tres Reges, de dromedariis et equis eorum multimode ornatis descendentes, tanto timore et tremore fuerunt perteriti et concussi, quod de omnibus ditissimis et nobilissimis ornamentis que secum ad offerendum domino detulerunt ex thesauris tunc apertis nichil [nisi] quod vnicuique primo ad manus eius deuenit recepit; videlicet Melchior rex Nubie et Arabum sumpsit triginta denarios aureos et paruum pomum aureum quod manu concludi †potuit infantulo Ihesu deuote optulit; quem sequens Baltasar rex Godolie et Saba thus optulit sicut ad manus eius deuenit; et deinde Iaspar rex Tharsis et insule Egrisculle [optulit] mirram lacrimose. Et tanto tremore erant hij tres Reges perteriti et tam deuoti et

† Salamonis] Salamonis optulit et. † potuit] potuit et.

astonyd and brennyng in deuocion of her offryng that they conciderid nothing to the wordis of Marie savyng þat she to euery Kyng in his offryng bowyng mekely with her hede she seyd humbly, '*Deo gracias*'.

And the appil which Melchior wiþ þe .xxx. pens offrid was sometyme Kyng Alisaundris the Grete, and it was no more in quantite but as hit might al be closyd in an honde. And it bytokenyd al þe world, which of so smale parcelles the tribute of all the provinces of the world was broght to his honde. And [f. 238^{r}] he held it evyn in his honde, as al þe world was includyd in his power. And this appil with othre riche ornamentis left in Ynde. And why that Melchior offrid þe apple some clerkis discusse. For as rowndenesse of þe round apple hath non ende ne bygynnyng but includith þe spere of all the world, so his power the vniuersal hight of hevene and the deppest of hell compacith al the endis of the world. Also some bokys seyn that þe gold offrid was the subleuacion of þe pouerte of Marie and of her child Ihesu. But thogh almighty God le[te] put hym in freelte of manhode and for vs be born pore ȝet he nedid noght of þe ȝeftis of þe Kyngis to helpyng of his pouerte, *quia ipse dixit et facta sunt.* For

15 lete] left L.

ardentes in oblacione effecti quod in omnibus verbis que tunc beata virgo Maria protulerat quasi nichil considerabant sed quod ad vnumquemque Regem offerentem inclinato capite dixit humiliter, Deo gracias.

Pomum autem aureum quod Melchior rex cum triginta denariis optulit quondam [fuit] Alexandri magni, et non fuit maioris quantitatis quam totaliter manu concludi potuit. Mundum significa[ui]t, quod ex minimis particulis auri omnium tributorum mundi et omnium prouinciarum †compleri fecit; et ipsum semper in manu portauit, [f. 25^{r}] velut sua potencia totum mundum in sua manu conclusit. Et ipsum pomum in India cum aliis ditissimis ornamentis permansit quando de paradiso terrestri reuersus fuit. Horum trium Regum munerum interpretacio et significacio et exposicio multis libris est diuersimode exposita per diuersos doctores et declarata, sed quare Melchior rex pomum aureum optulit †discussum ab aliquibus sic reperitur. Nam ipsius pomi rotundi rotunditas immensa significat quod sicut aliquo[d] rotundum absque principio et sine fine speram mundi concludit, sic vniuersalem altitudinem celi et nouissima inferni sue potencie volubilitate et velocitate circuit fines terre†. ... Iterum de auro thure et mirra que ipsi tres Reges domino optulerunt plures libri diuersimode loquntur; nam aliqui libri continent quod aurum oblatum fuisset ad Marie et infantuli inopiam †subleuandam. ... [f. 25^{v}]

Licet omnipotens dominus in nostra f[ragili]tate et humanitate vt exinaniuit semetipsum pauper propter nos fuerat natus, tamen hiis omnibus trium Regum muneribus non indiguit ad aliquam inopiam subleuandam, quia ipse dixit et omnia facta sunt. Nam

† compleri] conflare. † discussum ... terre] *archetypal corruption.* † subleuandam] subleuandam et thus propter fetorem stabuli et mirra ad vermes infantuli depellendos.

the appil which was by Alisaundre mightly ordeynid and so prowdly made, whil Melchior offrid hit to the child Ihesu, anon in þe same moment hit turnyd to poudre and to noght.

And aftir þat þes thre Kynges with offryng of her yeftis had wurshipid Ihesu þe child, and in the tyme of all her comyng fro so ferre contres of þe Este by al her way her peple and her bestis into the tyme of her comyng to offre to þe child kept hem fastyng without mete, drink, or slepe, than aftir tyme of her offryng aftir þe kynd of manhede they toke her reste of slepyng. And all þat night folowyng and a day in Bedlem þei refresshid and confortid hem, and all the peple there þe cause of her so ferre comyng from her londis by ledyng of the [f. 238v] sterre so merveillously mekely they declarid and expownyd, that þe more confusion to þe mysbyleve of þe Iewis and more solace of byleve to alle þe peple shold arise. And þan, as þe gospell seith, *Et responso accepto in sompnis ne redirent ad Herodem, per aliam viam reuersi sunt in regionem suam.* And þan the sterre which byfor in her comyng ledde and went byfor hem fro þat tyme apperid to hem no more, but they turnyd homward to her kyngdomes & by the wey toke her herborowyng on nyght. And thes .iij. Kynges which of her ferre londis and kyngdomis so ferre beyng atwynne so merveillously and sodenly mettyn togidir so they to her londis & kyngdomys togidir went ayen. And

pomum aureum oblatum per Alexandrum tam potenter congregatum et arroganter conflatum dum ipsum Melchior infantulo Ihesu optulit, extunc in momento statim fuit in puluerem et fauillam contritum et ad nichilum redactum. ... [f. 26r]

Postquam vero ipsi tres Reges dominum adorassent et sibi munera optulissent et omnia ad que de oriente dominum quesiuissent gloriose perfecissent, extunc †satis ipsi Reges et eorum exercitus equi et animalia et alia eorum + iumenta que ibidem ex remotis et longinquissimis finibus terre et orientis per omnem viam absque aliquo cibo potu et pabulo manserunt, extunc more suo et mortalium †hominum dormire ceperunt, et per totam illam diem in Bethleem et aliis circa locis quiet[i] et solacio se [de]derunt; et omnibus causam quare de finibus terre et de extremis mundi partibus stella eos miraculose duxerit humiliter dixerunt et exposuerunt, vt Iudeis maior confusio et gentilibus maius credulitatis exinde solacium orietur. Iterum prout ait euangelium: Et accepto in sompnis responso ne ad Herodem redirent, per aliam viam reuersi sunt in †terram suam. Et extunc stella que eos prius precedebat vltra non apparuit; sed reuertentes ad terras et regna sua humano more hospicia die ac nocte in via capiebant. Et ipsi tres Reges qui ex tribus viis et longinquissimis suis terris et regnis remotissime distantibus miraculose exinopinato conuenerunt, tunc in vnum ad terras et ad regna sua simul redierunt. Et

† satis] statim. † hominum] hominum esurire et sitire et. † terram] regionem.

by all þe londis, regions, & provinces by which Duk Olofernes with all his ostis & cariage from þe Este and Chalde went into Ynde, by the same londis the thre Kyngis wiþ alle her ostis and ordenance went, so that the peples of the londis and regions by which þei passid by the hering of her passage went Oloferne þat tyme to have passid ayen by that way, and in all citees, townes, and placis they were of all peple benigly receyvid. And al þat they had seyn, done, and had happid hem seth þe tyme of the comyng of hem from her londis they prechid and shewid mekely to the peple, and in euery place as kynges worshipfully were receyvid, so that her mekenes, vertew, and good fame in all þe contres and provinces of the Iewys was neuere seth foryeten. And of all her vitailes which they toke with [f. 239[r]] hem in her londis at her comyng out for hem and for her peple and her bestis into the tyme of her comyng home ayen to the hill of Vaus & to her londis and kyngdomys had they no failling ne defaute but hole and sound wiþ all her peple and ordynaunce safly come home. Bvt her iourne which þei in the goyng outward thurgh lede of þe gloriouse sterre they perfourmyd in .xiij. dayes in her passage homward ayen with grete travaill by leders and gydes they vnnethe perfourmyd in twy yeer, that þei and all oþir peple shold vndirstonde and knowe the difference bytwene Goddis wor<ch>yng and mannys.

per omnes terras ac regiones et prouincias per quas olim Olofernes cum suo exercitu et expedicione ab oriente et Caldea transijt et in †I[ndi]am peruenit, per has terras et [f. 26[v]] vias ipsi tres Reges cum eorum comitatu et diuersa expedicione ex improuiso transierunt, quod omnes homines parcium illarum et regionum secundum auditum antiquum et relatum putabant Olefernem iterato pertransire, et ab omnibus villis et ciuitatibus et ab vniuersis populis benignissime sunt recepti. In quibus omnia que viderant egerant et audierant et que ipsis acc[i]derant post egressionem terrarum suarum omnibus humiliter predicabant. Et ad quecumque loca peruenerunt †ab omnibus populis more regio benigniter et benefici recepti† fuerunt. Vnde eorum virtutes humilitas et meritorum fama a Iudeis in omnibus †ipsorum terris et prouincijs postmodum nunquam potuit aboleri. Et de omnibus cibariis et necessariis que de terris et regnis suis secum sumpser[a]nt, tam ipsis quam eorum exercitu[i] †eciam eorum equis animalibus et iumentis quousque ad predictum montem Vaus et ad terras et regna sua perue[ne]runt penitus nil defecit, sed sani et incolumes cum omnibus suis ad propria sunt reuersi. Sed in ipsa via quam de tribus regnis eorum in tresdecim diebus stella duce perfecerunt, per biennium in redditu per †ductores interpretes laboriose permanserunt, vt ipsi [+] et alij h[omine]s scirent distanciam inter operacionem diuinam et humanam.

† Indiam] Iudeam. † ab omnibus ... benigniter et benefici recepti] omnibus ... benigni et benefici. † ipsorum] illis. † eciam] quam. † ductores] ductores et per.

But Herode and þe eldremen and þe scribis by mich way of her iournes folowid hem and of <e>nvie many of Tharcenses, which mych prechid herof, they distroyed and her shippis and all the lond vndur his power by which þei made passage he distroyed. And Herode & þe seniours and þe scrybes and Iewes se[w]id thus thes thre Kyngis for they herd telle of her merveillouse passage by all londis by night & by day wiþ so mich clernesse of light, and specially of the sterre that was to hem ledere so wondurfully whil they perfourmyd her iourne in .xiij. dayes, and how þei with so mych trauaille aftir the lesyng of þe sight of þe sterre by leders and gydes they fulfillid her iourne homward. For all þe peple by whos cuntres the thre Kyngis had passid outward with her oostis [f. 239v] couthe not suffise to telle with how mich mervaille night and day the .iij. Kyngis passyd þurgh her regions and londis.

And to voyde vttirly þe inexcusable envy and mysbyleve of þe Iewes, and the helpyng and techyng of the feiþ of all peple, almighty God which in all his werkys euere is merveillous and in his mageste gloriouse, willyng þe knowyng of þe difference bytwene þe workyng of God and of man in ledyng the .iij. Kynges from her cuntrees without lettyng and all her peple

5 sewid] seid L.

Iterum Herodes et seniores et scribe ipsos per multam viam fuerunt secuti †per vniuersam terram per quam transierunt. Et quia Tharsens[e]s predicare specialiter† Cilicie reperit post ipsos declinare et eorum virtutes ac merita [f. 27r] declarare, ipsis Tharsensibus ex inuidia culpam imponit quod ipsos fluuium Siler transire permiserunt, eorum naues combussit, et totam terram que sub eius fuit potestate per quam transierant multum destruxit. Iterum Herodes [seniores] et scribe et Iudei ipsos Reges fuerunt secuti quia ab omnibus audierant quod ipsi tam miraculose per omnes terras die ac nocte cum magna claritate et luce et specialiter stella duce miraculose in .xiij. die[bu]s absque aliquo impedimento transierunt, et quam laboriose stella amissa per ductores et interpretes recesserunt. Nam omnes gentiles et gentes per quarum terras ciuitates et loca ipsi Reges et eorum exercitus in exitu transierunt cum maxima admiracione plene narrare non sufficiebant quam miraculose die ac nocte per eos et eorum terras et loca [et] regione[s] trans[iu]issent. ... [f. 27v]

Ad tollendum ergo omne dubium in premissis et ad extirpandum radicitus inexcusabilem Iudeorum inuidiam et perfidiam et ad erudiendum gencium ignoranciam et eorum infirmitatem adiuuandam et nostram fidem roborandam, omnipotens deus, qui semper est mirabilis in sanctis [suis] et [in] sua maiestate gloriosus, †omnibus scire voluit que qualis et quanta esset distancia inter operacionem diuinam et †operacionem humanam. Nam †ipsi tres Reges cum omni ipsorum exercitu expedicione

† per ... specialiter] et universam terram per quam transierunt et specialiter Tharsenses. † omnibus] *archetypal corruption.* † operacionem] omnem operacionem magicam vel. † ipsi] ipsos.

and bestis without mete or drynk to Bedlem in .xiij. dayes, which way þei couthe vnnethe homward perfourme with trauaill yn two ȝeer. For if byfor all fel to hem in prosperite in her wey, aftirward with trauail faylid hem with aduersite. But he wold his name, þat byfor his natyuite in Ynde was vnknowyn, among alle peple aftir fro the rysing of þe sonne into the west shold be worshipid and praysid.

And whan thes .iij. Kynges with her peple and ordonances with grete trauaill to the hill of Vaus aftir þe two yeer were come, than they lete make a chapell in worship of þe kyng of Iewys born which they had so soght and wiþ her ȝeftis so worshipid, and with all ornementis deuoutly storid, and þer in euery ȝeer with othir princes and kynges in that chapell in worshipyng of that child so born had her metyng, <an>d in the toun which was vndur þe hill o<f he>r long travaill restyn. And ther they chosyn þe place of her sepulture by on acorde. And a litil tyme aftir the Kyngis & princis of all þe londis and kyngdomes [f. 240r] ny about hem and her peple in that chapell þere hem mettyn and hem in her homecomyng as was conuenyent receyvid, and of her ayencomyng mych ioying, heryng what

5 fro] r *perhaps altered from* o L.

et comitatu absque cibo potu [et] pabulo in Bethleem in .xiij. diebus absque [f. 28r] aliquo impedimento de oriente et regnis eorum miraculose cum stella potestate et operacione diuina perduxit, per quam viam in biennio laboriose vix poterant perficere per interpretes et ductores operacione humana et ad propria redire et peruenire. Nam si aliqua †res prius in viis [pro]speris affuisset, eciam in viis eorum laboriosi[s] et aduersis postmodum non defuisset. Sed omnipotens deus hoc natiuitatis sue misterium semper notum voluit esse populis vniuersis, quod nomen suum gloriosum, quod prius vsque ad natiuitatem suam tantummodo in †I[ndi]a latitabat, ipsum omnes gentes tribus et populi ab ortu solis vsque ad occasum vnanimiter collaudarent. Sed vt ad propositum redeatur.

Postquam vero ipsi tres Reges cum exercitibus et expedicionibus eorum (vt dictum est) cum maximis laboribus per ductores et interpretes ad montem Vaus victorialem post biennium peruenerunt, extunc capellam in honore regis Iudeorum nati quem itaque quesierunt et ei munera optulerunt laboriosissime et ditissime fieri fecerunt et multimode more regio ornauerunt. Et in oppido quod subtus montem situm fuerat a laboribus itineris quieuerunt; et ibidem locum eorum sepulture concorditer elegerunt, et deinde singulis annis cum aliis eorum regibus et principibus ibidem †conuenerunt condixerunt et firmiter promiserunt.

Vnde post modicum tempus omnium terrarum et regnorum eorum principes nobiles et honorati ac vniuersi populi ipsis [ibidem] obuiauerunt et ad ipsos [f. 28v] vnaminiter confluxerunt et ipsos prout decuit solempnissime receperunt. Et de aduentu eorum multum gratulantes, et audientes que

† res] ars. † India] Iudea. † conuenerunt] convenire.

thingis God had wroght for hem, with drede and also love merveilyng, and in more wurship, drede, and love havyng hem for þe worchyng of God for hem. And so thes thre Kynges, yevyng thonkynges to God, her testamentis and willis disposyd, eche of hem with al hys to his owne londe in hele and ioy were come home, wiþ her bodyes for a tyme and noght her hertis disseuerid. And to all peple al þat they had seyn and done and had fallyn to hem humbly they prechid and shewid, and in all her londis and templis the fourme of the child and of þe sterre and þe signe of þe crosse above as þei had byfor sight þerof they dede grave and peynt, wherof meny of þe peple ther, levyng her ydols and errours, worshipid the child to whom the thre Kyngis had offrid deuoutly with yeftis. And that chapell þat þei had made on þe hill of Vaus peple of diuers nacions from ferre come to visite and to worship. For aftir þat þe .iij. Kyngis were come home they wax more meke & devowte þan eny othir, and nacions of all regions and londis in the Est suffisid not to telle þan of her vertu, humilite, and deuocioun. And so in laudable lyf and honneste conuersacion þei bode vnto the assension of our Lord and into the comyng of Seynt Thomas the Apostle.

And aftir the departyng of the .iij. Kyngges [f. 240v] from Bedlem whan þei had offrid her ʒeftis to our Lord, than our Lady with our Lord her child Ihesu byleft in that cave ther he was borne. But aftir growyng of the fame

et qualia deus per eos et cum eis esset operatus mirabilia, timore et amore obst[u]puerunt et in maiori reuerencia honore et timore ex hiis ipsos habere ceperunt. Et sic tunc ipsi tres Reges, testamentis ipsorum dispositis et ordinatis, deo gracias agentes quiuis cum om[n]ibus suis ad terras [et] ad regna sua sani cum gaudio sunt reuersi, et corporibus non cordibus abinuicem ad tempus †separati. Et omnibus populis ea que viderant et audierant et ipsis acciderant humiliter predicabant. Et in omnibus eorum terris et templis [stellam] cum infantulo et desuper signum crucis per modum et formam prout ipsis apparuit honorifice fieri et sculpere fecerunt. De quibus quamplurimi gentiles relictis suis erroribus et idolis infantem cui ipsi tres Reges deuote munera optulerunt ipsi adorauerunt, et capellam super montem Vaus factam ex longinquissimis partibus homines diuersarum nacionum deuotissime visitauerunt. Nam postquam ipsi tres Reges ad propria sunt reuersi omnibus hominibus humiliores et deuociores sunt effecti, et vniuersarum †terrarum regionum naciones in oriente de eorum virtute humilitate et deuocione plene non sufficiebant narrare. Et sic in laudabili vita et honesta conuersacione vsque ad ascensionem domini et aduentum beati Thome apostoli laudabiliter permanserunt.

Post recessum ipsorum trium Regum de Bethleem quando domino munera optulerunt, extunc beata [f. 29r] virgo Maria cum infantulo suo Ihesu in tugurrio et spelunca in qua natus fuit homo per modicum tempus permansit. Sed crescente

† separati] sunt separati. † terrarum] terrarum et.

of her birthe and of the .iij. Kyngis than she went fro thens to anothir cave vndur erthe corve out of the stone with her sone Ihesu for drede of the Iewis and þere abode ynto the tyme of the day of her purificacion. And [for] diuers men and wymmen, old and ȝonge, lovyd our Lady and her sone Ihesu, in as mych as they might þei counceilid hem and fond hem euere lyvelode as hem nedid. And of þat same cave aftirward, encresyng the Cristyn feith, was made a chapell in worship of Seynt Nicholas and of the .iij. Kyngis, and hit is sene ȝet a stone wheron Marie was wont to yeve her child soke. And on a tyme, of chaunce, happid a lytil mylk of her pappis fall on that stone, of which mylk the tokenyng and fourme is yet sene into this day. And the more the stone is trodyn and defoulyd, the more þe sight of þe milk wexith. And such mylk of our Lady is shewid in meny chirches and of pilgrymes wyde born abowt. And whan Marie wiþ her child Ihesu fro þe cave in which he was born went for drede of the Iewes so spedely and hyingly and fled vnto þat othir cave vndur erthe forsayd, than left she and foryate in the cave þer the child was born [f. 241^{r}] her sherte and the clothis in which Ihesus was wrappyd and lappyd yn in the hey in the cracche, which vnto the tyme of Seynt Eleyne, modir of Constantyne, as God wold in the same place and cracche left hole and

4 for] *om.* L.

de ipsa et tribus Regibus tam mirabili fama + extunc de ipso tugurrio et spelunca in aliam speluncam subterraneam ex rupe factam cum infantulo Ihesu metu Iudeorum intrauit, et vsque ad diem sue purificacionis in ea permansit et latitauit. Et quia, prout decuit, vtriusque sexus homines senes et iuuenes beatam Mariam diligebant et suum infantulum Ihesum, in quantum poterant diligenter celabant et ipsis necessaria quibus indiguerunt pie ministrabant. Et ex eadem spelunca in qua beata virgo Maria itaque cum infantulo suo Ihesu latitauit postmodum crescente fide christiana facta est capella in honore trium Regum et beati Nicholaij consecrata. Et videtur per ipsam capellam communis transitus fuisse, et quondam duas ianuas habuisse; sed nunc vna ianua lapidibus est obstructa. Et in illa capella adhuc videtur lapis super quem beata virgo semper sedere consueuit quando suum infantulum Ihesum lac[ta]uit. Et quadam vice ex casu modicum lac de sua mammilla super illum lapidem cecidit, cuius lactis species super eundem lapidem in presentem diem permansit. Et quanto plus abraditur, tanto plus accrescit. Et tale lac beate Marie in quampluribus ecclesijs demonstratur et a peregrinis vndique deportatur. Et postquam beata virgo cum infantulo suo Ihesu de spelunca in qua Ihesus fuit natus metu Iudeorum tam celeriter [f. 29^{v}] et festinanter exiuit et [in] hanc speluncam subterraneam de qua dictum est fugit et intrauit, extunc camisiam suam et pannos quibus Ihesus fuit inuolutus in feno et presepe pariter inuolutos fuit oblita. Qui vsque ad tempus venerabilis Helene matris Constantini prout deo placuit recentes et integri in eodem loco in presepe permanserunt.

fresshe. For the Iewis þat place yn which Crist was born fro þat tyme long tyme had yn despyte and envye and held hit for a cursyd place, bywicchid and acursyd, so that they wold not suffre childryn, bestis, ne her seruauntis come in that place, and so thrette all peple, ȝong and old, of goyng into that cave that none durst entre theryn, for they held euery man that come þerin acursid. And whil Marie her child Ihesu in her purificacion af[ti]r þe lawe of Moyses offryd white turtles and Symeon toke hym into his hondis seying, '*Nunc dimittis seruum [tuum], domine, secundum verbum tuum in pace*', the same Symeon and Anna aunte of þat same Ihesu in presence of meny prestis and scrybes prophecied meny thinges, as the gospel seith. And þan of the relacion of the Iewis that were þat tyme present in the temple the fame of Marie and of Ihesu of new more acresyd so that for drede of the Iewis and Herowde Marie myght no lenger dwelle in that cave with her child. [And] aftre that, as þe gospell seith, *Angelus domini [ap]p[a]ruit in sompnis Ioseph dicens, 'Surge, accipe puerum et matrem eius, et fuge in Egiptum, et esto ibi vsque dum dicam tibi; futurum est enim vt Herodes querat puerum [ad perdendum eum'. Qui consurgens accepit puerum] et matrem* [f. 241v] *eius [nocte], et cecessit in Egiptum, et erat ibi vsque ad obitum Herodis.*

6 aftir] afor L. 8 tuum] *om.* L. 14 And] *om.* L; apparuit] comperuit L. 17 ad ... puerum] *om.* L. 18 nocte] *om.* L.

Nam Iudei ipsum locum quo natus fuit Ihesus ab illo tempore postmodum per longa tempora ex inuidia habuerunt pro loco prophanato sortilego et maledicto, ita quod nec pueros pecora vel gentiles ipsum locum intrare permiserunt, et tantum timorem senibus et iuuenibus [et omnibus] incuciebant quod ipsum locum nullus intrare fuit ausus. Nam omnem intrantem habuerunt pro contaminato. Iterum dum in purificacione sua beata virgo infantulum suum Ihesum secundum legem Mo[ysi] in templo cum turturibus optulit, et ipsum Simeon in vlnas suas recepit dicens, 'Nunc dimittis seruum tuum †in pace secundum verbum tuum†', prout dicit scriptura, et eodem tempore tam ipse Simeon quam Anna annicula de ipso infantulo Ihesu †deo pluribus Iudeis et eorum sacerdotibus presentibus et scribis astantibus plurima prophetabant prout dicunt euangelia, †et tunc† de relacionibus Iudeorum qui itaque tunc aderant in templo fama Marie et infantul[i] Ihesu de nouo tantum accreuit quod pre Iudeis et Herode in ipsa spelunca vel in aliquo alio loco beata virgo cum infantulo suo diucius non potuit latitare. Et extunc prout ait euangelium: Angelus [f. 30r] domini apparuit Ioseph in sompnis dicens, '†Surge, accipe puerum †cum matre† eius, et fuge in Egiptum, et esto ibi [vsque] dum dicam tibi: futurum est quod Herodes querat puerum ad perdendum eum'. Qui consurgens accepit puerum et matrem eius nocte et cecessit in Egiptum; et erat ibi vsque ad obitum Herodis.

† in pace ... tuum] domine secundum verbum tuum in pace. † deo] *om.* † et tunc] extunc. † Surge] Surge et. † cum matre] et matrem.

And how that our Lady with her child Ihesum went ynto Egypte and come ayen thens pleynly is founde in the book of the childhede of Crist. But by meny perilouses places and wildirnessis of men and bestis they went, for aftir tyme that Ioseph was warnyd of the aungell in Bedlem in his slepe that he shold take Ihesu his sone and Marie his modir and go into Egipt for drede of Herowde, Ioseph aftir the byddyng of þe aungell risyng toke his child wiþ his modir and by nyght passid into Egipt. And they went by meny diuers perilous places and weyes for perilouse men and bestis in the deserte. And in euery place of her restyng by the weyes goyng into Egyptward and also in her comyng ayen, and nowher ellis in þat cuntre, for a tokyn into euerlastyng remembraunce growyn yet rosis drye which al about ther be callyd rosys of Ierico. And the wymmen Sarazins gladly vse þes roses in her beryng of childrin. Of the whiche rosis men that be kepers of bestis ther in deserte, which [men] be clepyd Bedewyns, gadryn and for her brede sellyn in grete plente to men of the cuntre and to pilgrymes, which pilgrymes and men of þe cuntre also selle hem forth, and so they be bor[ne] thurgh þe world.

And the place in which our Lady with her sone and Ioseph dwellid in Egypt that tyme from Bedlem is but .xij. iournees wher she dwellid .vij. ȝeer into the dethe of Herowde. And [f. 242r] the place wher they dwellyd

4 aftir] H *begins, with the running title* Ioseph. 5 his(1)] her H. 8 for] for diuers H. 9 the(2)] her H. 14 men] H, *om.* L. 17 borne] bore H, *in* L *only the first three letters can be read at the line end due to the tightness of the binding.* 20 And] And in H.

Et quomodo et qualiter beata virgo cum infantulo Ihesu in Egiptum peruenerat et inde redierat in libro de infancia Ihesu plenius reperitur. Sed per plurima loca multum periculosa hominum siluestrium et animalium periculosissimorum per deserta transierunt. Et pro intersigno in omnibus locis et viis per quas in exitu et redditu beata Maria cum infantulo suo Ihesu transiit adhuc crescunt rose aride que vndique rose de Iherico vocantur; et hiis mulieres saracene multum libenter vtuntur in partu. + Iterum locus quo beata virgo cum infantulo suo Ihesu [f. 30v] itaque in Egipto habitauit distat a Bethleem xij dietas per viam itaque per quam beata virgo transiit; et non alibi nisi per illam viam crescunt ille rose de Ierico in memoriale sempiternum. Et ipsas rosas colligunt homines qui ibidem Bedewyni vocantur, qui de loco ad locum in ipso deserto cum pecoribus vagantur, et pro pane ipsas vendunt in maxima multitudine et quantitate hominibus incolis et peregrinis, per quos vlterius venduntur et per mundum deportantur.

Iterum locus quo beata virgo cum infantulo suo Ihesu in Egipto per septennium vsque ad Herodis obitum habitauit

was ny þe citees of Babyloyne and Alchaye, in which now is the dwellyng of þe sowdan. And þes two citees be but lytil atwyn, and they be passyng grete citees; but yet Alchaya is mych more than Babyloine, and hit is hold more than xij sithe the toun of Parys. And in þe same place wher our Lady dwellid with her child is now the gardyn of bawme, noght a stonys cast thens. And in that same gardyn bene .vij. wellis of noble watre of which our Lady was wont whan she dwellid þere to take and to wesshe her child and her clothes and also bathe h[y]m. And bycause of tho wellis þat gardyn is opyn, vnwallyd and vnclosyd. And in that gardyn growyn busshys in manere as rosers, of the which busshis growyn the bawme, and droppith out of the twyggis of the busshis whan they be kutte as watir out of the cuttyng of vynes whan they be cutte. And th[o] busshis be but of an elle lengthe of height, and the levis of hem aftir the shap of a thre levyd grasse, and euery busshe haþ a keper in speciall, a Cristynman which be of þe sowdans prisonners, and euery man kepith his busshe as his owne body, and they cl[en]se hem and pyke hem. And þer may no man kepe hem but Cristynmen, for if eny oþir than a Cristynman kept hem anon they shold drye vp and dye, as hit hath be oft yprevid. And euery yeer in [f. 242v] Marche the sowdan in propre persone is i[n] that gardyn, and þan in his

1 citees] citee H; and] and of H. 3 Babyloine] Babyloyne H, *possibly* Babylonie L; hold] *om.* H. 7 to take and to wesshe] *trs.* H. 8 also] also to H; hym] hem LH. 10 as] as busshes of H. 12 whan] whan that H; tho] the L, þese H; but] but as H. 15 and ... kepith] which kepe euery man H; his(2)] her H. 16 clense] H, close L; hem(2)] hem clene H; hem(3)] tho forseyd busshes of baw<m>e H. 17 than a Cristynman] men þan Cristynmen H. 18 drye ... dye] shrynk & dryen vp H; oft] dyuers tymes opynly H. 19 in(1)] in his H; in(2)] H, is L; þan] þere H.

fuit iuxta ciuitates Babiloniam nouam et †Alchaie, qua† nunc est habitacio soldani. Et iste ciuitates modicum distant inter se; et sunt maxime ciuitates, set †Alchaie est† maior Babilonia et reputatur maior quam septem ville parisienses. Et in ipso [loco] quo itaque beata virgo per septennium cum infantulo suo Ihesu habitauit nunc est ortus balsami, qui non est ad iactum lapidis magnus. Et in ipso orto sunt septem fontes aquarum in quibus beata virgo infantulum Ihesum lauare et balneare et sua vestimenta et infantuli lauare et mundare consueuit. Et propter ipsos fontes ortus est disperse situs et non muratus nec munitus. Et crescit et effluit balsamus ex virgis quarum rubus est modicum alcior vna vlna et in modum rubi rosarum †formatilis, et folia eius quasi trifolia sunt formata. Et vnusquisque rubus habet custodem specialem christianum, aliquem de [f. 31r] captiuis soldani, qui ipsum rubum quasi corpus suum custodit irrigat et mundat. Et in mense marcij tunc soldanus continue personaliter est presens in hoc orto. Et tunc

† Alchaie qua] Alcayre que. † Alchaie est] Alcayr est. † formatilis] formatus.

presence the busshis of this bawme be kytte in manere as vynes be [kytte]. And þan the kyttyngis-of and the twyggis be bound togidir with cotoun, and vndir hem þan be set smale vessels of syluer, and the kyttyngis and the twiggis be hangyd ovir tho vessels þat the bawme may droppe out of the kyttynges, as watir droppith out of kyttyng of vynes. And whan the bawme is all droppyd out byfor the sowdon thus, than is it put out of tho vessels into a siluer pot that is callid ther *serra*, which is litil more þan a potell of wyne, which pot þan wiþ the bawme vnneþe is fillyd. And than þe sowdon gothe with the pot of bawme and kepith [it] hyms[elf] in grete specialite. And if eny messager come from eny· kyng or eny grete lord $^{+}$ to the sowdon for eny of this bawme, than the sowdon yevith hym a litil in a litil glasse of the michilnes of a mannys fyngir full. And aftir that euery [keper] takith þe kuttyngis and [þe] twigges of his busshe, which he kepith aftir that the sowdon is gon with his bawme, and sethe hem in a clene pot. And þan the bawme which þan sethith out of the twiggis and boylith swymmith above the water as it were fat, and [þis bawme] is sumwhat thik and colourid as brasyll, and they gadre that þan and put hit saf in a vessell. And if eny man of an hye fall be broke withyn [f. 243^{r}] or brosyd and be

1 the] þes H; kytte] H, *om.* L. 6 thus] *perhaps* þis H. 9 it hymself] H, hym soft L; specialite] specialite and vndir stronge wardis þat no man may come þerto but he H. 10 eny(3)] eny oþir H; lord] H, lord come L. 11 sowdon] sowdon of Babyloyne H. 12 the] the shappe & H; full] for a grete deynte and a dereworth presente H; keper] H, kyng *apparently cancelled and* man *written above in the same hand* L. 13 þe(2)] H, *om.* L; he] H, `he´ L. 14 his] the principall H; sethe] sethith H. 15 the(2)] *possibly* tho L, þe H. 16 fat] oyle or oþir fatt licour H; þis bawme] H, hit L. 17 colourid as] it is also colourid as it were H; they ... vessell] þan þei gadir þat togidir wel preciously and puttyn hit fayr & savely in vessels H. 18 eny ... (83/1) bawme] þer be eny man þat be brostyn or brosyd of eny hye falle lete hym be anoyntid anone wiþ that bawme and H.

virge balsami in modum vitis scinduntur et vulnerantur, et ipse scissure bombice circumligantur, et subtus bombicem et scissuras parua vascula argentea tunc penduntur in quibus balsamus per scissuras et bombicem sicut aqua ex vite per stillas effluit. Et ex illis vasculis funditur †ad amphoram argenteam que ibi †serra vocatur, que modicum maior est quam sextarium vini possit intrare; que tamen extunc balsamo vix impletur. Et tunc soldanus rec[i]pit omnem balsamum solus. Sed cum legatus alicuius regis mittitur, ipsi dat paruum vitriolum in modum digiti magni balsamo plenum. Et itaque omni balsamo exstillato soldanus recedit. Et tunc vnusquisque rubi custos sumit virgas de suo rubo scissas et ipsas in mundissima olla bullit. Et balsamus qui tunc ex virgis ebullit sicut pinguedo supernatat, et talis balsamus est spissus et vt braxina coloratus. Et dum aliquis homo ab equo vel aliqua altitudine cadit et intus rumpitur et quassatur

† ad] in. † serra] zerra.

anoyntid with þat bawme, they shul be hool anone, and if eny woundis be anoyntid therwith, they shul be helid þat þei shul not be sene. And of this bawme thes kepers take and selle to men and to pilgrymes, and þus it is borne into all þe world. But ȝet it is not of so mych vertu nowher ny or [of] noblesse as the bawme which stillith out of his owne kynde. For if a drope of þat bawme þat stilliþ out of his owne kynd be droppid or leyd on a mannys honde, anon hit passith thurgh and swetith on þat othir syde, and the place þat hit droppith on or was wet þerwith [shall neuere aftir be corrupt ne scabbid]. And it is in colour as hit were grene wyne thinne and sumwhat troubly [+], and þat is callid rawe bawme; and þat bawme þat is boyllid is callid [bawme coct, þat is to sey] sodyn bawme. And they byleve þere þat this gardyn hath that vertu to bring forth so þat bawme for our Lady dwellid so þere .vij. ȝeer with here child, & herself, her child, and her clothis ofttymes þere wysshyn in the wellis of þat gardyn.

3 to men and to] þerof to trauaylyng men and H. 5 of(1)] H, *om.* L; the bawme which] þat bawme is þat first H; of(2)] by H; a] o H. 6 of(2)] by H. 7 swetith ... syde] on þat oþir syde hit swetiþ þurgh H. 8 shall ... (1.9)scabbid] H, is vnpercid and vnsene L. 9 in ... thinne] of colour grene as it were thenne wyne H. 10 troubly] troubly colouryd L, troubly and thik H; is(2)] is so H. 11 bawme(1) ... sey] H, *om.* L; bawme(2)] bawme And þis bawme þat is sode and al þe profyt þat comith þerof longith to þe forseyd Cristynmen þat be kepers of þe bawme to do her best þerwiþ H; And] Also H. 12 so þat] this H; for] by vertw and cause þat H. 13 so] *om.* H; child(1)] H *ends, adding* Amen.

et cum illo balsamo lotus perungitur, statim efficitur sanus. Et cicatrices vulnerum cum †non sint cooperte, si cum tali balsamo perungantur modicum non apparent. Et talem balsamum custodes ruborum tunc vendunt hominibus et peregrinis et vndique per mundum deportatur. Sed in nulla comparacione est tante virtutis et nobilitatis sicut balsamus qui naturaliter stillat ex vite. Nam dum talis [f. 31[v]] balsam[i] gutta in manum ponitur, ipsam penetrat et ab altera parte resudat, et ille locus incorruptibilis permanebit in eternum. Et est quasi vinum viride tenue aliquantulum turbidum coloratus, et vocatur ibidem balsamus crudus; et alter balsamus bullitus vocatur ibidem balsamus coctus. Et de aliis balsami nobilitatibus et virtutibus longum esset enarrare. Et creditur firmiter in oriente et in omnibus partibus illis quod ille locus adhuc ex eo hab[ea]t talem virtutem quod in eo balsamus crescit quod beata Maria cum suo infantulo Ihesu per septennium in illo loco habitabat et in ipsis fontibus se et suum infantulum Ihesum frequenter eorumque vestimenta lauabat. Sed ad maius signum ipsum ortum nullus omnino hominum nisi sit christianus colere potest vel custodire, quod sepius est expertum: si alij homines gentiles ipsum colerent, extunc rubi balsami et eius virge statim arescerent [et perirent]. Sed vt ad propositum redeatur.

† non] *om.*

And ye shul vndirstond as of the presentis and offringes which the thre Kyngis of the orient offrid to our Lord that Melchior, kyng of Nubye and Arabye, offrid to our Lord an appil of gold þat was some tyme grete kyng Alisaundris, as mich as hit myght be hold in hond and closyd; which appil in the offryng vanysshid and come to noght. And þis Melchior was the lest in stature of the thre Kynges. Balthasar, kyng of Godolye and of Saba, which to our Lord offrid [f. 243v] ensens was but of mene stature & persone. Iaspar, kyng of Thars and *insule Egrisculle,* which offrid to our Lord mirre was most of hem in persone, and an Ethiope and blak. Melchior the ȝeer of his age .C. and .xvj. afor all þe peple in bowyng of his heed wiþout eny dissese so dyed. And þe f[if]t day than next folowyng, in the feest of þe Epiphanye, Baltazar the yeer of his age a .C.xij. dyed. And the .vj. day than next folowyng Iaspar the yeer of his age a .C. & .ix. dyed. Melchior offrid also to our Lord on the Epiphanie .xxx.d of gold which Abraham, whan he went out of the lond of Caldee, toke with hym in his pilgrymage and yn Ebron, which was callyd þan Arabie, broght with hym, and wiþ tho .xxx.d a feld for sepulture of hym, his wyf Sare, and his sonys Isak and Iacob he boght. And as hit is red, Thare, Abrahams fadir, for the kyng of Mesopotane þat was callyd Nynus made the money of þo .xxx.d. And aftir, in Iacobis tyme, Ioseph was sold of his bretherin to the Ismaelites for tho .xxx.d. Aftir þat, the bretherin of Ioseph broght þe .xxx.+ pens ayen to Ioseph for whete which þei boght of hym in Egipte whan they

11 fift] fyst L   21 xxx] xxxd L.

Iterum de muneribus que ipsi tres Reges domino optulerunt est sciendum prout in aliis libris continetur quod Melchior rex Nubie et Arabum optulit domino paruum pomum aureum quod, vt dictum est, in oblacione in fauillam et ad nichilum fuit redactum. Item rex Melchior optulit triginta denarios aureos, quos Abraham egrediens de Caldeorum terra in peregrinacione sua secum sumpsit et in Ebron (quod tunc †Arabia vocabatur) portauit, et cum ipsis agrum in sepulturam suam et Sare et filiorum suorum Ysaac et Iacob [f. 32r] comparauit. Et horum denariorum monetam legitur fecisse Thare pater Abraham ex parte regis Mesopotanie nomine Nynus. Et deinde temporibus Iacob + pro eisdem triginta denariis †Hismaelitis Ioseph a suis fratribus fuit venditus in Egiptum. Post hec fratres Ioseph filij Iacob pro frumento reportauerunt eosdem ad Egiptum.

† Arabia] Arbea (Gen. xxiii.1).   † Hismaelitis] Hismaelitis filijs eius a quo Abraham agrum in sepulturam emit.

had derthe of corne in her londe. Aftir this [the same .xxx.d] aftir the dethe of Iacob were sent to þe qwene Saba for oynementis for the sepulture of Iacob by Ioseph and þan by the quene Saba put ynto the kyngis tresour. And aftir that, in þe tyme of Salamon, the same .xxx.d with me[f. 244r]ny othir ornementis into the temple of Ierusalem were offryd by the qwene Saba. And aftir, in the tyme of Roboam, Salamons sone, in the tyme of þe takyng of Ierusalem and of þe spoyling of the temple ther the same .xxx.d come into the hondis of the kyng of Araby wiþ help of the Egipciens and with othir ornementis of the temple were put into þe tresour of the kyng. And aftir þat in the byginnyng of the Newe Testament, aftir the birthe of our Lord in Bedlem, Melchior, that was kyng of Nubye and Araby, wiþ meny othir ornementis and vessels of gold of þe temple and othir meny riche yeftis which he toke wiþ hym to offre to our Lord þes .xxx.d of þe fynest gold of Arabye, which was hold the fynest gold in eny tresour, purposid to offre. But yet at the tyme of his offryng in the fest of þe Epiphanye he might fynd no mo of all his ornementis or iewels to offre but only þes .xxx.d, wiþ the appil of gold which anon was turnyd to noght, for whiche mervaile, drede, and haste all þe othir yeftis and iewels which he had purposid to offre to our Lord he foryate and left vnoffrid. And ye shul vndirstond that whan þe thre Kyngis come byfor our Lord to offre her iewels and yeftis they had no power to fynd þan eny othir yeftis to offre of all her tresour but tho þe which they offrid (þat was, gold, encense, and myrre), notwiþstondyng þat þei [f. 244v] broght with hem meny oþir iewels and yeftis to offre and to have offrid to our Lord. Wherfor sodenly astonyed, for drede and for wondring of þe brightnes o<f> þe sterre and of othir merveillis þat þei sawe with grete deuocion the first iewels which come first to honde of her tresours þei offrid.

1 the same xxxd] *om.* L.

Post hec ijdem denarij post obitum Iacob ad regnum Saba pro aromatibus ad sepulturam Iacob a Ioseph fuerunt missi et in thesauros regios repositi. Et post hec temporibus Salamonis ijdem triginta denarij cum quampluribus aliis ornamentis in templ[um] domini in Iherusalem a regina Saba fuerunt oblati. Et deinde tempore Roboam filij Salamonis in capcione Iherusalem et templi domini depredacione ad manus regis Arabum qui tunc temporis fuit in adiutorio Egipciorum peruenerunt et cum aliis ornamentis templi aureis spoliatis in thesauros regios reponebantur. Et post hoc nouo testamento inchoante, nato domino in Bethleem, extunc Melchior rex Nubie et Arabum cum quampluribus aliis ornamentis aureis et vasis templi et aliis variis et ditissimis muneribus que secum sumpserat hos triginta denarios ex auro Arabie purissimo, quia antiquitus nobilius aurum in thesauris non reperitur, hos domino cum aliis predictis ornamentis offerre proposuit; et solummodo hos denarios optulit, et alia ornamenta timore pretermisit, vt est supradictum.

And aftir that þes .xxx.d of Melchior were offryd, $^{+}$ as our Lady bare hem thurgh þe desert into Egiptward for drede and thoght of þe Iewis and of Erowde, as þei were bound in a litil lynnyng clout by the way she lost hem. Which .xxx.d a shephard that kept shepe þer in deserte, on of hem which be clepid Bedewyns, in his walkyng fonde and into a litil tyme byfor þe passion of our Lord held hem in his owne kepyng. And than þe shephard fil into an incurable sikenes. And whan he had soght from meny londis for to come to Ihesu for the grete fame þat he herd of hym — þat wiþ o word he helyd meny diuers siknessis and infirmites — he come at last to Ierusalem and by his good byleve þere he receyvid his hele of God. And þer he was conuertyd and cristenyd, and þere þes .xxx.d wiþ the encens and mirra in Ierusalem wiþ grete deuocion he offrid to God on the auter in þe temple. And for offrynges of iewels were þat tyme selde and deynte, the pres[t] of þe temple brent þe encense on the auter in tokyn of so wurshipful an offryng and he toke þe .xxx.d and þe mirre and put hem into her tresorie þat they clepyd *gazophilacium*. And aftir þat a litil while, [f. 245^{r}] the .iij. day byfor [þe] passion of our Lord, the prince[s] of prestis and the Iewys, that they be ind<i>fferent of his passion and deþe, toke þe .xxx.d out of þe tresorie and of her comune purse out of the temple and yaf

1 offryd] offryd `&´ L. 14 prest] prestis L. 17 þe] his L; princes] prince L.
18 indifferent] *a letter (perhaps* p*) has been partially erased under the second* i.

Cum autem beata virgo Maria metu Herodis fugit in Egiptum, extunc hos triginta denarios [f. 32^{v}] cum aliis muneribus thure et mirra sicut sibi fuerunt oblata in panno lineo ligatos in deserto amisit. †Qui quid[a]m pastor, vnus ex ho[mini]bus qui ibidem Bedewyny vocantur, degens in ipso deserto qui cum gregibus suis de loco ad locum in pascuis vagabatur repperit, et vsque ad modicum tempus ante passionem domini apud se retinuit. Et extunc idem pastor cecidit in incurabilem infirmitatem. Et cum fama de Ihesu quod diuersas infirmitates et varios langores solo verbo curaret per omnes terras volaret, extunc idem pastor Iherusalem se transtulit et per fidem suam a domino sanitatem recepit. Mox est instructus et conuersus. Extunc idem pastor hos triginta denarios aureos cum aliis muneribus thure et mirra prout prius domino in sua infancia in Bethleem per tres Reges fuerunt oblata idem pastor prout in deserto repperit denuo in Iherusalem tunc domino optulit cum deuocione. Que dominus agnoscens iussit pastorem vt ipsa munera poneret super altare in templo. Vnde sacerdos domini qui tunc sorte exiit in signum tam honorabilis oblacionis thus super altare incensorum accendit; et quia munera erant rara et gloriosa hos triginta denarios cum mirra in gasophilacium misit. Et post hoc per modicum tempus, tercia videlicet die ante passionem domini, principes sacerdotum et omnes Iudei, vt indifferenter †principes essent in †passionem domini et eius morte, triginta denarios $^{+}$ ex communi bursa et gazophilacio ex templo domini sumpserunt et

† Qui] Que. † principes] participes. † passionem] passione.

hem to Iudas Scaryot for to bytraye Ihesu his maystre and lord. And of þe mirre a parcell they medlyd wiþ eysel to ȝeve Ihesu to drynk whan he hyng on þe crosse, and the remenaunt of the mirre Nichodemus, prince of þe Iewes, wiþ aloe and oþir precious o[yne]mentis kept for þe sepulture of our Lord. And aftir þat Iudas in the temple threw at the feet byfor þe Iewes þe .xxx.d whan he had repentid hym of his treson. And þan þe Iewes yave .xv.d of þo .xxx.d to the knyghtis for to kepe the sepulcre and wiþ þe oþir .xv.d [boght] þe feld of a potter for pilg[r]imes to be byried yn. And ȝe shul vndirstond that þat feld is ny to Ierusalem, vnnethe a stonys cast þens, and hit is a longe feld and a grete. And merveillith not þogh þo .xxx.d in þe gospell be callyd *argentei*. For they were of þe purest and fynest gold of Araby, but by custome and comune name þei were clepid *argentei* as of diuers money of gold some be clepid scutes, some motons, some floreyns. And þe printe and lyknesse of þat money lastid in that cuntre from the tyme of Abraham into þe tyme of destruccion of Ierusalem by Titus and Vaspasyan. And in no londe toward the [f. 245v] Est is eny money

4 oynementis] ournamentis L. 8 boght] *om.* L; potter] *after* po *a letter (or letters) has been underpuncted and altered to* tte; pilgrimes] pilgimes L.

ipsos Iude Scarioth discipulo domini vt eum traderet tradiderunt. Et [f. 33r] partem mirre vino quod or[i] domini in cruce optulerunt miscuerunt et †reliquam mirre Nichodemus princeps Iudeorum cum aloe et aliis aromatibus condidit ad domini sepulturam. Et postquam Iudas hos triginta denarios retulit et ad pedes Iudeorum in templo proiecit, extunc Iudei dederunt xv denarios militibus qui sepulcrum domini custodierunt. Et cum reliquis quindecim denariis emerunt agrum figuli in sepulturam †peregrinorum. + Et [est] sciendum quod ager figuli est prope Iherusalem situs et vix ad semi[iactum] lapid[i]s, longus et magnus. Et temporibus quando Iherusalem fuit christianorum extunc de ipso agro profundissima facta et effossata est spelunca, et ab omni parte sursum a fundo circummurata et desuper testudinata; et desuper in testudine sunt foramina per que corpora mortuorum in profundum mittuntur et proiciuntur. Nec moueat aliquem quod ijdem denarij in + euangelio argentei vocentur quia fuerunt ex auro Arabie purissimo, sed communi nomine argentei vocabantur sicut denarij aurei nunc scutati mutones vel floren[i]. Et similitudo horum denariorum in nomine et moneta in illis partibus a temporibus Abrahe vsque ad destruccionem Iherusalem per Titum et Vaspasianum permansit. Et in omnibus partibus orientis nu[n]quam

† reliquam] reliquam partem. † peregrinorum] peregrinorum vnde ait euangelium Et consilio inito emerunt ex hijs agrum figuli in sepulturam peregrinorum.

chaungyd in weight or yn value. And eche of tho .xxx.d were of þe valew of þ[r]e floreyns, and in the prynte of the to syde of the money is an heed of the kyng crownyd, and on þat othir syde be lettris of Caldee which men now can not wele reed or discreve.

Thus (þat is, encence) perteynith to sacrifise, gold to trybute, and mirre to sepulture.

Whan aftirward Marie with her child was revokyd out of Egypt by the aungell as the gospell seith, *Defuncto Herode ecce angelus domini apparuit in sompnis Ioseph dicens, 'Surge, accipe puerum et matrem <eius>' &c.* And what thinges and what manere and how gret our Lord Ihesu in tho tymes wroght and suffryd [yn]to the tyme of his passion, resureccion, and assension [+] hit is opynly seyn and knowyn by the gospellers. And whan our Lord aftir his assencion sent Thomas his apostle specialy into the parties of Ynde to occupie and perfourme þer the office of prechyng in which londis tho .iij. Kyngis which to our Lord in his childhod offrid þe ʒeftis

2 þre] þe L.   11 ynto] þat to L.   12 assension] assension as L.

mutantur monete pondere vel valore. †Et similitudo horum triginta denariorum ex auro vel cupro in similitudine pondere [f. 33v] quantitate et forma et similitudo in longitudine et latitudine cum tunica domini inconsutili multum artificialiter facta in oriente apud quamplurimos principes et nobiles adhuc hereditarie permanserunt in presentem†. Et vnus illorum triginta denariorum circa tres florenos habuit in pondere et valore, et in vna parte talis denarij in nummismate stat capud regis laureatum impressum et [in] alia parte sunt littere Caldaice que ab hominibus modernis non possunt legi vel discerni. ...

[f. 34v] ... Cvm elapso tempore quando beata virgo Maria cum infantulo suo Ihesu ex Egipto reuocabatur, prout ait euangelium: Defuncto Herode ecce angelus domini apparuit †Ioseph dicens 'Surge, accipe puerum et matrem eius, et vade in terram Israel; defuncti sunt enim qui querebant animam pueri'. Qui consurgens accepit puerum et matrem eius et venit in terram Israel. Audiens quod Archelaus regnaret in Iudea pro Herode patre eius timuit illuc ire. Et †annuncians in sompnis secessit in partes Galilee et habitauit in ciuitate Nazareth, vt adimpleretur quod dictum est per prophetam dicentem: Quoniam Nazareus vocabitur. Et que qualia et quanta in hiis et ab illis temporibus dominus Ihesus in sua deitate et humanitate egerit et fecerit vel passus fuerit vsque ad eius passionem resurreccionem et ascensionem in euangeliis plenius continetur. [f. 35r]

Cum autem dominus post [suam] gloriosam ascensionem specialiter ad partes Indorum Thomam suum apostolum in sorte predicacionis miserat in quibus ipsi tres Reges gloriosi qui domino in sua infancia munera optulerunt

† Et similitudo ... in presentem] *archetypal corruption.*   † Ioseph] Ioseph in somnis.
† annuncians] ammonitus.

dwellyd, enhabitid, and regnyd, althogh Thomas toke on hym aȝens his will þe office of prechyng, which Thomas aftir the resureccion of our Lord whom he wiþ touchyng of his fyngris knewe [...] and our Lord by Thomas meny merveilles had shewyd and wroght by diuers langours and infirmites helyng and curyng and meny othir miracles worchyng, whan Thomas goyng about all the yles and provinces of Ynde, fyndyng in all þe temples of þe ydoles þere the sterre wiþ the child and the ...

... [f. 246r] yong from diuers cuntres ferre to this chapell on this hill of Vaws in worshipyng and offryng. And thes thre glorious Kyngis for her hye deuocioun made in þe fote of þat hille a noble cite and callid hit Sculla, whiche is now into this day hold on of the noblest citees and the ricchest in all þe parties of Inde and of the Est. And in this cite is þe habitacion of þe lord of Inde which is callid Pretre Iohn, and also of Thomas, þe patriarke of Ynde.

And whan Thomas in all þes parties and kyngdomes had baptisid and

3 *see note.* 7 *a lacuna of one folio follows* L.

habitabant et regnabant, licet Thomas [inuitus officium] predicacionis in ipsis partibus regnisque susceperat, tamen ex magna prouidencia ipsius lapidis angularis qui fecit vtraque vnum estimatur fore factum †qui Thomas [post]† passionem domini et eius resurreccionem qu[e]m digitis palpauit †missus agnouit† vt hanc ipsis Regibus et gent[i] predicaret et annunciaret †qui eciam eiusdem domini infanciam de remotissimis et longinquissimis orientis partibus et mundi quesiuit et vidit et muneribus [veris] et misticis deuotissime adorauit et honorauit. ...

Iterum [cum] Thomas apostolus in partibus et regnis Indorum euangelium domini fideliter predicasset et vniuersas illas insulas et prouincias circuisset et demones signo crucis effugasset [f. 35v] et diuersos languores et infirmitates curasset et dominus ibidem per eum quamplurima [miracula] fecisset et quamplurimas gentes ad euangelium conuertisset, reperiens in omnibus ydolorum templis stellam cum infantulo et signo crucis prout ipsi tres Reges in omnibus eorum terris et regnis et eorum templis fieri et sculpere fecerunt et preceperunt quando de Bethleem fuerunt reuersi. ... [f. 37r]

Et facta est leticia magna in populis, ita quod vtriusque sexus homines paruuli et adulti qui tunc presentes in comitatu non fuerunt de longinquis partibus ad hunc montem Vaus et capellam deuotissime peruenerunt. Et propter talem ac tantam deuocionem ipsi tres Reges maximam ac nobilissimam ciuitatem in pede huius montis construxerunt fecerunt et ditissime consummauerunt, et ipsam ciuitatem vocauerunt †S[cull]a, que adhuc nunc est maior et dicior ciuitas in omnibus partibus Indie et orientis in presentem diem. Et in hac ciuitate est habitacio domini Indorum qui presbiter Iohannes vocatur ac Thome Indorum patriarche.

Iterum postquam Thomas in omnibus istis partibus et regnis [f. 37v] omnes populos

† qui Thomas post] quod Thomas. † missus agnouit] *om.* † qui] que. † Sculla] Seuwa *(so generally).*

conuertyd þe peple to the faith, than thes thre glorious Kyngis he consecrate into erchebisshopes. And þan tho thre Kyngis, so made archebisshopes, chese and ordeynid othir bisshopes and prestes vndur hem to serve all the peple, and all her temples in wurship of God and our Lady his modir halowid, and yaf to hem largely possessions. And Thomas to þo Kynges and archebisshops and othir bisshopis and prestis ʒaf the ordre of masse syngyng and expressid to hem the wordis which our Lord yaf in þe concecracion of his body and to[ʒt] hem also the paternoster and yaf hem specialy þe ordre of bapteme, commaundyng hem neuere to foryete þat sacrament of bapteme. And þan Thomas aftir þe conuertyng of all the peple by his preching and merveill[e]s worchyng to God endid his lyf gloriously in martirdom, as hit is red in his passion. And all manere peple which are born in þe londis in which Seynt Thomas was martrid by kynd have visaiges [f. 246v] lyk to howndis shapyn and wondur rogh into this day; and yn euery lande of Ynde growyn and are born meny diuers men, bestes, and herbis, of whom in speciall hit were now to long to telle.

And aftir the dethe of Thomas Apostle than the thre Kyngis made erchebisshoppis + wente in cumpace in alle the citees, townys, and londis, in which they foundid and ordeynid meny cherches and ordeynid hem

8 toʒt] toke L. 11 merveilles] merveillous L. 18 erchebisshoppis] erchebisshoppis and L.

ad dominum conuertisset et baptiza[sse]t, extunc ipsos tres Reges in archiepiscopos consecra[ui]t. Et ipsi tres Reges archiepiscopi effecti alios episcopos et presbiteros sine macula in omnibus populis elegerunt et ordinauerunt et omnia ydolorum templa in honore dei et sue genitricis matre consecrauerunt, quibus omnibus et aliis dei ministris dona predia et possessiones large donauerunt. Vnde beatus Thomas ipsis Regibus et archiepiscopis et aliis episcopis et presbiteris ordinem missam celebrandi et verba que dominus in cena in sui corporis et sanguin[is] consecracionem expressit et dominicam oracionem tradidit et de hiis omnibus fideliter instruxit et informauit. Et specialiter ordinem baptismatis ipsis dedit, et ipsum baptisma nullo modo vnquam debere obliuisci monuit et hortabatur et precepit. Et itaque beatus Thomas ibidem omnibus populis ad dominum conuersis †varia mirabilia operatus† vitam ibidem martirio sicut in passione eius legitur laudabiliter consummauit. Et omnes homines vtriusque sexus qui nascuntur in ipsis terris quibus beatus Thomas fuit martirizatus naturaliter facies habent in modum canum formatas, sed †[irsutas valde]†, in presentem diem. Nam †semper in vnaquaque terra et insula in India semper nascuntur et crescunt et sunt homines herbe et bestie et alia specialia de quibus per singula longum esset narrare.

Post recessum et decessum beati Thome appostoli extunc ipsi tres Reges in archiepiscopos ordinati omnes gentes ciuitates villas et terras circuibant, in quibus quamplurimas ecclesias fundauerunt et in ipsis

† varia mirabilia operatus] ad superiores partes Indie ad predicandum verbum dei se transtulit et. † irsutas valde] non hirsutas. † semper] *om.*

bisshopes, prestis, and mynistris, yevyng hem largely possessions, and levyng all vanyte of the world chosyn hem a perpetuel mansion in the cite of Sculla atte the foot of the mount Vaws. And with the help of God and of othir bisshopes and prestis they gouernyd so, all her londis and kyngdomes boþe in the spiritualte and also in the temperalte noght althing with drede but with love, noght as to her lordis but as to her fadris in alle thingis obeying and wiþout faynyd charite lovyng.

And in the second ȝeer next byfor her resolucion and departyng owt of this world thes thre Kyngis made archebisshopis lete gadre and mete in o place alle the kyngis, princes, and lordis, bysshopis, prestes, and mynistris in convocacion, whan they were þat tyme wery in age and had no childryn ne heres ne neuere had wyves ne concubynes, as is þe maner in that cuntre. And [+] hit is trowyd in all þat landis that they were virgines ynto her dethe. And as affermen some bokys [+], as they weren *primicie gencium* in the faithe, right so were they [f. 247r] the first of the peple which had virginall dignyte and offryd hit to God – as some bokis expownyn that they offrid gold in signe of virginal deuocion, dignyte, and chastite, and encence in signe of virgynall deuocioun and orisoun, and mirre in signe of þe mortificacion of the flesshe which nature denieth, aftir the seying of the wyse man

13 And] And as L. 14 bokys] bokys þat L. 15 they] *catchword* þe first L.

episcopos presbiteros et dei ministros ordinauerunt, quibus predia [f. 38r] et possessiones large per omnia contulerunt. Et relicta huius mundi vanitate in ciuitatem S[cull]a quam in pede montis Vaus fundauerunt perpetuam mansionem elegerunt. Et cum adiutorio dei et aliorum episcoporum et presbiterorum terras et regna sua in spiritualibus et temporalibus adhuc gubernauerunt et rexerunt, quibus omnes gentes non timore sed amore, non vt dominis sed vt patribus in omnibus et per omnia obediuerunt et caritate non ficta eos dilexerunt.

Anno [vero] secundo ante felicem eorum resolucionem extunc ipsi tres Reges archiepiscopi ordinati omnes alios reges et principes nobiliores ac maiores natu de terris et regnis eorum et omnes alios [episcopos presbiteros] et ministros dei in vnum locum conuenire et conuocari fecerunt. Et erant iam †longeui et decrepiti†, fessi, nec habebant aliquos liberos vel heredes nec, vt communis omnium illarum parcium consuetudinis est, vnquam habuerunt reginas vel concubinas. Et estimatur et firmiter creditur ab omnibus libris in oriente eos virgines fuisse et eos vsque ad mortem sic permansisse. Et asserunt quidam libri quod sicut fuerunt primicie gencium in fide, ita eciam fuerunt primi gencium qui virginalem dignitatem optulerunt, prout eciam quidam libri [in] eorum muneribus que domino optulerunt inter cetera ex superfluo exponunt, scilicet aurum optulerunt in signum virginalis †deuocionis dignitatis et castitatis, thus in signum virginalis deuocionis et oracionis, et mirram in signum mortificacionis carnis quam natura negauit, iuxta [dictum] sapientis

† longeui et decrepiti] longo senio et decrepitu. † deuocionis] *om.*

þat seith *In carne viuere sine carne est vita angelica, [non humana].*

And whan thes thre Kynges had in gadryng togidir alle the kyngis, bisshopis, princes, and peple forsayd, byddyng hem to abyde stable in the feiþ which þat Thomas had prechid to hem and þat þei shold þan chese an able and a conuenient man, trew and stable in þe feith, to succede in the place of Thomas in spiritualte to all þe peple. And he þat all þe peple as to her fadir shold obey to in wurship of Seynt Thomas into perpetuel memorie shold be callid Thomas and of all peple be wurshipid. And aftir decece euermore of euery patriarke so chosyn, alle þe bisshopis, erchebisshops, and prestis in his place shold chese aftir her concience to whom al þe peple as to her heed shold obeye. And to hym þei ȝaf þan (all the kynges, princes, and lordis) the tithes of alle her londis and possessions and assignyd. And so they chosyn at that tyme all on Iacobus of Antioche, a straungere which had into þat cuntre folowid Seynt Thomas Apostle, and chaungyng his name put to hym þe name of Thomas. And euere seth þe men of Ynde to such a patriarke callyd so Thomas obey as we obeye to our pope. [f. 247v]

And also þes þre gloriouse Kynges, havyng þat tyme no childryn ne

1 non humana] *om.* L.

sic dicentis: In carne viuere sine carne est vita angelica, non humana. [f. 38v]

Cum itaque tres Reges (vt dictum est) omnes reges episcopos et nobiles et omnes populos in vnum fecerant conuenire, extunc omnes hortabantur vt in fide quam ipsis Thomas predicauit fideles et stabiles permanerent, et quod ipsi tres Reges episcopi et presbiteri nobiles et uniuersi populi ibidem in vno congregati vnum virum ydoneum voluntatem in fide habentem ex omnibus populis ibidem congregatis communi †loco et vnanimi assensu el[i]ger[e]nt qui loco beati Thome apostoli in spiritualibus omnibus populis preesset et cui omnes populi vt patri in omnibus humiliter obedirent qui eciam in honore beati [Thome] apostoli in memoriale sempiternum patriarcha Thomas ab omnibus perpetue appellari deberet et ab omnibus venerari. Et post decessum talis [vnius] patriarche sic electi extunc omnes archiepiscopi episcopi et presbiteri deberent in vnum locum conuenire et alium loco defuncti secundum eorum conscienciam concorditer eligere, cui vniuersi populi vt priori per omnia deberent obedire. Et ipsi Reges tunc tali patriarche decimas omnium terrarum et regnorum perpetue dabant et assignabant. [Tunc] ipsi tres Reges + et omnes alij episcopi presbiteri et vniuersi populi concorditer elegerunt Iacobum Antioch[en]um aduenam qui ad ipsas partes beatum Thomam fuit secutus in primum eorum patriarcham †elegerunt, cui nomine mutato nomen Thomas imposuerunt. Et post hoc Indi tali patriarche qui Thomas vocatur vt nos pape obediuerunt in presentem diem.

Iterum predicti tres Reges gloriosi qui liberos et

† loco] voce. † elegerunt] *om.*

eyres, with o comune [+] counseill and assente of all þe peple þat tyme þan gadrid chosyn þe most noble, doughty, and worthy man which shold from þat tyme in her kyngdomes in temperalte for euermore be gouernour, that if eny rebellid to þe patriarkes, bisshopis, or prestis or yn þe feithe varied or erryd, þat by þe arme of seculer temperalte þei myght þan to þe right wey be compellid. And þis lordship perpetuelly durid by eyris. And such a gouernour yn temperalte shold not be callid as kyng or emperour, but of all peple shold be callid Prestre Iohn. And Prestre Iohn he shold be callid for this cause, for þer is no man worthier þan a preest in þe world, vndur whos power to rightful and vnrightful hevyn is shet and opynid and yn whos lyftyng of his hondis or strecchyng knees and nekkis of all emperours, kyngis, princes, and peples bowe and obeye; which is lord of all þe Indes, writyng into this day in his lettris and epistles many diuers vertues & dignitees. And þe lettris and epistlis which he writith to kynges & prynces be rolles foldyn & wounde in which he writith in name of salutacions blessynges of all þe childrin, wyves, seruauntes, handmaydenes, bestis, feldis, cornes, wynes, and al oþere goodes of hem, þe prynces or kynges or lordis, to whom at þat tyme [he writith]. And he writith to hem

1 comune] *after* comune *follows* co *plus 4 minims hyphenated at the line end, then on the next line* ne L.   18 he writith] *om.* L.

heredes [f. 39r] non habuerunt extunc eciam ex communi [cons]ilio et vnanimi consensu omnium populorum ibidem congregatorum ex omnibus populis ibidem congregatis elegerunt tunc virum strenuum nobilem et illustrem qui omnibus terris et regnis suis in temporalibus perpetue preesse deberet, vt si aliqui maliuoli et malefici patriarcham episcopos seu presbiteros non curarent vel ipsis rebellarent seu a fide apostatarent quod per brachium seculare ad viam rectam possent cogi et compelli. Et illud dominium perpetue deberet †exercere per heredes et durare. Et talis rector et gubernator in temporalibus non vt rex vel imperator deberet vocari, sed ab omnibus populis presbiter Iohannes imperpetuum deberet appellari. Nam presbiter Iohannes ex eo vocari deberet quia presbitero nullus sit dignior in mundo, cuius potestate hominibus iustis et iniustis celum clauditur et aperitur, et in cuius extencione manuum siue eleuacione omnium imperatorum regum et principum et populorum genua et colla curuantur. Et quamplurimas virtutes et alias dignitates idem presbiter Iohannes qui est dominus Indorum in suis litteris et epistulis specialiter scribit et exprimit in presentem diem. Et littere et epistule sue quas regibus et principibus mittit sunt rotuli [inuoluti], in quibus in principio scribit et mandat pro salutacionibus benedicciones omnium puerorum seruorum et ancillarum armentorum animalium agrorum et vinearum et specialiter vxorum et concubinarum et omnium que ille rex vel princeps seu homo possidet in domibus vel in campis. Et

† exercere] succedere.

as they be of condicion, sendyng for salutacions blessynges. [f. 248^{r}] And he hath in his selis and baners Goddis right honde blessyng in a cumpas with sterris yn cumpas enpeyntid. Also þe same lord of Ynde Prestre Iohn shal be clept of twey causes, þat is to sey of Iohn Euanglist þat was a prest and byfor alle other moost chosyn and lovid. Also þe same lord of Ynde shal be callid Prestre Iohn þurgh name and wurship of Iohn þe Baptist which baptisid our Lord, afor whom among alle childrin of wymmen rose not a more (as Thomas þe Apostle hem byfor had enfourmyd and prechid). And þes thre gloriouse Kynges to all kyngis, princes, & lordis, bysshopis, prestes, and all þe peple þes Thomas þe patriarke and Prestre Iohn as for her lordis and gouernours in spiritualte & temperalte assignyd for eueremore to whom al manere peple humbly shold do obedience and reuerence and to her ledyng and power submytte hem. And aftir þat þan, glad and ioying with miry hert, þes þre Kynges of al þat euere þei had seyn & herde enactyng and recordyng turnyd eche of hem to his owne cuntre and goodes. And so þe forseyd gouernours of þe Ynde cuntrees in spiritualte & lordis in temperalte þes patriarke Thomas & Prestre Iohn be callid in all þe world into þis day.

And also þes Kynges þan to oþir princes of her kyn and kyngly blood meny diuers londis & yles yaf & assyngnid in heritage which shuld be called princes of [Vau]s foreuere in perpetuell memorie, and ȝet this kyn-

21 Vaus] Waies L.

secundum quod ille est condicionis cui litteras suas mittit, secundum hoc sibi scribit et demandat pro salutacionibus benedicciones. Et habet dexteram dei benedic[ent]em in giro cum stellis ornatam in suis sigillis et vexillis. [f. 39^{v}] Item idem dominus Indorum presbiter Iohannes deberet vocari a duobus, videlicet a Iohanne euangelista qui fuit presbiter et a domino pre ceteris magis dilectus et electus. Item idem dominus Indorum Iohannes deberet nominari nomine et honore Iohannis baptiste qui dominum baptizauit, quo eciam non surrexit maior inter natos mulierum, prout Thomas apostolus per omnia [ips]os informauit. Item hij tres Reges gloriosi omnibus regibus principibus et nobilibus, episcopis et presbiteris ac omnibus populis Thomam patriarcham et presbiterum Iohannem in eorum dominos et rectores in spiritualibus et temporalibus tunc imperpetuum assignabant, quibus tunc vniuersi populi obedienciam et reuerenciam humiliter fecerunt et se eorum ducatui et potestati subiciebant. Et leti ac gaudentes ac alacri corde super omnia que viderant et audierant et acciderant et acta et ordinata fuerant ad propria sunt reuersi. Et sic ijdem domini et gubernatores Indorum in temporalibus et spiritualibus patriarcha Thomas et presbiter Iohannes in vniuerso mundo sunt vocati in hodiernum diem.

Iterum hij tres Reges de premissis itaque dispositis et ordinatis + extunc aliis principibus de sanguine eorum regali quamplurimas alias terras et insulas dederunt et iure hereditario assignauerunt, qui principes de Vaus imperpetuum deberent vocari in memoriale sempiternum. Et adhuc hec progenies

rede which is callyd þe kynrede of Vaus [f. 248v] is þe most, myghtyest, and noblest kynrede ȝet in Ynde and in + þe Est ȝet into this day. And þis forseid kyn hath made a castell in Acon for þe merveilles which were euery day þere bysily shewid, and meny of þe princes of hem for her noblete have weddid wyues yn diuers londis, of whos sede the ȝeer of our Lord a .Ml.CCC.lj. were worthy princes of lyve, ambaciatours in the c[ourt]e of Rome.

And whan all thinges by þes gloriouse Kynges wurshipfully were perfourmyd in the manere forseide, þan þei turnyd hem holy perpetuelly to dwelle in þe cite of Sculla, and aftir þe ful parfite takyng & vndirstondyng of þe feiþ þei ouerlyvid ij ȝeer. And a litil afor þe feste of þe Natyuite of our Lord a newe, straunge, vnsene sterre aperid ouer þe citee, and by þat sight þe ny resolucion of her lyf þei vndirstodyn and shewid to all peple þat þei were callid of God. Wherfor þei lete ordeyne for hem in that chirche þere her entoumbyng as to kyngis shold perteyne and on þat feste of Natiuite lete do solempnily dyvine servise. And the viij day aftir þe Natyuite Melchior, kyng of Araby & Nubye, þe ȝeer of his age .C.xvj. aftir þe full endyng of dyvine seruise dyed in bowyng of his heed wiþout dolour or dissese. Whom þe oþere two Kynges and oþere hyest & worthiest princes [f. 249r] and lordes and all þe peple [in her] pontificall and also

2 in] in to L. 6 courte] cuntre L. 20 in her] *om.* L.

que de Vaus vocatur est maior potencior ac nobilior progenies in India et in oriente in presentem diem. Et hec progenies [f. 40r] (vt supradictum est) in Acon propter diuersa mirabilia que ibi cotidie et assidue videbantur et audiebantur castrum fecerunt, et ex illis quamplurimi alij principes propter eorum nobilitatem in diuersis terris vxores duxerunt, de quorum semine anno domini millesimo trecentesimo [quinquagesimo primo] adhuc strenui principes fuerunt superstites in curia romana ambassatores.

Cum itaque omnia per ipsos Reges essent laudabiliter disposita et ordinata, extunc ad ciuitatem Scullam ad perpetue manendum tunc se transtulerunt. Et †post perceptam fidei plenam noticiam† duobus annis superuixerunt. Et extunc modicum ante festum natiuitatis domini quedam stella noua rara et insolita super illam ciuitatem apparuit, per quam eorum felicem resolucionem instare intellexerunt et quod a domino vocabantur omnibus intimabant. Vnde ibidem in ecclesia per ipsos regaliter facta tumilum sibi more regio preparari fecerunt, et per illud instans natiuitatis domini festum diuinum officium solempniter peregerunt. Et octauo natiuitatis domini die, extunc Melchior rex Arabum et Nubie diuino officio sollempniter celebrato anno etatis sue centesimo decimo sexto coram omni populo inclinato [capite] absque dolore in domino obdormiuit. Cuius corpus alij duo Reges et alij principes et nobiles ac vniuersi populi vestimentis pontificalibus

† post ... noticiam] *om.*

regal vestimentes *cum aromatibus* and all manere regale reuerence and duete lete entere and byrie as hit best semyd. And aftir þis the fift day, [+] þe feste of Epiphany, Baltazar, kyng of Godolye and of Saba, on þe ȝeer of his age a .C. & .xij. aftir þat þe masse was solempnly done dyed byfor all þe peple wiþout eny dissese. Whom the [iij Kyng] and oþir moost noble princes and lordis and al þe peple wurshipfully enterid byside þat Kyng Melchior. And not long aftir þat, þe vj day next sewyng, Iaspar þe thrid Kyng, kyng of Insule, þe ȝeer of his age an hundrid & .ix. aftir fulfillyng of dyvine seruise folowid þe oþer Kynges afor all þe peple. And whan þe body of hym was bore wiþ reuerence as byfallid to be biried bytwene þe oþer two Kynges, seyng al þe peple þe bodyes of hem departid, remevyng and receyvyng bytwene hem þe body of þe thrid Kyng in þe middis of hem. And so þes thre glorious Kynges as þei lovid in her lyf togidir so in her deþe were þei not departid. And the forseid sterre which byfor her deþe aperid, into þe tyme þat her bodyes were translatid into Coloyne left alwey stable and vnmeble, as Yndes seyn, aboue þe same citee.

†ouere þo Kynges† þat in her lyf lovyd h[e]m in so meny wises honourid hem aftir her dethe. For diuerse peple for diuers infirmites &

2 day] day aftir L. 5 iij Kyng] thre Kynges (s *apparently partially erased)* L.
17 ouere þo Kynges] *see note;* hem] hym L.

et regalibus cum aromatibus more regali prout decuit in tumilum posuerunt. Et post hoc quinto die (qui est festum Epiphanie domini) extunc Baltasar rex Godolie et Saba [f. 40v] anno etatis sue centesimo duodecimo celebrata solempniter missa coram omni populo absque aliquo dolore ibidem in domino quieuit. Quem †cicius alter† rex et omnes alij principes ac nobiles et populi iuxta corpus prioris Regis defuncti eodem modo et cultu regio in tumilo honorifice posuerunt. Et non post multum temporis, videlicet sexto die sequente, extunc Iaspar tercius Rex Tharsis et †Insule anno etatis sue centesimo nono diuino officio deuote peracto coram omnibus astantibus sine dolore alios duos Reges ad dominum sequebatur. Qui dum more regio prout decuit iuxta corpora duorum priorum Regum ad sepeliendum defferretur extunc coram omnibus populis astantibus corpora duorum priorum Regum in sepulcrum posita quodlibet in parte cessit et corpus tercij Regis in medio receperunt. Et hij tres itaque gloriosi principes quomodo in vita sua dilexerunt †itaque in morte non sunt separati. Et stella rara et insolita que ante eorum obitum apparuit quousque eorum corpora Coloniam transferentur, prout dicunt Indi, immobilis supra †[eandem] ciuitatem† permansit.

Post decessum et obitum trium Regum gloriosorum extunc deus qui eos in vita dilexit ipsos eciam post mortem quamplurimum honorauit. Nam diuersos vtriusque sexus homines quacumque infirmitate dolore vel angustia siue

† cicius alter] tercius. † Insule] Insule Egrisoulle. † itaque] se ita et. † eandem ciuitatem] ciuitatem Seuwa.

tribulacions from ferre and ny, by londe and by watir come for to seke helpe by þe merites of þes Kynges [f. 249v] gloriouse and by her merites of God euidently were delyuerid, confermyng so þe fey which þei prechid in her lyf wiþ Seynt Thomas wiþ meny vertues and signes. And her bodies lying in þe sepulcre in her regale vestimentis and also pontificall vestimentis noght lyke as dede but as slepyng & better colourid þan in her lyf semyd to all þe peple, of which þei praysid God and worshipid.

Longe aftir, whan þe Cristyn feith more and more florisshid, þe enemye of all good sewe among þe corne cokkill in that cite of Sculla and all þe parties of the Orient, þat is to sey, heresies, opynions, & errours among þe Cristyn feiþ, so þat þe bodies and þe relikes of thes Kynges of all straungers were had in lasse reuerence and worship; for her londis and regions aftir þan were odyously devidid in her feith. And þan the bodies of þes Kynges which had left so long into þat tyme incorrupte and hole and as slepyng fro þens turnyd anon into poudir, chaungyng & departyng þe flesshe fro þe bones. Wherfor þe peple of þe kyngdomis of Nubye, Arabye, Saba, & Go[d]olye, Tharse & of Insule born in which þes Kynges regnyd weren devidid in the feith. And whan þe kyngdomys of þes Kyngis and þe cuntres of þe Este weren þus corrupt & in þe feiþe wiþ heresie þus

17 Godolye] Gololye L.

tribulacione detinebantur longe vel prope in terra vel in mari positos, qui auxilium ipsorum trium Regum implorabant et deuote inuocabant deus per eorum merita euidenter eos liberauit, ita quod ex longinquis [f. 41r] partibus per terram et per mare populi in maxima multitudine ad eorum reliquias confluebant, et fidem quam cum beato Thoma in vita predicabant eciam maioribus virtutibus et signis in morte et post mortem confirmabant. Et ipsorum corpora vestimentis regalibus et pontificalibus in sepulcro posita non quasi mortua sed vt dormiencia et melius quam in vita colorata omnibus populis apparebant, in quibus deum benedixerunt et laudauerunt.

Post multum vero temporis, cum itaque fides christiana in ipsa nobili ciuitate Sculla et vniuersis partibus et regnis orientis floreret, extunc inimicus omnium bonorum seminauit inter triticum zizannium, scilicet inter fidem catholicam diuersarum specierum heresim opiniones et errores, propter quod corpora et reliquie ipsorum trium Regum ceperunt ab omnibus indigenis minus in reuerencia haberi et minus venerari; nam terre et regna eorum in fide diuidebantur odiose. Et tunc statim ipsorum trium Regum corpora, que (vt dictum est) vsque ad illud tempus quasi dormiencia [et incorrupta] permanserunt, extunc + eorum carnis materia de eorum ossibus soluebatur et more suo in puluerem reuertebatur. Vnde homines de regno Arabie et Nubie Saba et Godolie Tharsis et Insule nati in quibus ipsi tres Reges regnabant in fide sunt diuisi.

Cum itaque horum trium Regum regna et vniuersa plaga orientis essent corrupta et in fide et + heresi essent

odiously devidid and of þe patriarke Thomas and of Prestre Iohn myght not be reuokyd from her erroures, þan þe peple bygan fast to drawe to ydolatrie, and þe childrin of blessid men in þe citee of Sculla dwellyng were odyously dyvidid in þe feith. And þan euery partie of euery cuntre, [f. 250^{r}] of envye and also of reuerence, þe body of her Kyng toke out of her sepulcre, for þei wold not have hem restyng among hem of her parties aduersaries, [and] led into þe moost hyest and wurshipful places of her landis; which were receyvid of all peple wiþ all reuerence & worship [as] whan þei come fro Bethlem, and yn toumbis reuerently enclosid, dwellyng so long tyme.

And whan it plesid to God þat þe cokkill were departid fro þe corne, and gloriouse Emperour Constantyn by Seint Siluestre þe pope by signes and tokenys to þe feiþ þe ȝeer of our Lord a .M^{l}.CC.xxxiiij. was conuertid, clensid of the lepre of his gentilite and ydolatrie, þe same tyme Eleyne, his modir, among þe fals Iewis in the parties of þe Orient was infect and corrupt in her fals and Iewis perfidie, but wondurly aftir turnid to þe feith of God, as is pleynly foundyn in the bokis of þe Inuencion of þe Holy

7 and] *om.* L. 8 as] *om.* L.

odiose diuisa, et propter nimiam multitudinem distanciam et discordiam †per potenciam a patri[f. 41^{v}]archa Thoma et presbitero Iohanne ab erroribus non possent reuocari $^{+}$, extunc in regnis et in terris illis in hac dissensione cepit gentilitas reuerti et ydolatria repullu[l]are, †et beatorum nati qui in ipsa ciuitate Sculla potenter habitabant eciam in fide odiose fuerunt diuisi. Et tunc queuis pars tam ex reuerencia quam inuidia corpus sui Regis de sepulcro sumpsit, quia cum parte aduersa esse et quiescere id [n]oluit, et ad loca maiora sue partis reduxit. Que ab omni populo prout quando viuentes de Bethleem venerunt cum ymnis et laudibus et reuerenciis maximis sunt recepta et in loculis diuersimode ornatis reuerenter sunt inclusa; et in hiis per tempora longiora permanserunt.

Cum autem placuit deo quod triticum et semen fidei itaque longo tempore laboratum quod eciam per zizannia seminatum et aliis persecucionibus et impedimentis dudum latitauit in terra et talibus variis frigoribus et tempestatibus transactis eciam in germine appareret: vnde circa annum domini †millesimum ducentesimum tricesimum quartum dum gloriosus Constantinus imp[e]rator in occidente per sanctum Siluestrum gracia dei signis et prodigiis ad fidem esset conuersus, a lepra carnis gentilitatis et idolatrie mundatus, et in nouum hominem vita et moribus in melius esset mutatus, eodem tempore Helena sua mater inter perfidos Iudeos in oriente conuersabatur et iudaica perfidia quasi iam esset infecta et corrupta, sed mirabiliter ad dominum [f. 42^{r}] conuersa, prout hec omnia in libris de inuencione sancte

† per] et discordancium. † et] vnde in tali miseria homines de regnis istorum trium Regum. † millesimum] *om.*

Crosse. And from þens, as myche as [byfor] Eleyne was lyvyng in þe Olde Testament in mysbileue, aftir in þe Newe Testament was bysily studying in þe euangelies and lawe of God. And all places which in þat cuntre God had wiþ his godhede, myght, and manhode halowid, and she hem by þe cumfort and suggestion of þe Iewis lawe held as for vnclene and in hate, aftirward wiþ all ricchessis wurshipyng deuoutly visitid. Wherfor þe wurshipful Eleyne, aftir þat she had found þe crosse and þe nayles by grace and myracle of God aboue, ouer þe same place of þe mount of Caluarie & þe sepulcre of Crist, and þe place also wher þe thre [f. 250v] Maries stood whan þei sawe remevid þe stone from þe monument, and þe place in which Crist apperid to Marie Magdeleyn yn liknes of a gardyner, and meny oþir holy places lete make a faire chirche in whiche she closid al þe places forseid. And aftirward Prestre Iohn and þe folk of þe regne of Nubye born (which in þo parties be callid Nubyans) lete make vndur þe mount of Caluarie out of þe hard roche a chapell which þei did halowe in worship of þo .iij. glorious Kynges and memorie þat Melchior, kyng of Arabum and Nubye, restid þere vndur þe cloude whan he soght to wurship our Lord in his childhode. And þat chapel is into þis day clepid þe chapell of Nubyans, but þe Sarazins now have stoppid þe dore of þat chapell with stones for envie.

1 byfor] *om.* L.

crucis plenius reperiuntur. Et extunc venerabilis Helena, quanto magis prius in veteri testamento iudaica perfidia insistebat, tanto magis postmodum in nouo testamento + in euangeliis studiosius estuabat. Et omnia loca sancta que in illis et in aliis partibus Ihesus sua deitate et humanitate ac †potencia consecrauit, que prius ex suggestione Iudeorum ipsa Helena prophanata et odiosa habuit †incontaminata, hec omnia loca Helena postmodum ad laudem dei et con[fusio]nem Iudeorum humiliter visitauit et deuotissime honorificauit ditauit et ampliauit. Vnde postquam venerabilis Helena crucem et clauos domini nutu dei miraculose inuenit, extunc super eundem locum †in monte† Caluarie, et sepulcrum Christi, et locum quo tres Marie steterunt et lapidem de sepulcro reuolutum †viderunt + , et locum in quo Ihesus [Marie Magdalene] apparuit in specie ortolani, super hec omnia loca et alia sancta loca Helena pulcherimam ecclesiam construxit in [qua] hec omnia loca supradicta insimul comprehendit et inclusit. Et postmodum presbiter Iohannes et homines de regno Nubie nati, qui in illis partibus Nubiani vocantur, subtus montem Caluarie ex rupe de durissima petra capellam exsculpere fecerunt, quam in honore trium Regum consecrari fecerunt in memoriale quod Melchior rex Arabum et Nubie ibidem in caligine et nebula resedit quando dominum in sua infancia adorandum quesiuit. Et vocatur illa [f. 42v] capella Nubianorum ad Reges in presentem diem; sed saraceni nunc prout patet ianuam ip[s]ius capelle lapidibus ob inuidiam obstruxerunt.

† potencia] presencia. † incontaminata] et contaminata. † in monte] et montem.
† viderunt] viderunt et locum quo Ihesus in cruce matrem discipulo commendauit.

And also þis Eleyne made in all places + which God in his manhode and presence halowid wiþ signis and mervailles many mynstres & cherches, ordeynyng in hem bysshopes, abbotis, and prestes & goddis mynistres, endowyng hem wiþ meny diuers possessions and tithes. And þan aboue þe place where þe aungel aperid to þe shiphardis, denouncyng to hem wiþ multitude of hevynly knyghthode and brightnesse þe natiuite of our Lord, she lete make a double cherche which she lete calle Gloria in Excelsis, and into þis tyme in þ[o] cuntres hit is callid Gloria in Excelsis. And in þat chirche she lete ordeyne a college of chanons which of spe[f. 251r]ciale priuilege at all her ouris and servise bygynne wiþ *Gloria in excelsis*, as in þis cuntre we bygyn with *Deus in adiutorium meum intende.*

And aftir þat þis cherche was fully made, than she come ynto Bedleme into þe cave wher þe child Ihesu was born which into þat tyme by þe envie of Iewis (as God wold) was shet and lettyd from þe entring of eny man, holding þat place as for acursid and prophane; in which Eleyne fonde þe cracche in which Ihesus þe child afor the oxe and þe asse lay lappid couchyng in hey, and tho cloþes yn which Ihesus was woundyn, þe hey, and þe smok of our Lady which she left in þe crecche whan she fled out

1 places] places in L. 8 þo] þe L.

Iterum in omnibus locis que deus in humanitate sua presencia signis et prodigijs consecrauit et illustrauit in ipsis venerabilis Helena monasteria et ecclesias honorifice fundauit, et in hiis patriarchas archiepiscopos episcopos abbates et presbiteros ac dei ministros instituit et ordinauit, quibus predia et possessiones ac decimas habundanter erogauit. Extunc eciam Helena supra locum quo pastoribus angelus cum multitudine milicie celestis cum claritate natiuitatem domini annunciauit pulcherimam duplicem ecclesiam construxit, quam Gloria in Excelsis vocauit, [et] adhuc in omnibus partibus orientis Gloria in Excelsis vocatur in presentem diem. Et in ipsa ecclesia quondam fuit ditissimum collegium canonicorum qui ex speciali priuilegio omnes horas canonicas cum Gloria in excelsis inceperunt, sicut in partibus istis cum Deus in adiutorium; et adhuc incipiunt horas ibidem cum Gloria in excelsis in presentem diem.

Postquam hec ecclesia fuit facta et perfecta extunc †veniens Bethleem ad speluncam et tigurrium in quo deus fuit homo natus, et, vt est predictum, in ipsum locum (scilicet speluncam et tigurrium) post natiuitatem Christi vsque ad tempus illud sicut eciam deo placuit ex inuidia Iudei nullum hominem vel animal intrare permiserunt, nam ipsum locum pro loco [f. 43r] maledicto et prophanato habuerunt †et pro contaminato. Et in ipso loco tunc Helena presepe in quod Ihesus infantulus in feno ante azinum et bouem fuit positus et ipsos pannos quibus Ihesus fuit ibidem inuolutus et fenum et camisiam beate Marie quam in presepe dimiserat oblita quando cum infantulo Ihesu

† veniens] *archetypal corruption.* † et] et omnem intrantem habuerunt.

of þat cave for drede of the Iewis, & al þat she þere fonde, save þe crecche, she caried wiþ her into C[o]nst[a]ntinople and leyd hem reuerently in the chirche of Seynt Sophie. And þere þei left into þe tyme of Kyng Charles, which, while he toke and conquerid Ierusalem and meny oþir citees Cristien and Zacharie the patriarke and oþir Cristynmen out of þe Sarazins hondes, comyng home wiþ hostis by Constantinople he toke þan our Ladies smok, þe hey, and þe cloþes in which Ihesus þe child was lappid by askyng and graunting of Eleyne and broght hem home wiþ hym to þe citee of Acon wiþ meny oþir reliqs, in þe chirche of our Lady levyng; which be into þis day from meny diuers cuntres visitid, soght, & wurshipid.

But of þe lengthe and brede of þis sherte meny folk merveile. And vndirstondith þat in þe este [f. 251v] cuntres growiþ miche flex twies in þe ȝeer, of which is made cloþe good and fyne and of good chepe. & in all þo cuntres for þe more partie mennys cloþes and wyves be long and brood & wyde and wondur white and clene for þe grete hete of þe sonne, and lenger þei are þan eny of [her] o[þi]r cloþes, namely of wymmen. And þat passith ouer þe clothis in lengthe of wymmen of wurship and astate be

2 Constantinople] Canstontinople L. 17 her oþir] our L. 18 þe] þe oþer *struck through* L.

de spelunca fugit metu Iudeorum et recessit [reperit et †inuenit]. Que excepto presepio omnia secum in Constantinopolim transtulit, et ibidem in ecclesia sancte Sophie reuerenter collocauit. Et ibidem vsque ad tempus Karoli permanserunt. Qui dum Iherusalem et alias ciuitates christianorum et Zachariam patriarcham et alio[s] christianos de manibus saracenorum eripuisset et per Constantinopolim in redditu cum suis excercitibus tran[si]sset, extunc camisiam beate Marie et fenum et pannos quibus Ihesus infantulus fuit inuolutus peciit et obtinuit. Que cum aliis reliquiis quibus ibidem et alibi fuit honoratus secum sumpsit et Aquisgrani (id est Akne) in ecclesia beate Marie quam ibidem fundauit honorifice collocauit. Que ibidem a fidelibus ex longinquis partibus visitantur et honorantur in presentem diem.

Set de longitudine et latitudine huius camisie multi homines mirantur. De qua est sciendum quod in partibus vltramarinis et orientis nimis multum crescit linum bis in anno, vnde efficitur pannus lineus multum bonus et subtilis [et] optimo foro. Et in omnibus partibus illis omnia vestimenta virorum et mulierum pro maiori parte †sunt multum longa lata et larga et vltra modum alba et munda propter intollerabilissimum solis ardorem sunt facta. Et specialiter camisie mulierum [f. 43v] in quibus aliqua vis consistit sunt tam longe qu[od] fimbrias omnium aliorum vestimentorum quasi circa tres vel quatuor vel quinque vlnas †excedit. Et illa pars camisie que sic excedit

† inuenit] inuenit prout beata virgo ibidem oblita dimisit et reliquit. † sunt] sunt linea et sunt. † excedit] excedunt.

richely set wiþ gold and good stones aftir þe power and astate of þe wymmen. And whan eny mayde child is þere borne of a riche mannys, the modur letith make such smokkis and shetis and othir ornementis to her dowyng and weddyng. And whan eny wurshipful woman ridith by þe strete, þan some wurshipful man or her seruaunt or a knyght on foot shal bere þat ilk smok abrood bytwene his hondis. And oþir pore wymmen þat may not have such smokkis so arayed wiþ stones þei have þogh large smokkis white, lenger þan eny of her othir vestimentis, wiþ diuers swete herbes sauerid and wiþ rose watir wesshyn, as the odour may be felid whereuere they ride or go. And our Ladies smok as aftir þe comune custome of þ[o] cuntres and aftir the stature was þoght wondur short. And our Lady, as bokis þere seyn, was a woman yn party fully, flesshy, and broun.

And aboue þis cave and þe place also wher the thre Kynges offrid her yeftis, + which [f. 252[r]] place to þe Iewis was so odyous, Eleyne lete make a faire cherche richely with gold & stonys adornyd, in manere of a castell

11 þo] þe L. 15 yeftis] yeftis to L.

auro margaritis et aliis preciosis lapidibus secundum facultatem †mulierum portantur ditissime ornata†. Et dum alicui nobili vel diuiti mulieri filia nascitur, extunc mater inmediate incipit facere filie tales camisias et linthiamina et alia ornamenta ad dotem et ad nupcias necessaria et apta; que vix potest perficere vsque ad tempus sue filie maritacionis et desponsacionis. Et dum aliqua sponsa vel nobilis seu diues domina in plate[i]s equitat, extunc aliquis nobilis vel famulus seu miles pedester portat illam [partem] camisie ornatam suis brachiis extensis. Et dum tales domine et mulieres vadunt extunc recipiunt partem camisie sue anteriorem subtus brachia et posterior pars camisie per aliquem militem seu famulum vel pedissequam leuatur et portatur vtrisque brachiis et manibus extensis. Et alie mulieres que non habent camisias preciosas et ornatas hee tamen habent camisias multum longas mundas et albas omnia alia vestimenta multum excedentes, diuersis aromatibus et herbis odoriferis fumatas et aqua rosacea lotas, ita quod vbicumque equitant vel incedunt eorum odor et fragrancia per totam plateam sentitur. Vnde camisia beate Marie que est Aquisgrani secundum communem consuetudinem parcium illarum et secundum staturam tunc temporis hominum videtur fuisse et esse multum breuis et humilis. Et in omnibus libris [f. 44[r]] et in partibus illis eciam legitur quod beata Maria fuit puella aliquantulum grossa et carnosa et fusca.

Super hanc speluncam tugurrium et locum in Bethelem in quo deus homo fuit natus, in quo eciam tres Reges munera domino optulerunt, qui locus, vt supradictum est, itaque Iudeis fuit odiosus, super hunc locum venerabilis Helena nobilissimam et pulcherimam ecclesiam fundauit opere m[usa]ico et marmoribus et auro sub vitris diuersimode optime et ditissime et regaliter ornatam, et in modum castri

† mulierum ... ornata] mulieris portantis ditissime est ornata.

strengthid, not sclattyd but aboue tymbre of cedre helyd wiþ lede. And out of þis cherche is a wey descendyng ynto þe cave wheryn Crist was borne, which is right vndur the chef hye auter of þe quere. And a litil fro þe autur, in a [wal]le, is þe c[rec]che of lengþe of thre or four fete ynto which our Lady lappid her child in hey byfor the oxe and þe asse, and in þe same place byside the cracche þe .iij. Kyngis worshipid þe child, offryng to hym her yeftis. And in þat cave Seynt Ierome, Seynt Poule, and Eustas, nobles and lordis of Rome which lyvid wiþ Seynt Ierome, be þere byried. And in þat faire cherche bene about .lxx. pylers of marble beryng & susteynyng þe housyng and þe tymbryng, and þe ȝeer of our Lord a thowsand .CCC.xlj. Sarazins wold have take doun þe fairest pilers and have put hem in her templis, but þei were ferid wiþ an horrible noyse and sight [and] lete hem stond still. And þis cherche wiþyn & wiþout riche & nobly is made. And Eleyne in þat chirche ordeynid an erchebishop, chanons, prestis, & oþir ministres which of special pryuilege yn all her massis & servise seid and song *Gloria in excelsis deo*, and in alle festis and houris. But aftir þat

4 walle] vale L; crecche] cherche L. 12 and(2)] *om.* L.

propugnaculis factam; set non est testudinata, set super ligna et tigna cedrina, et est plumbo cooperta. Et in hac ecclesia ante chorum descenditur in speluncam et locum in quo deus homo erat natus. Et directe subtus maius altare quod est supra chorum apud speluncam est altare in loco in quo deus homo fuit natus. Et non longe ab hoc altari est presepe lapid[e]um †in quodam muro† circa tres vel quatuor pedes longum, in quod beata Maria infantulum Ihesum ante bouem et asinum in feno posuit pannis inuolutum. Et in eodem loco iuxta presepe tres Reges deum adorauerunt et eidem ibidem munera optulerunt. Et in ipsa spelunca sanctus Ieronimus Paula et Eustochium nobiles Romane qu[e] ex deuocione ibidem cum beato Ieronimo deguerunt sunt sepulte. Et in ipsa nobilissima et pulcherima ecclesia sunt circa lxx columpne marmoree tecta et ligna et alia susten[f. 44v]tantes et portantes. Et anno domini millesimo trecentesimo quadragesimo primo saraceni pulcriores columpnas †accipere voluerunt et in templo eorum proposuerunt ponere; set horribili visione perteriti ipsas stare permiserunt. Et vltra modum hec ecclesia intus et foris est ditissime nobilissime et regaliter facta consummata et perfecta. Et venerabilis Helena in ipsa ecclesia archiepiscopum et canonicos presbiteros et alios dei ministros instituit qui ex priuilegio speciali in omnibus missis et eciam missis animarum Gloria in excelsis deo cantabant, et in festiuitatibus omnes horas canonicas cum Gloria in excelsis incipiebant. Et quamplurimas alias †reuerencias prerogatiuas habuit hec ecclesia pre aliis et habet prout decet, de quibus per singula longum esse[t] narrare. Set postquam

† in quodam muro] vt ibidem est moris. † accipere] excipere. † reuerencias] reuerencias et.

the Holy Lond fill into þe hondis of þe sowdon, euery Cristynman þat wold come into þat chirche payed to þe soudons officers two Venician pens. And now Grekis have the quere and þe chef autour for a certeyn pension to do þere her servise.

And in þe night of þe Natiuite of our Lord all manere peple of all langages [f. 252v] þat be vndur hevyn comyn, fillyng all herbergages wiþin Bedlem and without. And for þat, þe soudon suffriþ none excepte officers to enhabite þere but Cristinmen. Also all manere peple of all tunges in þat night þer gadrid and herbo[ro]wyd, þogh þei be in þe feithe & yn her tunges dyvidid and odiouse, ȝet euery secte & parte of Cristien have a special place ordeynid by hemself in which þei may sey her servise aftir her right and custome solempnily as bysemith. And the Latynes, which have hem most aftir þe feith of þe courte of Rome, done her seruise in þe cave at þe autir where the child Ihesus was bore. And than many diuers songes, spechis, lettris, and melodies be in diuers langages & tunges herd, and ȝet no man lettiþ oþir in her songe. And þan aftir syngyng of þe masse þat bygynniþ *Dominus dixit ad me* þei go þan to þe double cherche wher þe aungell apperid to þe shepherdis denouncyng to hem the natiuite of our Lord [and þer] þei begyn & syng þe masse þat bygynnith *Lux fulgebit*. And

9 herborowyd] herbororowyd L. 19 and þer] *om.* L.

terra sancta ad manus et potestatem peruenit soldani, quicumque christianus ipsam ecclesiam intrare voluerit dat officiario soldani ibidem duos denarios venicianos. Et nunc Greci sub certa pensione pro se habent chorum et maius altare ad diuinum officium eorum peragendum. In nocte natiuitatis domini extunc omnium ydiomatum et linguarum †omnes peregrini et christiani qui sunt sub celo in ipsa ecclesia conueniunt. Et tunc hospicia in Bethleem peregrinis intus et extra sunt plena; et propter hoc lucrum soldanus exceptis †officiatis non permittit ibidem nisi christianos habitare. Iterum omnes christiani qui ibidem in ecclesia in nocte natiuitatis domini conueniunt, licet in fide et linguis sunt †odios[i] diuisi, tamen queuis pars et secta omnium christianorum in ipsa ecclesia per se suum habet locum specialem [f. 45r] deputatum, in quo secundum ritum eorum diuinum officium faciunt et agunt tunc solempnissime prout decet. Vnde Latini qui se habent ad fidem ecclesie romane agunt diuinum officium suum in spelunca in altari et loco quo deus homo fuit natus. Et tunc in ipsa nocte diuersa ydiomata littere et cantus et melodie in variis et diuersis linguis audiuntur; tamen [nu]llus homo impedit alium in suo cantu vel aliquo †versu vel cathenatu†. Et tunc celebrata missa que incipit Dominus dixit ad me tunc vadunt omnes ad ecclesiam duplicem que Gloria in Excelsis vocatur, vbi angelus domini pastoribus natum d[omin]um annunciauit, et ibidem celebrant missam que incipit Lux fulgebit; et

† omnes] homines. † officiatis] officiatis suis. † odiosi] odiose. † versu vel cathenatu] risu vel cachinatu.

þe two cherchis be þer in twyn but a litil half myle. And aftir þe singyng + of þat masse all peple with ioy turne aȝen to Bedlem to þe hye masse, and þere þei rede al þe gospelles which be red in þat holy cherche. And þan all peple of all tunges, ȝung and olde, þat day syng þe anteme in Latyn *Hec [est] dies quam fecit dominus* which þei kun in all þat cuntre in Latyn by vse. And þe Iewis of envie callid Eleyne "stabularie", for she had made so noble a chirche on a stable and ovir so foule [f. 253r] a place foundyd and edified which was to hem so odyouse. Wherfor euery Cristemesse nyght a table of þe merites and preisynges of Eleyne is þere hangid, þus bygynnyng, *Venerabilis Elena fuit bona stabularia que [h]ic presepe domini sui fideliter quesiuit.* And oþir meny of [the] merites & vertues of Eleyne in that table be writyn.

Also in the feste of þe Epiphanie concours of all peple, tungis, and nacions comith þere þat þe thre Kynges wurshipid our Lord, offryng to hym her yeftis, and a sterre nobly ouergilt þei were wont to honge, drawyng hit al þat day wiþ cordis craftily from place to place in þat cherche. And of all þe noble customes, priuileges, and prerogatyues which

1 singyng] singyng of þe L. 5 est] *om.* L. 10 hic] sic L. 11 the] her L.

hee due ecclesie distant per modicum dimidium miliare. Et ibidem illa missa celebrata extunc omnes populi cum magno gaudio et cantu redeunt in Bethleem ad summam missam. Tunc in eisdem ecclesiis omnia euangelia ibidem specialiter leguntur, de quibus †tamen vniuersa ecclesia catholica de longinquo loquitur et testatur. Et tunc vtriusque sexus omnes homines quarumcumque linguarum vel scolarum existunt paruuli et adulti in ipsa ecclesia per totum illum diem cantant illam antiphonam in latino Hec est dies quam fecit dominus, quam in illis omnibus partibus in latino cordetenus sciunt ex vsu. Et est sciendum quod Iudei ex inuidia inter se stabulariam Helenam vocauerunt, quia huiusmodi nobilissimam ecclesiam supra stabulum et tam vilem locum eis exosum fundauit et edificauit. Vnde omni nocte natiuitatis domini tabula de laude et meritis [f. 45v] venerabilis Helene de digitis beati Ieronimi scripta iuxta presepe in spelunca †pend[i]tur, que sic incipit: Venerabilis Helena fuit bona stabularia que hic presepe domini fui fideliter quesiuit. Et alia quamplurima de meritis et virtutibus venerabilis Helene in hac tabula sunt conscripta.

Item in festo Epiphanie domini est eciam in ipsa ecclesia maximus omnium linguarum populorum concursus. Et in loco iuxta presepe quo tres Reges dominum adorauerunt et eidem munera optulerunt magnam stellam optime deauratam pendere consueuerunt, que per totum illum diem artificialiter de loco ad locum in ecclesia cordis trahebatur et regebatur. Et de hiis huius ecclesie in Bethlem nobilibus consuetudinibus et specialibus priuilegiis et prerogatiuis que

† tamen] tunc. † penditur] pendebatur.

bene in þat chirche it were to long to telle. But how þe fest of þe Epiphanye is þer wurshipid shal be declarid heraftir.

And aftir þat þes chirches were þus complete, þan Eleyne went her to Nazareth, which is a delitable cite and myrie, set in a valey ful faire, vnwallid, fer departid here and þere of þe habitacions and houses þerof. And in þat citee Eleyne lete founde a faire cherche, ordeyning þerin an erchebisshop, chanons, prestis, and Goddis mynistres, [and] wiþ diuers possessions endowid. And in þis chirche on þe right side b[y] þe quere Eleyne enclosid þe chaumbre in whiche was our Lady whan þe aungell grette her, and þere is made a chapell in þe whiche sto[nt] þe pilere by which þe aungel stode and knelid, and his ymage is ympressid in þat pilere as hit were in a sele. And afore þe dore of þat chaumbre & chapel toward þe [est] is þe welle of which our Lady was wont oft to [f. 253v] drawe her watir, and þere þe aungel oft confortid her and grette her. And of þis welle pilgrymes bere her watre into diuers cuntres and ȝet done so into this tyme, and meny sike folk þerof receyve her hele. Wherfor of envye þe Sarazins stoppid þe welle, and ȝet þe more hit is stoppid, þe more hit wellith out. Ne þe Sarazins to no þing wol ocupie þat watir, and meny infirmytes yet þurgh hit is curid. And in þat chapell were ordeynid speciall prestis and

7 and(2)] *om.* L. 8 by] byfor L. 10 stont] stode L. 13 est] chapell L.

hec ecclesia pre aliis ecclesiis prout decet [habet] singulariter longum esset narrare. Et qualiter festum Epiphanie ibidem honoratur et celebratur inferius audietur.

Iterum postquam hee ecclesie itaque essent complete, extunc Helena se transtulit Nazareth; que est ciuitas multum delectabilis et amena et val[l]e florida sita, et non est murata, et habitaciones eius et domus sunt hinc inde disperse. Et in ipsa eciam ciuitate magnam et pulcherimam ecclesiam fundauit, in qua archiepiscopum et canonicos et presbiteros et dei ministros instituit et ordinauit, et prediis et possessionibus quamplurimis specialiter ditauit et ampliauit. [f. 46r] Et in eadem ecclesia Helena de dexteris prope chorum cameram beate Marie conclusit, in qua fuit et stetit quando ei Gabriel archangelus dominum concipiendum annunciauit. Et ex ipsa camera nunc facta est capella, in qua est columpna †circa quam angelus stetit et reclinauit, et eius ymago in columpna sicut in sigillo [est] impressa. Et ante ianuam illius camere et capelle versus orientem est fons de quo Maria frequenter aquam haurire et afferre solebat, et ibidem angelus ipsam sepius salutabat et confortauit. Et ex hoc fo[n]te peregrini ad longinquas partes afferebant aquam, et quamplurimi infirmi ex ea sanitatem receperunt. Vnde ob inuidiam saraceni ipsum †fontem obstruxerunt; et quanto plus obstruebant tanto plus erumpebat. Nec saraceni a[d] aliqua adhuc vtuntur ipsa aqua; set a peregrinis ad longinquas partes affertur et portatur, et ex ea varie infirmitates depelluntur. Et in ipsa capella fuerunt speciales ministri et

† circa] contra. † fontem] fontem sepius.

mynistres which euery day þe seruise of þe Annunciacion of our Lady wiþ her offises & houris songyn and seyde. And byside þat chapell and chaumbre is a stonyn piler yn which from þe day þat Mary was grett wiþ þe aungell [a tokyn] hath byleft into þis day, and þe same hour euery day þat þe sonne heliþ þat tokyn afor the goyng doun of þe sonne is and was that tyme in which þe aungell gret our Lady, denouncyng God for vs of her to be bore man. And in þe tyme whan hit was Cristyn were ordeynid mynistres in þat chapell & chaumbre þat, whan þe sonne touchid and helyd þat signe in þe pilere, þan þei drowe thries a litil belle which hyng aboue þat pilere, and þan al þe peple wiþ knelyng deuoutly sey[d], *'Ave Maria';* [...] and of meny Cristyn folk is into þis day of ferre cuntres visitid. And þei seyn in þo cuntres eche to oþere, 'Go we for indulgencis of Nazareth to Ave Maria'. And in þat chirche and chapell all her houris + bygunne with *Aue Maria*, as in þis cuntre [f. 254r] we begynne with *Deus in adiutorium.*

And þis cite of Nazareth is set in þe londe and lordship of Galilee, and beside þe marchis of Galile is an hye hill, not grete but wondur hye, which is callid *mons Thabor*, on whom Ihesus sate with his disciples whan he was

4 a tokyn] *om.* L. 10 seyd] seyn L. 11 *see notes.* 13 houris] houris be L.

presbiteri qui omni die dominica[m] annunciacione[m] cum omnibus eius officiis et horis diei et noctis cantabant et celebrabant. Et iuxta hanc capellam et cameram est columpna lapidea in qua a die postquam angelus Marie dominum annunciauit vsque in presentem diem signum permansit. Et dum per totum annum sol †t[eg]it illud signum ante eius occasum tunc fuit et est hora quando Gabriel Mariam salutauit et deum de ipsa pro nobis hominem nasciturum annunciauit. [f. 46v] Et temporibus christianorum fuerunt in ipsa camera et capella speciales ministri quando sol tetigit signum illud in columpna qui tunc ter trahebant paruam campanam que supra columpnam pependit; et extunc omnes homines cum genufleccione dicebant ter deuote, Aue †Maria. Et illa capella vocatur ibidem in omnibus partibus orientis Aue Maria, et a fidelibus de longinquissimis partibus visitatur in presentem diem; vnde dicunt ibidem [et] in omnibus partibus illis alterutrum, Eamus pro indulgenciis Nazareth ad Aue Maria. Et in illa capella et ecclesia in qua ipsa camera beate Marie est inclusa omnes hore canonice cum Aue Maria incipiebantur, sicut in partibus istis [cum] Deus in adiutorium meum †intende. Et ista ciuitas Nazareth est in terra et principatu Galilee sita, et iuxta fines Galilee est mons non magnus set vltra modum altus qui vocatur mons Thabor, super quem Ihesus coram discipulis suis fuit

† tegit] tetigit. † Maria] Maria et exinde per vniuersum mundum peruenit in consuetudinem quod ante solis occasum ter trahitur campana et dicitur a fidelibus ter cum genuflectione Aue Maria. † intende] *see note.*

transfigurid, as hit is conteynid in þe gospell. And on þat hill Eleyne foundyd a grete, strong, and passyng fair mynstre and in manere of a castell with touris and defence al about strengthid yt, in which þe abbot of þe ordre of Seynt Benet vsyd crose, mytre, ryng as a bisshop, and bulle of lede. And the feest of Transfiguracion of our Lord fallith euere o[n] þe day of Seyntis Syxti, Felicissimi, & Agapiti, and in all þo cuntres massis be seyd wiþ newe wyne, and all metropolytane cherchis & cathedrall be dedified in þe worship of þe transfiguracion. And þe masse is begunne wiþ *Dominus dixit ad me* and *Alleluia, h[i]c dies sanctific[a]tu[s]* and þe gospell *Assumpsit Ihesus discipulos suos et ascendit in montem excelsum et transfiguratus est ante eos*. And kyngis, princes, lordis, barons, knyghtis, and all prelatis of þat diocise comyn to þat dedicacion of þat chirche, & al þei do put and stike aboue þe chirche the baners of her armys and al þe peple þat nyght of þe dedicacion wacchyn wiþ all ioy, & wiþ all ornementis wurshipyn. And all metropolitan cherchis & cathedrale in þat cuntres be callyd cherchis of Seynte Sophie. And Thabor is from Ierusalem but thre day iournes and an half, and bytwene þat mount and Ierusalem is a wey in [f. 254v] which Ihesus went with his disciples in his manhood and toght hem, and ferrere þ[an] bytwene þat mount & Ierusalem and þe placis

5 on] of L. 9 hic dies sanctificatus] hec dies sanctificetur L. 13 stike] i *perhaps over erasure* L. 19 þan] þere L.

transfiguratus, prout in euangelio continetur. Supra illum montem + venerabilis Helena magnum et pulcherimum et fortissimum monasterium fundauit et in modum castri turribus [et muris] et propugnaculis vndique firmauit. Cuius abbas ordinis [beati Benedicti] infula anulo baculo pastorali ac bulla plumbea vtebatur. Et occurrit semper illud festum transfiguracionis domini die sanctorum Sixti Felicissimi et Agapiti; et tunc in omnibus partibus orientis celebrantur misse cum vino nouo. Et omnes ecclesie metropolitane et cathedrales in oriente in honore transfiguracionis domini sunt consecrate. Et ipso die [f. 47r] in omnibus ecclesiis in missis cantatur introitus Dominus dixit ad me et Alleluya hic dies sanctificatus et euangelium Assumpsit Ihesus discipulos suos et ascendit in montem excelsum et transfiguratus est ante eos. Et ipso die omnes reges principes et nobiles barones et milites et omnes in ipsa diocesi prelati ad dedicacionem ecclesie sue cathedralis conueniunt, et omnes eorum vexilla cum eorum armis supra ecclesiam figere et ponere faciunt. Et omnes populi illam noctem in ecclesiis cum gaudiis et leticiis ducunt insompnem, et multum ornant ecclesias suas diuersis et variis ornamentis. Et omnes ecclesie metropolitane et cathedrales in omnibus partibus orientis vocantur ecclesie sancte Sophie (id est V[e]rbigene); et est titulus omnium ecclesiarum cathedralium quod Ad sanctam Sophiam vocantur. Et [distat] hic Thabor a Iherusalem tres dietas cum dimidia. Et inter Iherusalem et illum montem via fuit per quam Ihesus iuit cum discipulis suis in humanitate, [in] qua docuit et signa fecit et predicauit, et vlterius quam inter Iherusalem et illum montem et loca

set bytwene went not Ihesus as man. And þat Mount Thabor aboue is of no more brede þan þat mynstre may comprehende. And þe Sarasins byfor þe takyng of Acres occupied þis mynstre and tokyn and madyn a castel þerof. And ayen hem þe Cristynmen at þe foot of þe mount made anoþer castell from which þei defendid þe Sarazins passage vp or doun, callyng þat castell Blansagarda. And of þat castell aftir come a noble kynrede and progenye which were callyd þe noblis and kynrede of Blansagarde, and so be callid into þis day. But now þat castell and mynstre aboue þe mount is distroyed and desert.

And whan Eleyne in all þes places had ordeynid erchebisshopis, bisshopes, abbotis, prestes, and oþir mynistres and al done þat she myght semyng to þe wurship of God, þan she had streitly in thoght þe bodies of þe thre gloriouse Kynges which offrid to God, wurshipyng hym wiþ yeftis; and went her into þe londis and provinces of Ynde, which was yet at þat tyme sugget to þe empire of Rome, with a grete multitude of peple wiþ her. In which londis all þe temples yn whiche regnyd ydolatrie as ferre as she myght she distroyed and instede of hem in the honour of God foundid chirches & ministres, ordeyning in hem erchebisshopis, bisshopis, abbotis, prestis, and mynistres for fulfillyng of Goddis seruise in strengthing of Goddis worship. And þe Christyn feith, which was yn [f. 255r] þo cuntres

inter ea sita vt homo non iuit vel processit. Et ipse mons Thabor desuper non est maioris capacitatis quam illud monasterium comprehendit. Et ante capcionem Acon saraceni hoc monasterium ceperunt et occupauerunt et ex eo castrum fecerunt. Contra quos christiani in pede montis aliud castrum fecerunt a quo saracenis ascensum et descensum †defendunt; cui nomen Blansagarda imposuerunt. Et ex illo †castro nomine maxima et nobilis progenies surrexit [f. 47v] qui ibidem nobiles de Blansagarda vocantur in presentem diem. Set nunc illud castrum et monasterium supra montem sunt destructa et deserta.

Cum itaque venerabilis Helena in hiis et in omnibus locis quibus e[i] expedire videbatur archiepiscopos episcopos et abbates presbiteros et alios dei ministros instituisset et ordinasset, et omnia ad laudem et honorem dei rite perfecte et laudabiliter perfecisset, extunc de corporibus et reliquiis ipsorum trium Regum qui d[e]um ibidem adorauerunt et ei munera optulerunt cepit anxia cogitare. Et ad terras et prouincias que circa Indiam adhuc romano imperio permanserunt cum nobili et maximo comitatu se transtulit. In quibus omnia templa et aras ydolorum vbi ydolatria et gentilitas pullulauerat prout potuit destruxit, et pro hiis in laudem et honorem dei ecclesias et monasteria fundauit, in quibus archiepiscopos episcopos et abbates et alios dei ministros instituit et ordinauit, et cultum dei in omnibus partibus illis in omnibus et per omnia reparauit et amplificauit et fidem christianam, †quam in illis partibus prius

† defendunt] defenderunt. † castro] castro et. † quam] que.

hatid and detestable, she mych encrecyd and honourid, enhauncyd, and glorified. To whom al Cristyn peple come wiþ one acorde, for they herde of þe merveilis of her in fyndyng of þe cros, þe nayles, our Ladyes smok, þe hey, & þe clothis in which God in his manhede and childhode was lappid. Wherof all peple were comfortid, but þe Iewis and þe gentiles and wurshipers of ydolatries herof were sorowyng and confoundyd. And whan Eleyne of þe kyngdomes of þe .iij. Kynges and of her lyf and dedis by hem done so pleynly was enfourmyd, she þan more diligently þoght & enquerid of her bodyes and reliqes. And her desire God fulfillid, *qui [semper prope est] omnibus inuocantibus eum in veritate.* For he þat to Eleyne byfor þe crosse and þe nailes so depe vndur þe erthe hid cowd shew by reuelacion, the same God also þe bodies and reliques of þe thre Kynges couthe shewe to her. Of which Kynges þe bodies of two, þat is to sey, of Melchior and Balthasar, in amplificacion of þe wurship of God merveilously and wiþ grete studye wan hem wiþ askyng of þe patriarke Thomas and Prestre Iohn.

9 semper prope est] est prope L.

detestabatur, tunc multum honorauit Helena exaltauit et glorificauit. Ad quam tunc omnes christiani et catholici vnanimiter venerunt. Nam audierant quanta mirabilia et magnalia deus de inuencione sue crucis et clauorum ac camisie beate Marie virginis feni et pannorum quibus deus in sua humanitate et infancia fuit inuolutus per ipsam venerabilem Helenam †dominus fuit operatus. In quibus Helene [f. 48r] omnes congratulabantur vnanimiter et in fide confortabantur, et Iudei et gentiles, ydolatre et heretici de hiis multum dolebant et confundebantur. Et extunc †eciam ipsis superioribus partibus quamplurimis ecclesiis et monasteriis fundatis vndique et reparatis et [in] hiis dei ministris de nouo institutis et omnibus christicolis in fide confortatis extunc venerabilis Helena de corporibus et reliquiis trium Regum beatorum cepit inquirere et diligenter inuestigare. Et cum de ipsorum trium Regum [regnis] et ipsorum vita et gestis per ipsos Reges factis et ordinatis Helena plenius fuit instructa, extunc de eorum corporibus et reliquiis cepit studiosius et ardencius cogitare et diligencius laborare. Cuius desiderium imple[uit] omnipotens deus qui semper prope est omnibus inuocantibus eum in veritate et †quia prius ipse Helene crucem suam ac clauos sub terra profundissime absconsa reuelauit ipse Helene eciam corpora et reliqui[a]s trium Regum beatorum monstrauit. Quorum duo corpora, scilicet Melchior et Balthasar, a patriarcha Thoma et domino I[nd]orum presbitero Iohanne et aliis illarum terrarum et parcium principibus et prelatis ad ampliandum honorem dei et diuin[um] cultum miraculose et studiose impetrauit. Et quia tunc pro parte romano imperio pertinebant, et omnes vnanimiter audierunt et sciuerunt quanta mira et magnalia deus per Helenam fuisset operatus, sibi ipsorum duorum Regum corpora benigne et reuerenter tradiderunt et dimiserunt.

† dominus] *om.* † eciam] eciam in. † quia] qui.

But the body of þe thrid Kyng, Iaspar, þe peple of his londe (callid Nestorynes, in þe londe and kyngdom of Iaspar borne) kept among hem, duryng in her eresies, errours, and wykkidnes, and translatyng & havyng to þe best, strengest, and grettest yle of Ynde which is clept Egriscull (of which Iaspar also was kyng & lord callid), & þere þat body priuily hyd. And whan Eleyne had þe bodyes of þe two Kyngges, willyng not þe bodies of þes thre Kynges [f. 255v] to be departid or devidid, by solempne legatis and messagers and grete yeftis of þe moost myghty potentis Nestoryns of þe londe of þe Insule for chaunge of þe body of Thomas þe Apostle, which she had wiþ her þan lyng, she gate þe body of Iaspar the þrid Kyng. Which body of Thomas þe Apostle fro þes Nestoryns twies aftir þat was byreft, & of certeyn causis to her londe of Nestoryns restorid; & into þis day yet in all þo parties of Nestorynes is a comune profecie þat þe body of Seynt Thomas þe Apostle yet þe thrid tyme shal be byreft & to Coloyne to þe bodies of þe thre Kynges restoryd & translatid and þere perpetuelly abyde. And while þe body of Iaspar þe thrid Kyng was broght from þe yle of Egrisculle & ioyntly couchyd to þe bodyes of þe toþir two Kyngis, such an odour & so grete swetnesse was saveryng of hem þat all þe peple of ferre cuntres of þat odour felt and þerof were fillid.

Corpus vero Iaspar tercij Regis Nestorini [f. 48v] de regno ipsius Iaspar Regis nati sub eorum potestate habuerunt, et in sua nequicia et heresi perdurantes suum sanguinem dare resisterunt ob inuidiam et negauerunt. Nam illud ad meliorem et forciorem et maiorem insulam Indie nomine †Egrosilla (de qua Iasper eciam rex Insule vocabatur) suum corpus transtulerunt et secretissime absconderunt. Venerabilis Helena dum itaque habuit duorum Regum corpora, nolens ipsos tres Reges pati diuisos, per multos solempnes legatos precibus importunis et muneribus multis apud potenciores Insule †ipsos Nestorin[o]s optinuit et† corpus Thome apostoli, quod tunc eciam ibidem impetrauit, pro corpore Iaspar tercij Regis dedit et permutauit. Et id ipsum corpus Thome apostoli a Nestorinis bis est ablatum et ex certis causis ipsis totidem restitutum. Set in presentem diem adhuc est commune vaticinium in omnibus partibus illis quod adhuc corpus Thome apostoli eis tercia vice debeat auferri et Colonie ad trium Regum corpora transferri et ibidem perpetue permanere (prout adhuc inferius a[u]dietur).

Iterum dum itaque corpus Iaspar tercij Regis de Insula portaretur et aliis Regum corporibus iungeretur, extunc talis et tanta fragrancia odoris et suauitatis ab eis exiuit quod omnes de longinquo suauitate[m] odoris senciebant [et] ipso replebantur.

† Egrosilla] Egrisoulla *(so generally)*. † ipsos Nestorinos optinuit et] et ipsorum Nestorinorum ordinauit et obtinuit quod.

Than Eleyne þe bodyes of þes þre Kynges in a riche toumbe in the noblest citee þat than her son had made and foundid, Constantinople, which is the heed of all Grece, wiþ grete ioy and reuerence wiþ meny oþir diuers reliques which she had fro diuers placis gotyn she broght and translatid, and of al peple þer for þat same cause callyd and gadrid togidir wiþ ympnes and all wurship, as hit best bysemyd, were resceyvid þere in the chirche of Seynt Sophye in Constantinople; which is aboue all þe cherches of all þe world passyngly [f. 256r] myche and large, so þat a passyng grete ship [wiþ her veiles spred abrood] may esyly turne [her in] her and cumpase. And þat cherche in Grege is callyd Verbygene. And all þe cathedrall chirches and metropolytane in þe Est be callyd and obeying to þe cherche of Seynte Sophie — which Constantyn foundyd, and þe moost and hugest marble pylers wiþ þe helpe of a child alone leftyd, and þat cherche wiþ meny diuers ornementes wurshipid. And yn þat cherche is *tunica inconsutilis*, and on of þe naylis of our Lord, and a partye of þe pilere to which Ihesus was boundyn and scourgyd, and meny oþere diuers reliques of which Grekis recche noght. And in þe tyme ȝet of Lowis, kyng of Fraunce, þe verrey croune of God left þere. And þat tyme þe Turkis and Sarazins mych distroyed þe citee of Costantynople and þe lordship of

9 wiþ her veiles spred abrood] spred abrood wiþ her veiles L; her in] *om.* L.

Et extunc venerabilis Helena ipsorum trium Regum corpora in loculo ditissimo in maiorem et nobiliorem filij sui ciuitatem quam fundauerat Constantinopolim [f. 49r] (que est caput Grecie) cum maxima exultacione et reuerencia cum aliis diuersis reliquiis quas hinc inde impetrauerat et congregauerat transportauit, et om[n]ibus populis ibidem ad hoc specialiter congregatis et conuocatis cum ymnis et laudibus prout decuit multum honorifice sunt recepta et ibidem in ecclesia sancte Sophie in Constantinopolim; †[que] est vltra modum pre omnibus aliis ecclesiis in mundo magna et lata, ita quod nauis magna omnibus velis suis explicatis et extensis in ea [se] posset commode vertere et girare. Et ipsa †ecclesia sancte Sophie quod in greco dicitur Verbig[e]ne; et (vt supradictum est) omnes ecclesie metropolitane et cathedrales in oriente ad sanctam Sophiam vocantur. Quam Constantinus fundauit et eius maximas marmoreas columpnas cum adiutorio dei cum infante solus leuauit et diuersis aliis ornamentis plurimis decorauit. Et in ipsa ecclesia est tunica domini inconsutilis, et clauus domini, et pars columpne ad quam Ihesus fuit ligatus et flagellatus, et quamplurime alie et diuerse reliquie venerande de quibus Grecis non est cura. Et temporibus Lodowici regis Francie adhuc corona domini spinea in ea remansit. Et tunc temporis Thurci et saraceni Constantinopolim et imperium Grecorum multum destruxerunt.

† que] reuerenter collocata et est sciendum quod ecclesia sancte Sophie in Constantinopolim. † ecclesia] ecclesia vocatur ibidem ecclesia.

Grekis, and þe emperour þat tyme þan bysoght þe help of Lowys, þe kyng of Fraunce, and many placis lost þan recouerid wiþ þe help of God and of hym. And for h[is] costis þe kyng Lowis took yn wed and yn payment [...] wiþ myche sorow of þe Grekis and grete ioying of þe Frensshe men by ship broght home to þe citee of Parys; which crowne þe Grekis yet hope to recouere into this day. And in þis cherche stont a pylere of marble grete, on which stondiþ an ymage of þe emperour – of which spekiþ Maundevile &c, wherfor no more here.

Whan Eleyne þes bodies of þes thre Kynges by þis same pilere had couchid, than from all diuers londis of all peple þei were wur[f. 256v]shipid and long tyme visitid. And God to her reliques meny yeftis of grace and mercy ha[s] yevyn by shewyng of meny mervailes þere, so þat al in þe Cristyn feith on londe or on watir were visitid wiþ eny tribulacions were †wiþ by sekyng of her helpe and merytes.

Þan aftir þe deþe of Eleyne, regnyng Iulyan þe Apostata, ydolatrie and mysbyleue regnyd, and myche hard persecucion of Cristynmen þat tyme durid, as ys foundyn and red in þe passions of many diuers martris. Cesyng

3 his] her L. 4 *see note.* 12 has] had L. 14 wiþ] *see note.*

Et imperator tunc auxilium sancti Lodowyci implorauit; qui multa perdita et deuastata cum auxilio dei recuperauit. Et pro suis expensis tunc imperator sancto Lodowyco ipsam coronam spineam tradidit et obligauit, et cum Grecorum maxima lamentacione exultacioneque Francorum in crastino sancti Laurencij ad nauigium fuit ducta [f. 49v] et ad villam parisiensem translata; quam Greci adhuc recuperare sperant in presentem diem. Iterum in hac ecclesia sancte Sophie magna stat columpna marmorea, super quam stat ymago imperatoris equestris erea optime deaurata; et habet pomum rotundum more imperiali in sinistra, et contra orientem rebellantibus saracenis quasi minans dextera. Et iuxta et subtus hanc columpnam venerabilis Helena ipsorum trium Regum corpora in loculis diuersimode ornatis honorifice et specialiter collocauit. Et cum ista trium Regum corpora in hac ecclesia et ciuitate itaque essent collocata, extunc a longinquis terris et partibus ab omnibus populis humiliter et deuote sunt visitata et longo tempore venerata, et ad eorum reliquias confluentibus deus dona sue misericordie multimode est largitus et per ea multa mirabilia operatus. Nam omnes qui in fide et deuocione †in terra vel in mari detinebantur eorum merita et eorum auxilium implorabant in quacumque tribulacione† deus liberauit eos.

Post obitum et decessum gloriosi Constantini et venerabilis Helene, Iuliano apost[a]ta regnante, extunc ydolatria et gentilitas repullulauit et grauissima persecucio gladij in christianos et martires temporibus longis durauit, prout in passionibus diuersorum martirum et aliis libris plenius continetur et reperitur. Et

† in terra ... tribulacione] eorum auxilium implorabant a quacunque tribulacione in terra vel in mari detinebantur eorum meritis.

þan aftir þe persecucion of þe swerd ayen martiris of Crist, þan in al þe world bygan of newe anoþir persecucion, of heretikes and sismatikes, ayen þe truw peple of þe feiþ, and þat persecucion is seyd þat hit was more crwel þan þat oþir byfor. And in þis tribulacion þe Grekis, alþogh þei had þan many wurshipfull & holy doctours & popis of Rome of Grecelond born, yet þan fro þe articles of þe feith (as shal be seyd) they departid and disseuerid and þere ches[e] to hem a propre patriarke to whom from þat tyme in all as we to our pope obeyed. And duryng þis tempest þe bodyes of þes thre Kynges were left wiþout eny reuerence or wurship. Wherfor our Lord left all Grece and Ermeny into þe hondis of Sarazins & of hem of Pers, which distroyed mich þes londis; which Maurice, þe ferst emperour of Romayns, wiþ þe help of þe *Med[i]olanen[s]es* recouerid. And, as it is sayd, wiþ þe counceil of the same emperour þe bodies of þes thre Kynges [f. 257r] were þan wiþ other reliques translatid. And hit is red þat Manuel, Emperour of Grece, sent a wyse and discrete religious man, Eustorche, a Greke [of] ber[þ], in legacye to þe syte of Mediolane; whom þe *Mediolanen[s]es* [ch]esyn to her bisshop. And turnyng ayen to þe kyng,

7 chese] chesith L. 12 Mediolanenses] Medeolanences L. 16 of berþ] bery L. 17 Mediolanenses] Mediolanences L; chesyn] plesyn L.

ipsa persecucione gladij contra martires cessante, extunc cepit in vniuerso mundo alia de nouo persecucio hereticorum et scismaticorum diuersorum errorum contra catholicos et fideles; et ipsa persecucio hereticorum et errorum fertur durior et amarior [f. 50r] fuisse persecucione gladij †anterioris, vt fides christiana et catholica tanquam triticum crib[r]aretur, vt nullus puluis errorum in ea de cetero remaneret. Et in hac tribulacione Greci, licet habuissent quamplurimos sanctos et egregios doctores et romanos pontifices de Grecia natos, tamen ab ecclesia romana et articulis fidei (prout inferius audietur) recesserunt et sibi proprium patriarcham prefecerunt et elegerunt, cui ab illo tempore in omnibus et per omnia vt nos domino pape vsque in presentem diem obediuerunt. Et [in] hac tempestate corpora et reliquie ipsorum trium Regum absque aliqua reuerencia et in nullius cura permanserunt. Vnde dominus Grecia[m] et Armenia[m] tradidit in manus saracenorum et Persarum, qui has terras multum destruxerunt; quas Mauricius primus imperator Romanorum ex Grecis cum auxilio Mediolanencium recuperauit. Vnde (prout fertur) eiusdem imperatoris consilio ipsorum trium Regum corpora cum aliis reliquiis postmodum fuerunt translata. Et legitur quod Manuel Grecorum imperator Eustorgium virum religiosum et prudentem nacione Grecum in legacione misit Mediolanum †quia prudens erat quem† in episcopum elegerunt Mediolanenses. †Reuersusque ad regem

† anterioris] anteriori. † quia prudens erat quem] et quia prudens erat et apud Imperatorem potens ipsum. † Reuersusque ... imperatorem] et ipsorum precibus et incitacione ipsa trium Regum corpora de quibus tunc nullus curauit ab Imperatore.

axyd of hym þat he wold graunte hym some iewell for to lede with hym, noght expressyng certeyn in axyng. But aftir þe grauntyng of þe kyng he axid nempnyng þe bodies of þes thre Kynges. Which of þe emperour he had grauntyd, and so he broght hem reuerently to þe cite of Mediolane and in þe chef worthy chirche, which is now þe Frere Prechours, with ympnis and praysynges [l]eid, wiþ all þe peplis wurshipyng; where God þurgh her meritis, as he did in oþir placis byfor, oft wroght meny meruailes and vertues.

The yeer of our Lord a .Ml.C.liiij. the cite of Mediolane rebellid to þe ferst Emperour Frederike; which he þoght to distroy, and he bysegid hem. Wherfor the noblest of þe citee, fewe wytyng, hyd pryvely the bodyes of þes thre Kynges. And whan þe emperour wiþ help of Reynold, archebisshop of Coloyne, and oþir princes and lordis bysegid þe cite of Mediolane, and aftir toke and ouercome +, þan Reynold þe archebisshop þe paleys entrid of Assone, a lord whom þe emperour moost hatyd, and in his hondis þat paleys kept. Whiche A[s]so axyd a safe conduyte of comyng to þe erchebisshop Reynold. Which, while he come vndur seurte to þe erchebisshop, bysoght of hym þat, if he wold gete hym grace [and] good will of þe emperour, þan wold he yeve hym and shewe þe bodies of þe thre Kynges, privily hid, wiþ othir reliques. And whan þe archebisshop had

6 leid] seid L. 14 ouercome] ouercome and L. 16 Asso] also L. 18 and] of L.

peciit vt quoddam iocale secum + ducere posset; set quale non expressit. Set postquam rex anuit nomina[ui]t corpora Regum; que apud imperatorem† impetrauit. Et sic ipsa Mediolanum reuerenter transportauit, et in ecclesia speciali que nunc est fratrum predicatorum cum ympnis et laudibus cum omni populo honorifice collocauit. Vbi eciam deus [o]b ipsorum merita, prout in locis prioribus, multa mira[f. 50v]bilia et virtutes operatus est.

Anno vero domini millesimo centesimo sexagesimo quarto ciuitas mediolanensis Frederico imperatori primo rebellauit; quam imperator destruere proposuit, et circumvallauit. Vnde meliores et nobiliores et maiores in ciuitate, paucis scientibus, ipsorum trium Regum corpora secretissime absconderunt. Et cum imperator auxilio Reynaldi archiepiscopi coloniensis et aliorum principum et dominorum Mediolanum obsedit [cepit] et expugnauit, extunc Reynaldus archiepiscopus coloniensis palacium domini Assonis †decurij, quem imperator pre aliis omnibus exosum habuit, cepit et intrauit et ad manus suas optinuit. Qui dominus Asso secretum accessum + ad Reginaldum coloniens[em] archiepiscopum peciit. Qui dum securus et secrete ad archiepiscopum venisset, ipsum peciit vt, si sibi graciam apud imperatorem posset et vellet impetrare, extunc trium Regum corpora sibi cum aliis reliquiis vellet dare et absondita demonstrare. Quod cum Reginaldus archiepiscopus

† decurij] de Turri.

gotyn hym þis grace of þe kyng, he had of Asso [f. 257v] þes reliqes, which he led wiþ þe priuiest of his counceile secretely to Coloyne, and shewid aftirward to þe emperour, but þan first þo reliques axid of þe kyng, not shewyng hym in certeyn what þei were byfor þe tyme of þe kyngis grauntyng of hem to hym, doutyng hym to have gotyn þe grauntyng of hem of þe kyng. And þan þe erchebisshop translatid þo reliqes wiþ grete worship to Coloyne opynly, and of all peple with all ympnis and praysinges were receyvid and yn the cherche of Seynt Petre wiþ grete reuerence leyd; by which our Lord yet meny merveiles and vertues wurchith ynto þis day, and of meny diuers lordis and peple from ferre londis þei be soght & visitid and wurshipid.

And what reuerence and wurship is had of þe reliqes of þo þre Kynges in all þe londis of þe Orient of all kyngis, princis, lordis, and all peple of þat londes & provinces is clerely and opynly knowyn. And witith wele þat Prestre Iohn, lord of Ynd, and al kyngis and lordis vndur his empire obeying, and þe kyng of þe londe George þe Lowour, and all oþir kyngis Cristyn þere þe day of Epiphanye, as þei wold yn þe day of her coronacion, wiþ all manere regale vestimentis & ournementis in wurship of þe reliques of þe thre Kynggis be clad and crownyd. And þre tymes in

coloniensis fecisset, extunc sibi reliquias dedit et demonstrauit. Quas cum habuisset, extunc per suos fideliores et secreciores statim versus Coloniam direxit et destinauit; quod postmodum imperatori indicauit. E[t] tunc primo ipsas reliquias ab imperatore postulauit peciit et impetrauit; et distulit imperatori prius indicare, nam ipsas reliquias venerandas dubitauit se posse impetrare. Et extunc archiepiscopus ipsorum trium Regum corpora cum aliis reliquiis Colonie publice et honorifice transtulit, et ab omni populo cum ympnis et laudibus recepta et in [f. 51r] ecclesia sancti Petri ibidem reuerenter sunt collocata; per quas dominus ibidem quamplurima mirabilia et virtutes in presentem diem operatur, et a principibus et nobilibus †de diuersis populis deuote venerantur et a longinquissimis terris et partibus et prouinciis cum maximis reuerenciis queruntur et visitantur. ... [f. 51v]

Iterum in quali et quanta reuerencia hij tres Reges qui domino munera optulerunt †in honore habeantur in omnibus terris et prouinciis in oriente et ab omnibus regibus et principibus et nobilibus et omnibus populis ibidem †cognoscitur. Et† sciendum [est] quod presbiter Iohannes dominus Indorum et omnes reges sub eius imperio et rex †Georgie inferioris et omnes alij reges christiani hij omnes in die Epiphanie sicut in die coronacionis eorum vestimentis regalibus et aliis ornamentis [+] in honore trium Regum beatorum sunt induti et coronati. Et tribus vicibus in

† de] et. † in] et. † cognoscitur Et] venerentur. † Georgie] Georgie superioris et rex Georgie.

þe masse þei offre, þat is to sey, in þe bygynnyng of þe masse, at tyme of þe offertorie, and at tyme of þe comunnyon, and þei offre gold, encense, and mirre. And euerych oþir lord arraieth hem as he is of noblesse and faculte and offryn also thries in þe masse. And how myche þe sismatikes and heretikes have yn wurship and reuerence þes thre Kynges in þes [f. 258[r]] cuntres is merveile. And hit is to wyte þat in the parties of þe Orient and al þo parties beyend þe see þe Cristyn feithe is dyvidid into dyuers parties and sectes of men whos namys here folowyn: that is to sey, Nubyans, Soldynes, Nestorynes, *Latini, Indi, Armeni, Greci, Sir[i]ani, Georgiani, Iacobite, Nicholaite, Copti, Ismini, Maromini, Mandapoli.* And in all þes peple aboue all þes men and heretikes but in her owne londis and kyngdomes euere þe Indes bene þe principall, and be clepid þerfor þere Latines for ca[u]se þat þei sey and synge her masses, houres, & her offices and redyn in Latyne, as we done in this londe. But more solempnly þei seyn and do her masse and servise in þe day of þe Epiphanye þere þan we in þis cuntre, and s[yng] her gospell.

Also Nubianes be men of þe kyngdome of Arabie and Nubie in which

9 Siriani] Sirani L.   13 cause] can se L.   16 syng] seyn L.

missis offerunt oblaciones: videlicet in introitu misse offertorio et communione offerunt aurum thus et mirram cum maxima humilitate et deuocione. Et alij principes et nobiles se quiuis pr[e] alio ornat prout est m[ai]oris nobilitatis et †facultatis eciam offe[ru]nt ter in missis oblaciones. Item notandum [est] in quali et quanto honore et reuerencia hij tres Reges habeantur ab omnibus hereticis et scismaticis in omnibus prouinciis et partibus orientis qui adhuc ibidem degunt et permanserunt. Et sciendum [est] quod in oriente in omnibus partibus vltramarinis fides christiana in diuersas partes et hominum sectas est diuisa, secundum homines quorum nomina subsequuntur: Nubiani Soldini Nestorini Latini Indi Armeni Greci †Suriani Georgiani Iacobite Nicholaite Copti †Ysmini †Maromini †Mand[a]poli. Et ex hiis omnibus [f. 52[r]] christianis ibidem super omnes predictos homines et hereticos preter in ipsorum hereticorum propriis terris et regnis semper †Indi habent principatum. Et vocantur propterea ibidem Latini quia missas et horas et diuinum officium cantant et legunt et agunt in latino, sicut in partibus istis. Set multum solempnius in die Epiphanie domini diuinum officium peragunt quam in partibus istis, et cantant †euangelium.

Item Nubiani sunt homines de regno Arabie et Nubie, in quibus

† facultatis] facultatis et.   † Suriani] Siriani.   † Ysmini] Ysini.   † Maromini] Maronini.   † Mandapoli] Mandopoli.   † Indi] Latini.   † euangelium] evuangelium in missa per notas.

regnyd Melchior, lord & kyng of hem, which offrid to our Lord gold. Also the Nubyans myche folowe þe childis birthe in þe feith. For as gold put yn þe hote fire is not lessid ne by no rustyng may be consumyd or peyrid, so þes Nubians may wiþ non heresie be corrupte. Wherfor þei be callyd þere Nubyans, and have afor al Cristyn sectis þere prerogatif in wurship of her Kyng into þis day. And whidir þei go, they go togidir, and for special reuerence in all places of Cristyn þei have special chirches and chircheyerdis for her byrying, as the Frisons. And her prestis go to þe autir wiþ crounes of gold or ouergilte aftir her faculte, and þat they do yn tokyn þat þe Kyngis so reuerently crownyd offrid her yeftis to our Lord.

Also þe Soldynes be men of þe kyngdom of Godolye and of Saba yn which regnyd Balthazar, [f. 258[v]] which offryd to God encense. For þes were sumwhat corrupt in the feith of an heretike was clept Soldyne, and they have hem sumwhat aftir þe manere of Grekis, and they have a partie of heresye, and vsyn lettris of Calde, and have by hemself a propre langage. And þes have not þere so mych reuerence as þe Nubyans, for they kepe not so solempnly þe feith as Baltazar her kyng which offrid to God

regnauit Melchior dominus rex eorum qui domino aurum optulit. †Itaque Nubiani homines de regnis eorum natum† ipsum in fide splendide sunt secuti. Nam sicut aurum in camino ignis positum non minuitur nec aliqua rubigine potest consumi, sic isti homines Nubiani aliqua heresi non poterant corumpi. Vnde specialiter Nubiani ibidem vocantur, et in omnibus partibus ibidem christianorum volunt pre aliis habere prerogatiuam, et habent pre aliis christianis, in honore sui Regis in presentem diem. Et quocumque tendunt simul pergunt, et ob specialem reuerenciam in omnibus locis christianorum habent pro se ecclesias speciales et cimiteria in quibus specialiter sepeliuntur, sicut Frisones Aquisgrani. Et horum presbiteri cum coronis aureis vel deauratis secundum eorum facultatem ad altare coronati accedunt reuerenter, et hoc faciunt in signum trium Regum qui domino coronati reuerenter munera optulerunt.

Item Soldini sunt homines de regnis Godolie et Saba, in quibus regnauit Balthasar qui domino thus optulit. †Nam hij pro parte fuerunt in fide corupti et a quodam [f. 52[v]] heretico [nomine] Soldin[o] peruersi. Et †habent pro parte ad ritum Grecorum et partem habent heresis; et vtuntur litteris caldaycis, et habent per se proprium ydioma. Et hij in partibus orientis inter ceteros et pre ceteris christianis non habent talem et tantam reuerenciam sicut Nubiani. Nam [+] †ipsi fidem plene non custodierunt seu †seruauerunt [+] sicut Baltasar dominus rex eorum

† Itaque ... natum] nati hij pre ceteris Christianis in fide stabiles permanserunt et sicud Malchiar dominus rex eorum domino aurum optulit itaque Nubiani homines de eius regno nati. † Nam] nati. † habent] habent se. † ipsi] sicut ipsi. † seruauerunt] seruauerunt sed.

encense, whos odour wiþ mixture ne wiþ fire is not al don awey but as hit may [be] felid & sauerid; but þe feith in hem is not al clene voydit, þogh hit be yn hem sumwhat corrupt. And her prestis with gold and her dekenes wiþ encense & her subdekenes wiþ mirre gone to þe autir whan þei sey massis, yn signe þat þe thre Kynges offrid to God gold, encense, and mirre.

Also the men of þe kyngdom of Tharce and þe yle of Egrisculle yn which Iaspar regnyd, which offrid to God mirre, be callid in þo parties of þe Est Nostyrines, for they were corrupt and peruertid of an heretike was callid Nestoryne. Thes from þe feiþ of holy cherche vnresonabely by heresie as apostatas yn all departid. For as mirre which Iaspar offrid to God wiþ no manere oþere mixture may be swetyd, so þes Nestorynes of no doctours or prechours neuere myght or yet mowe be reuokyd from her heresie. And þei þes thre Kynges have in no manere reuerence; but whan her bisshopis ordeyne prestis, þei resceyve of [hem] othes þat þei shul curse al þo þurgh whos counceille þe body of Iaspar was takyn away. And þes in al þe parties of þe Est to all oþir sectis and Cristyn peple [f. 259r] bene hateful and yn despite, and wiþ her heresie about .xl. kyngdomes bene infecte. And for the more partie they be Ethiopes and blak, and yn her

2 be] *om.* L. 14 hem] *om.* L.

thus optulit, cuius odor in igne quibuscumque mixturis aliis totaliter non tollitur nisi ipsius odor senciatur et †adoletur, itaque tamen ab hiis Soldinis fides per heresim non est totaliter abolita, licet in ipsis aliquantulum sit corupta. Et presbiteri eorum cum auro et diaconi cum thure et subdiaconi cum mirra ad altare accedunt dum celebrare missam intendunt, et hoc faciunt in signum quod tres Reges domino aurum thus et mirram optulerunt.

Iterum homines de regnis Tharsis et insule Egr[isculle] nati in quibus Iaspar Ethiops qui domino mirram optulit in omnibus partibus et terris orientis Nestorini vocantur. Nam a quodam heretico nomine †Nestori[n]us fuerunt corupti et peruersi. Hij irracionabiliter a fide catholica per heresim totaliter recesserunt et apostatauerunt. Nam sicut mirra quam Iaspar rex cor[am] domino optulit nullis aliis mixturis potest obdulcorari, sic hij Nestorini a nullis doctoribus vel predicatoribus ab eorum heresi vnquam potuerunt vel adhuc possunt reuocari. Et hos tres Reges in nulla habent penitus reuerencia; set quando episcopi eorum consecrant et ordinant presbiteros, recipiunt ab eis sacramentum [f. 53r] quod omnes consiliarios et fautores debeant in omnibus missis eorum anathematizare et excommunicare quorum consilio et auxilio ips[is] corpus Iaspar regis fuit ablatum. Et hij in omnibus partibus orientis omnibus aliis christianis sunt exosi et despecti; et eorum heresi circa quadraginta regna sunt infecta. Et sunt pro maiori parte Ethiopes nigri. Et in

† adoletur] odoretur. † Nestorinus] Nestorius.

londis and her cherches they peynt God and our Lady his modir and þe thre Kynges and Seynt Thomas the Apostle blak and the develis white, in despite of all oþer.

Also yn Inde in þe kyngdomes of Prestre Iohn bene good Cristynmen born, and havyn a patriark namyd Thomas to whom þei obey in all thyng as we to our pope, emperour, or our kyng. And þes boþe (þe patriarke Thomas and Prestre Iohn) dwelle in cite of Sculla wher þe thre Kynges dyed and were from þens caried to othir places aftir þei were þere biried and enterid. And whan þes bisshopis of Ynde make prestis, they put in the fire a sharp yryn, blessyng þe fere, and wiþ þat hote yryn so sharp blessid þei marke the prestis in þe forhede & the noses doun into þe bare bone, and þat þei do in signe þat þe Holy Goost descendid ynto þe disciples. And of þes markynges and kuttynges prestis be knowyn and discernyd from oþere, as prestis in þis cuntre by þe crounys shavyn. And her prestis whil þei synge massis hang ovir the autir a goldyn croune or ovirgilt, and þan þe prestis, dekenys, and subdekenys seueraly from diuers weyes reuerently gone to þe auter, and þat þei do in signe that þe thre Kynges from her þre diuers kyngdomes by dyuers weyes for wurship of þe child with her yeftis byfor þe cracche togidir, wiþ o sterre her ledere, mete togidir in þre wayes

terris eorum †et [in ecclesiis eorum] pingunt deum et suam matrem et tres Reges et s[anct]um Thomam nigros et diabolos albos in despectum aliorum, prout inferius †plurima audientur.

Item †[in] India† de regnis presbiteri Iohannis nati sunt boni christiani; et habent per se patriarcham qui Thomas vocatur, cui ipsi in omnibus et per omnia obediunt vt †nos + imperatori vel regi. Et horum amborum habitacio est in ciuitate Sculla, qua ipsi tres Reges decesserunt et de sepulcro fuerunt †recepti et [ad] alia loca deportati. Et dum istorum [Indorum] episcopi ordinant presbiteros extunc benedicunt ignem in quem ponunt ferrum acutissimum, et cum ipso ferro benedicto et acuto f[er]uentissimo scindunt presbiteros quos ordinant per frontem et nasum deorsum vsque ad ossa nuda. Et hoc faciunt in signum quod spiritus sanctus in igne descendit in discipulos; ex hiis scissuris presbiteri in partibus illis discernuntur et cognoscuntur, sicut in partibus istis coronis rasis. Et horum presbiteri dum missas celebrant pendunt super altare coronam auream vel †deauratam, extunc presbiteri diaconi vel subdiaconi ex variis viis separatim reuerenter ad altare accedunt; [f. 53^{v}] et hoc faciunt in signum quod tres Reges de tribus regnis †in viis

† et] et regnis. † plurima] plura de ipsis. † in India] Indi. † nos] nos domino pape et presbitero Iohanni obediunt vt nos. † recepti] excepti.
† deauratam] deauratam et. † in] et.

at Bedlem. Also her prestis have wyues, and have longe [f. 259v] here, and they byleue not þe Holy Gost to procede of the Fadir and þe Son but of þe Fadir alone; also they byleue no purgatorie, and yn þes poyntes þei departe from þe feith of þe Cherche of Rome. And whil þei thenk to sey her masse, þei kerve out of a whete loof a foursquare oost which shal be consecrate, and put hit into a disshe of gold or of siluer, and above þat obley þei put a sterre helyd wiþ swete smellyng white cloþes. And aftir þe offretorie þei hold þe disshe wiþ þe obley and þe sterre þeron ovir þe prestis hede, goyng in procession about þe chirche wiþ grete deuocion wiþ candels and censers, goyng so to the autour, and þan all þe peple fallyn wiþ deuocion flat doun into the cherche. And þat þei do yn signe þat [þe] thre Kyngis wiþ her yeftis soughtyn God, wham þe sterre ledde to þe c[rec]che.

Also þe Cirions bene men of þe kyngdom of Ynde born, for þat londe which was callid sometyme Ynde is now callid Syrie, wherfor they be callyd Syrians. And they have not myche of heresie. And in þ<o> cuntres þei are callid Cristyn of the Girdyng, for they are gird wiþ lynnyn cloþe in prerogatyf þat þei be born of þe kyngdom of Ynde. And þei wurship mych þe evyn of Seynt Barbre in Babyloigne (wher þe soudons comunly lyen),

11 þe] *om.* L. 12 crecche] cherche L.

in Bethelem ad dominum adorandum ad presepe in †vn[a] stella duce simul conuenerunt. Iterum presbiteri †[e]orum sunt vxorati, et habent longos crines, et non credunt spiritum sanctum a patre et filio procedere set solum a patre, item non credunt esse purgatorium; in hiis articulis ab ecclesia romana sunt diuisi. Dum missam celebrare intendunt, extunc s[c]indunt a pane fermentato hostiam quadratam consecrandam; quam in discum aureum vel argenteum ponunt, et super ipsam oblatam ponunt stellam in †modum flexam cum pannis odoriferis et mundissimis tectam. Et post offertorium ponunt discum cum oblata et stella super caput, et cum turribulis et candelis cum maxima reuerencia ecclesiam circuiunt vsque ad altare; et extunc omnis populus in ecclesia pronus cadit in terram. Et faciunt hoc in signum quod tres Reges cum muneribus dominum exqu[i]siuerunt, quos stella ad prese[pe] perduxit.

Item Syriani sunt homines de regno †Indie nati†. Nam illa terra circa Iherusalem que olim †India vocabatur nunc †Syrus vocatur, vnde ipsi homines Syriani nuncupantur. Et non habent multum de heresi; et in partibus illis christiani de cinctura vocantur, quia panno lineo sunt cincti in prerogatiuam quod de regno †Indie sunt† nati. Et hij vigiliam beate Barbare †in Babiloniam vbi soldani quiescunt† cum maximo gaudio

† vna] vnum. † eorum] Grecorum. † modum] modum tripedis. † Indie nati] Iudee nati. † India] Iudea. † Syrus] Siria. † Indie sunt] Iudee sunt. † in Babiloniam ... quiescunt] cuius corpus in Babilonia soldani quiescit.

as we do here þe evyn of Seynt Martyn, and þei swere þere afor her iuges in domys by the thre Kynges, as we don here by oþir halowis, in wurship of þe thre Kyngis þat wurshipid God in þe kyngdom of Ynde wher þei were bore.

Also þe Armenes be doughty Cristynmen, and meny old errours have put away and [f. 260r] evil ritys have left. For on Estre evyn they were wont to ete flesshe, seying that on þe Saturday our Lord aros from dethe, and þe prestis were wont þere to put oyle to her wyne, but now euery day þei encrese to þe feith of þe Chirche of Rome. And her bisshopes and prestis be made and halowid Latynes and yn her massis syng þe melodye of Latynes, and indifferently vsyn in weryng of her clothyng and cappis on her hede into this day in manere and fourme as þe Kynges vsid whan þei soght God in Ierusalem and vsid al her lyf.

Also the Georgyens be men borne of þe kyngdom of George the Hyer. And þes for þe more partie have hem aftir the rite of þe Grekis, but þei be not obstinate in heresye, and þei be callyd Georgiens for þei go alwey togidir in cumpanyes as Frisons or Hungries and they have euere a banere of Seynt George peyntid. And they be Cristyn and doughty in armes, and

sicut in partibus istis vigiliam [f. 54r] sancti Martini deducunt; et vnus amicus mittit alteri caul[i]um et aliarum herbarum semina que in ipso anno in ortis debent seminari. Et hij coram iudicibus eorum iurant per euangelia et sanctos tres Reges, sicut iuratur in partibus istis ad sanctos in iudiciis; et hoc faciunt in honore trium Regum beatorum quia in regno †Indie, vnde ipsi sunt nati, dominum quesiuerunt et adorauerunt.

Item Armeni sunt †christiani strenuissimi, et multos antiquos errores postposuerunt et ritus peruersos iam dimiserunt. Nam in vigilia pasche carnes commedere consueuerunt, dicentes quod dominus sabbato surrexit a mortuis. Et presbiteri in consecracionibus ad vinum oleum addiderunt. Set nunc cotidie ad fidem romane ecclesie accrescunt. Et [episcop]i eorum et presbiteri ab episcopis †latin[i] consecrantur et ordinantur, et eorum missas et prefaciones cantant †melodiam latinorum. Et ipsi Armeni indifferenter vtuntur per omnia habitu vestimentorum et pilleis in capite in presentem diem in modum et formam prout tres Reges fuerunt vsi et induti quando in Iherusalem dominum quesiuerunt et in regnis eorum sunt vsi dum vixerunt.

Item Georgiani sunt homines de regno Georgie superiori nati. Et hij pro magna parte habent se ad ritum Grecorum set [in] heresi non sunt obstinati. Et vocantur ibidem Georgiani, nam quocumque tendunt semper in turmis vt Frisones et Vngarij simul inc[e]dunt et semper habent vexillum cum ymagine beati Georgij depictum. Et sunt christiani in armis strenuissimi, et

† Indie] Iudee. † christiani] christiani in armis. † latini] latinis. † melodiam] melodia.

they be ny to the citee of Michee wher lieþ the body of Machomete, profete of þe Sarasins; and they have a propre langage by hemself, and þe have an erchebisshop which is in þe mount of Syna, in þe cloystre of Seynt Kateryne, to whom þei obey as we do to our pope. And her religious ben in manere of þe ordre of Seynt Anthone or of Seynt Makary. And by all þe soudons londe they passe frely wiþout tribute, and þei be more frendly and meker þan oþir Sarasins ny marchyng about hem. And whereuere þei go or ride they syng songis of þe thre holy Kynges and of her [f. 260v] merites and signes, bothe seculere and religiouse.

Also þer be oþir Cristyn callyd Georgens born in þe kyngdom of George þe Lower þat now is callid þe kyngdom of Aboas, and men sey þat that is a lond all hilly, and sometyme hit was callid Armeny the More. And in þis lond is the hill on which aftir Noes flood restid Noes ship, and þei sey that þer is no goyng thidir for snow and othir horrible causes. But þe height of hym may be sey aboue þe height of all oþir hillis, and on þe cop of þat hill semith þe cop of a blak tree as hit were a grete tree brent, and þei byleve [þer] þat þer þe tre be ȝet bydyng of þe *archa Noe*. And in þis lond is anoþer londe which is clepid Henissem, of lengthe & brede of .v. myle, and þerby goth a flood, and hit is so clowdy wiþ derkenes þat at mydday

11 Aboas] o *possibly* e L. 17 þer(1)] *om.* L.

sunt vicini [f. 54v] ciuitati Mic[h]ee vbi habetur corpus Machometi saracenorum prophete. Et habent per se proprium ydioma, et habent archiepiscopum qui est in monte Syna in claustro sancte Katerine, cui ipsi per omnia obediunt vt nos domino pape. Et ipsorum religiosi habent se ad ordinem sancti Antonij vel Macharij. Et per omnem terram soldani transeunt sine tributo vel impedimento, †vel vicinis suis aliis saracenis sunt† amicabiliores et miciores. Et vbicumque incedunt, religiosi vel seculares, semper cantant canticum de tribus beatis Regibus et eorum meritis et signis.

Item sunt alij christiani qui eciam Georgiani vocantur, qui sunt nati de regno Georgie inferioris, quod nunc regnum †Aboas vocatur. Et dicunt quod sit terra per omnia montosa; et olim Armenia maior vocabatur. Et in hac terra est mons super quem post diliuium archa No[e] quieuit. Et dicunt quod pre niue et aliis causis horibilibus ad ipsum montem non sit via vel accessus, set eius cacumen vltra et supra omnia aliorum moncium cacumina discernatur et videatur, et super eius montis cacumen apparet quoddam lignum nigrum sicut sit arbor combusta magna. Et dicunt et credunt incole terre illius illud lignum ex archa No[e] adhuc ibidem permansisse. Et in hac terra est quedam alia terra que ibidem Henissen vocatur, et est in longitudine et latitudine circa quinque miliaria, et per istam terram transit fluuius, et †est tali et tanta caligine et nebula turbida sita quod

† vel ... sunt] vt ... sint. † Aboas] Abcas. † est] est in.

in the monþe of August þe sunne or hit passe that londe may not be seyn. And þei seyn ther þat hit is not writin in no boke or herde þat enybody goth yn or out of þat londe, and yet by the draght of an arblast þat lond is enhabitid yn cumpas about, ful of plente & lese, and þer is no lettyng to entre into þat londe but only the derkenes and thik cloudis. And in þat lond is dwellyng of men, for þerin is herd oft neying of hors and crowyng of cokkis, and by þe riuere which passith þurgh þat londe comith trees, strawe, and oþir thinges handilid wiþ men[nys] hondis. And hit is red in þo parties þat in þe tyme of Eracle Emperour, [f. 261r] which Machomete and þe Sarasins werrid, sleyng passyngly the Cristynmen and made fle, þat the Cristyn of þo parties fled to anoþir londe ful of hilles. Whom whan þe Sarazins had al aboute bysegid þat they myght nowher voyde, þan þe Cristyn bysoght the helpe of God that by þe merites of þe thre blessid Kynges, which þat tyme in all þe londis of þe Est were wurshipid, þei myght þat tyme be holpe. And þan anone in the place wher þe Sarasins wiþ her wyves, childryn, and bestis as to abyde þere were strengthid and gadrid

8 mennys] meny L.

in mense Augusti in meridie sol antequam ipsam terram pertranseat nunquam [f. 55r] potest videri vel discerni. Et dicunt homines et incole regni illius quod in aliquo libro non sit scriptum vel vnquam auditum quod aliquis homo ipsam terram tenebrosam intraret vel exiret; tamen ad tractum baliste est ipsa terra ab aliis hominibus et incolis vndique circum habita[ta]. Nam †ante illam sunt loca multa vberima et pascuosa, et non est aliquod obstaculum vel impedimentum illam terram tenebrosam †intrandi + nisi solummodo caligo et nebula densa. Et in ipsa terra tam tenebrosa est habitacio humana; nam in ipsa terra frequenter audiuntur hinnitus equorum et cantus gallorum, et cum fluuio qui per ipsam terram †transcendit descendunt ligna et stramina et huiusmodi alia manibus humanis facta et tractata. Et legitur in partibus illis quod temporibus Eraclij Romanorum imperatoris, dum Machometus et sar[a]ceni potenter †eripuissent et christianos vndique interfecissent et effugassent, quod christiani de †illis partibus et terris ad aliam† terram montosam fugissent. Quos cum saraceni in †omnibus circum† obsedissent quod ad dexteram siue ad sinistram non potuerunt declinare, extunc christiani auxilium dei inuocabant, †et per merita trium Regum beatorum, qui tunc temporis in oriente et in vniuerso mundo venerabantur, quod deus eorum meritis ipsis subueniret et liberaret. Extunc statim loco vbi saraceni simul cum vxoribus et paruulis ac pecoribus prout ibidem ad permanendum perpetue venerant fuerunt castrametati et congregati,

† ante] circa. † intrandi] intrandi vel exeundi. † transcendit] transit.
† eripuissent] erupissent. † illis ... aliam] alijs ... illam. † omnibus circum] in montibus. † et] vt.

a derk and a thik cloude helid hem and al þat place, þat from þat tyme neuere man went out of hem þens ne non oþere aftir þat went into hem into this day. Wherfor the Cristyn of þat kyngdom which be callid Georgyns, whereuere þei go or ryde, they go in cumpanyes, as Frisons, wiþ baners in which ymages of þe thre Kyngis be made, into þis day, for they were so myraclously delyuerid þat day thurgh her merites.

Also the Iacobytes be Cristyn and heretikes, in diuers londes here and þere among oþir Cristyn enhabytid. For they were peruertid of an heretik callid Iacob, and they byleve no trinyte but vnyte, yn witnes wherof þei make byfor [hem] a crosse wiþ o fyngir. And her prestis, dekenys, & subdekenys stonde togidir at her autir, aftir her ryte receyvyng togidir þe comunion, in signe þat þe thre Kyngis togidir and at onys offrid her yeftes in [f. 261v] the cracche to our Lord.

Also the Maronytes be Cristyn and heretikes, peruertid and corrupt of an eretyk callid Maro, dwellyng also here and þere in diuers regnis departid. And þes among oþir errours of litil cause hold her cherches prophane and pollute — as if a drop of reyne drop into þe cherche, or þe sonne by eny hole shyne yn, or if an arayne passe þerin, or such oþir light causes. And

10 hem] *om.* L.

ipsum locum tunc nebula tam densa [f. 55v] et caligo tenebrosa operuit et †artum dedit† quod ab illo tempore nunquam aliquis eorum exiuit et alius postmodum homo nunquam intrauit in presentem diem. Quare christiani de regno illo qui eciam †Georgiani vocantur, quocumque transeunt vel pergunt in turmis (sicut Frisones) incedunt cum vexillis in quibus ymagines ipsorum trium Regum facte sunt vel depicte in hodiernum diem, quia eorum meritis deus tam euidenter et tam miraculose eos liberauit.

Item Iacobite sunt christiani heretici hinc inde in diuersis terris et regnis inter alios homines habitantes. A quodam heretico nomine Iacobus fuerunt peruersi, et hij non credunt sanctam trinitatem set vnitatem, cuius signo ante se faciunt signum sancte crucis cum vno digito. Et horum presbiteri diaconi et subdiaconi stant simul in altari, et secundum ritum eorum pariter recipiunt communionem; et hoc faciunt in signum quod tres Reges simul et semel domino in presepio munera optulerunt.

Item Maroniti sunt christiani heretici, a quodam heretico nomine Maro corupti, eciam hinc inde in diuersis terris et regnis habitantes dispersi. Et horum presbiteri diaconi et subdiaconi sunt vxorati; et per totum annum nisi in festo pasche et natiuitatis domini non celebrant missas nisi de sancto Thoma et tribus Regibus alternatim. Et hij inter alios suos errores ex facili causa habent ecclesias eorum prophanatas, vt si gutta pluuie intus stillat, vel radius solis [f. 56r] aliquod foramen penetraret, vel si aranea pertransiret, et aliis huiusmodi leuibus causis. Et

† artum dedit] circumdedit. † Georgiani] Georgiani inferiores.

þes of þe assent of þat o partie disseuere matrimoigne, not callyng þat oþir partie.

Also Copti be Cristyn and heretikes havyng a secte by hemself, enhabitid as þes oþre here and þere among oþere and departid. And þe prestis in her chirches vsyn a book of talis reprevid of þe see of Rome, and they rede þe gospel of Nichodeme. And þei were her bisshopis copes as Frere Prechours, and þei seyn in her massis þe collectes of the thre Kyngis.

Also þe Ismini be Cristyn and heretikes in a secte by hemself, beyng for the more partie yn Egipte vndur þe ledyng of þe soudan. And her childrin, while þe prestis baptise hem, they kyt wiþ a crosse in þe forhede wiþ a sharp hote yrin, which crosse bydith in her forhede al her lyf tyme. And þei byleve fully þat þei shul yet encrece in so mych multitude þat wiþ strengthe þei shul go into Babyloigne wher þe soudon dwellith, and take euery man þerof a stone, þat for her multitude so þer shal not leve a stone. And her prestis aftir masse yeve blessyng to þe peple þat God lede and condyte hem as he led þe thre Kynges to Bedlem by þe sterre.

Also the Maromynes be Cristyn and heretikes havyng a secte by hemself, among oþer Cristyn and Sarazins here [f. 262[r]] and þere sprad and

hij ex consensu et voluntate vnius separant matrimonium, parte altera non vocata.

Item Copti sunt christiani heretici et sectam habent per se et †vt alij† homines hinc inde disperse habitantes. Et eorum presbiteri vtuntur in eorum ecclesiis quodam libro fabuloso a sede apostolica reprobato — et ipse liber Secreta sancti Petri vocatur — et in missis eorum legunt euangelium Nichodemi. Et episcopi eorum vtuntur capis sicut predicatores, et in omnibus missis addunt collectam de tribus Regibus.

Item Ysmini sunt christiani heretici in secta per se, et pro maiori parte degunt in Egipto sub †duce Soldani. Et eorum infantes dum baptizantur extunc presbiteri in frontibus eorum infancium scindunt [crucem] cum ferro †calido et acuto; cuius crucis signum in frontibus eorum omnibus diebus vite eorum permanebit. Et hij firmiter credunt quod adhuc in tantam crescent multitudinem quod violenter in Babiloniam qua soldanus habitat †pergunt, et vnusquisque lapidem †sumit, et pre multitudine eorum ibidem lapillus non debet remanere. ... [f. 56[v]] Et horum Ysinorum presbiteri post missam dant populo benediccionem quod deus eos regat et conducat sicut tres Reges quando ipsos per stellam in Bethleem ad suum presepe perduxit.

Item Maromini sunt christiani heretici, et sectam per se habent, inter alios christianos et saracenos hinc inde disperse

† vt alij] inter alios. † duce] dominio. † calido] candido. † pergunt] pergent. † sumit] sumat.

abydyng. And þei have [hem] for the more partie af[tir] þe custome of Nestorines, and þei be not circumcisid; and yet al þat þei do and begyn þei do in þe wurship of God and of þe thre Kynges.

Also Nicholaite are Cristyn and heretikes, the eldest in þe world: of þes is red in þe Apocalips. And among all her oþir errours þei holde and preche for a grete syn if a man pray a woman, or a woman a man, and þat on denye þat oþir þat askyng; and al manere [synnes] þat might fall herof [God] shold by his mercy foryeve and relece hem. And þei preche þat by al þe mercy of God the develis of hell shold be savid. And þes cursid heretikes, and specialy thes Nicholaites, strengthid hem in al þat þei myght aftir the dethe of Origene, þe wurshipful clerk, to defoule and empeire his name. For þei wrote al her errours and articles of her eresie in þe bokis of Origene, as hit shold seme þat he shuld consente to her errours. And þei afferme Origene to be dampnyd; but hit is not in eny mannys dome to deme eny man to be dampnid or savid. For hit is red in þe parties of þe Est þat aftir þe apostles was not found þat folowid so nye aftir þe lyf of þe apostles as Origenes was, for he werid þe heir aboue his flesshe and neuere

1 hem] *om.* L; aftir] afore L. 7 synnes] *om.* L. 8 God] *om.* L.

degentes. Pro maiori parte habent se ad ritum Nestorinorum, set non circumciduntur; tamen quecumque agunt vel agere incipiunt semper predicunt, In nomine dei et trium Regum beatorum.

Item Nicholaite sunt christiani heretici antiquiores in mundo: de hiis legitur in Apocalipsi. Et inter alios quamplurimos suos errores reputant et predicant pro inemendabili peccato vt si vir mulierem vel mulier virum †prorogaret si quis alteri denegaret; et quecumque peccata circa hoc et ex aliis possunt contingere et euenire deus remitteret cum misericordiis et relaxaret. Et predicant per omnem misericordiam dei demones adhuc esse saluandos. Vnde est sciendum quod isti maledicti et omnes supradicti heretici et specialiter isti Nicholaite post mortem Orig[e]nis magne auctoritatis viri eius nomen gloriosum obfuscare [et] denigrare [f. 57[r]] nitebantur et laborabant. Vnde omnes errores suos et heresis articulos in libris Origenis scripserunt, quasi erroribus eorum et heresi con[se]ntire videretur. ... [f. 57[v]] Et alie quedam omelie sine titulo super euangeliis leguntur in ecclesiis vniuersis quas aliqui Origeni ascribunt, asserentes ipsum esse dampnatum — ideo sine titulo leguntur. Set non attendunt quod pro tam autenticis in ecclesia catholica habentur sicut †qui cum titulis leguntur; et alicuius hominis iudicij non est Origenem vel aliquem hominem esse saluatum vel dampnatum. Nam in omnibus partibus orientis de ipso legitur quod post apostolos qui apostolicam vitam sicut Origenes sequeretur non sit inuentus. Nam super carnem semper cilicio fuit indutus, et nunquam

† prorogaret] pro concubitu rogaret. † qui] que.

ete flesshe ne neuere drank wyne or cithre or eny drink þat might make man drunk; and such as was his doctrine, such was his lyf. And þes Nicholaites, þogh þei be so shrewd heretikes, ȝet þer is none so pore of hem þat he ne ȝeviþ euery day thre almesses for hym, his wyf, and his childrin in wurship of þe thre Kynges.

Also in þe parties of þe Orient be men Cristyn right special which bene callid Mandapoli. Þes hold hem to [no] special rite or secte or heresie ne þei have among hem no prestis, but wiþ her childryn, assis, and [f. 262v] her bestis þei go in grete cumpanyes, ne þei neither sowe ne repe, ne in wyntir or somyr, cold or hete, night or day slepe [...] ne her wyues be delyuerid of child, but euere gone fro toun to toun, from place to place. And as long as þei dwel in o place or toun, þei wurche such as is to worke in þat place with her hondis. And ouer thre dayes may þei not dwelle in o place, for hit is oft seyn in experience þat if þei dwelle in o place ouere thre dayes or if þei slept yn eny hous be nyght, þei shold anone deye. And þei have wiþin hemself a name special þat none can vndurstonde, and þei vndirstond meny othir mennys langages. And þei have neuere amongis hem

7 no] *om.* L. 10 *see note.*

carnem comedebat, nec vinum ciseram vel omne quod inebriare potest nunquam bibebat. Et qualis erat sua doctrina talis erat [et] sua vita... . [f. 58r] ... Hij prefati Nicholaite, licet sint heretici tam peruersi, tamen non est aliquis tam pauper quin omni die dat pauperibus tres elemosinas per ipsum et vxorem suam et liberos osculatas in honore trium Regum beatorum.

Item in oriente in omnibus partibus vltramarinis sunt homines christiani multum speciales qui ibidem Mandopoli vocantur. Hij non se tenent vel habent ad aliquam specialem fidem ritum vel heresim, nec habent inter se presbiteros. Set cum vxoribus et paruulis et azinis in maximis turmis incedunt, et non seminant neque metunt, et nec in hyeme vel estate vel in pluuiis vel frigore vel inestimabili solis ardore die vel nocte in domibus dormiunt vel mulieres eorum in domibus pariunt, set de loco ad locum de villa ad villam per totum annum vagantur. Et quamdiu in vno loco moram trahunt, tunc cribra et huiusmodi de domibus et villis necessaria manibus operantur. Set [in] vno loco vltra triduum manere non possunt, et sepius est expertum: si in vno loco vltra triduum tenerentur, vel si per vnam diem in aliquibus domibus sub tectis morarentur vel dormirent, statim morerentur. Et hij homines inter se †nomen habent speciale quod nullus hominum nisi ipsi inter se possunt intelligere scire vel doceri; set ipsi quamplurima alia hominum ibidem sciunt et intelligunt linguas et ydiomata. Et nunquam habent inter se

† nomen] ydioma.

discorde yn woord or dede; or if eny of hem fynd oþere wiþ his wyf or doghtir lying, he wratthith not þerof, but whan he seth his tyme yeldith hym þe same. And þes to what places, tounes, or citees of Cristyn heretikes, Iewes, or Sarasins þei come, as long as þei be conuersaunt among hem, so long þei vse her rytes, lawes, maners, and customes in etyng, drynkyng, synggyng, ioying, or sorowyng, fastyng, wurchyng, and al þing doyng. And yn what place of eny sectes her wyves bere child, aftir her rytes þere her childrin be baptisid and make her confession, receyve her comunion, and be biried. And whereuere þei be on þe Sonday, wiþ her wyves, childryn, pipis & trumpis, leste and moste, fastyng wiþ deuocion at onys togidir þei go to chirche to [f. 263r] worship God, and þere þei lete syng a masse of the thre Kynges, that God by her merites by al þat woke folowyng save hem hole and sounde from all perils of bestis [and] wourmes as þei go by londis, mountaynes, feldis, or wildirnessis.

11 to(2)] *catchword* worship L.   13 and(2)] *om.* L.

discordiam verbis vel factis; seu dum †aliquis [f. 58v] alter[u]m cum vxore vel filia in adulterio vel concubitu reperit, non irascitur, set dum poterit reddit sibi tallionem. Et hij homines ad quecumque loca ciuitates vel villas omnium christianorum vel hereticorum omnium predictorum vel saracenorum seu †tartarorum vel quorumcumque hominum perueniunt, quam diu inter eos sunt et conuersantur, tam diu secundum omnem eorum ritum et legem mores et consuetudines se habent et viuunt; et vbicumque ieiunatur celebratur comeditur et bibitur operatur doletur plangitur gratulatur vel †gaudet, ibidem ipsi homines ieiunant et commedunt bibunt celebrant operantur dolent plangunt gaudent et gratulantur. Nec habent aliquos presbiteros nec habent se ad aliquam specialem legem fidem ritum vel heresim, set in quorumcumque christianorum vel hereticorum loco mulieres eorum pariunt secundum fidem eorum et ritum ibidem infantes eorum baptizantur, et quorumcumque christianorum vel hereticorum loco infirmantur secundum ritum eorum faciunt confessionem et recipiunt communionem, et mortui secundum ritum eorum traduntur ecclesiastice sepulture. Set in quibuscumque locis christianorum vel hereticorum sunt in die dominica, ibidem mane cum t[y]biis et †musicis omnes cum vxoribus et paruulis a minimo vsque ad maximum ieiuni deuote ad ecclesiam simul et semel perueniunt, multum humiliter deum adorando; et ibidem tunc semper missam de tribus Regibus faciunt celebrare, vt deus per ipsorum merita per totam septimanam per deserta campos et montana sanos ab omni periculo vermium et animalium perducat et conducat.

† aliquis] aliquis alteri prout ibidem est conswetudinis aliquid furatur vel aliquis.
† tartarorum] Turchorum.   † gaudet] gaudetur.   † musicis] musicis instrumentis.

And meny oþir rites and customes they have which were to long to telle but þo rytes wiþ which þei wurship þe thre Kynges, þat þei may be þe more of al oþere Cristyn wurshipid.

Also in þe parties of þe Orient weren othir worst heretikes which were callid Arriane; but þei had no þing þe thre Kynges in reuerence. And with her heresie al þe world was ynfecte; & þes now bene clene distroyed.

Also al þes sectis of Cristyn heretikes — þat is to sey, *Armeni, Georgeani, Soldini, Iacobite, Maronite, Siriani, Copti, Ysmini, Greci, Nestorini,* and *Mandapoli* — some of hem bene infecte wiþ heresie more & some lesse, but euery scole of hem hath oþir in hate, cursyng and condempnyng, ne none wole wiþ anoþere yn eny wise comune. And þe prestis of þes sectes obey to þe bisshopes of whos diocise þei or her fadris or modris be borne, þogh þei be neuere so ferre born or descendid. And yn all þe prouinces of þe Est is no cite þat þes sectes ne dwell þerin, and euery secte hath her speciall chirche, wher þat they dwell. And þei be for þe more partie wyse men, good leches and ficisians, riche marchauntis & bolde, þogh þei be þus odiously dyvidid in þe feith. But [f. 263v] in

Et [f. 59r] hij †omnes ac vniuersi heretici et scismatici supradicti quamplurimas alias habent consuetudines ritus et mores que pretermittuntur (nam de ipsis singulariter et specialiter dicere esset longum) nisi ea quibus ipsos tres Reges venerantur, vt e[o] magis et diligencius ab aliis catholicis honorentur.

Item fuerunt in oriente et alij pessimi heretici qui Arriani voca[ba]antur, set hij ipsos tres Reges in nulla penitus habebant reuerencia speciali. Et ipsorum heresi totus mundus fuit infectus; et hij nunc funditus sunt extirpati.

Item omnes predicti et supradicti christiani et heretici — scilicet Armeni Georgiani Soldini Iacobite Maronite Suriani Copti †Ys[m]ini Greci ac Nestorini et †Mand[a]poli — et omnes secte predicte, quedam secta ex eis est magis de heresi et quedam secta minus. Set qu[e]uis scola habet aliam odiosam execratam et condempnatam, nec vna secta vult cum alia aliqualiter communicare vel participare. Et istarum sectarum presbiteri obediunt episcopis de quorum diocesi ipsi vel parentes ipsorum sunt nati, licet remotisssime abinuicem s[i]nt separati. Et in omnibus prouinciis et terris orientis non est aliqua ciuitas quin ibi omnes predicte secte habitent in ea. Et queuis secta per se vbicumque degunt habent ecclesiam specialem. Et in quocumque loco degunt eorum decem oportet vt faci[a]nt obedienciam quia habent per se presbiterum specialem. Et sunt pro maiori parte viri discretissimi et optimi medici et ditissimi mercatores in temporalibus [f. 59v] et multum astuti et experti, licet hiis miseriis in fide et ritu sint tam odiose diuisi. Set tamen contra saracenos et in

† omnes] homines. † Ysmini] Ysini. † Mandapoli] Mandopolos.

wurshipyng of þe thre Kynges they be euere on and acordyng; and wiþ o procession gone to þe cherche, and þere þan may be diuers langages and melodyes herde.

Also all þes sectes sismatikes, religious & seculers, lewde and oþere, fastyn on Cristynmasse nyght into þe dawnyng, and þei sette euerich his borde wiþ mete and drynk as may suffise into þe day of þe Epiphanye, levyng þe borde helyd wiþ towails, as euery man is of faculte and power. And þei light a candel on Cristemasse evyn which þei lete stonde brennyng nyght and day into þe day of þe Epiphanye, and þei ete and drynk of þo vitailles wiþ most ioy fro þe Natiuite ynto þe Epiphanie. Also yn þe Epiphanie euery neighbor aftir the sonne goyng doun goth to his neyghboris hous wiþ a candele brennyng in his honde, and yn þe entryng euermore of þe hous he seith to his frend or cosyn, "Sir, good day to yow"; and if he answere to hym ayeen seying, "Good evyn", as for a grete wrong he wold accuse hym. And þei lede so wakyng al þat nyght from hous to hous, etyng & drynkyng, dauncyng and ioying, wiþ her candels in her honde, in memory þat the thre Kynges wiþ þe sterre brennyng which

veneracione trium Regum semper sunt vnanimes et concordes; et tunc in vna processione ad ecclesias vadunt, et tunc diuerse lingue et melodie audiuntur.

Iterum prefati christiani heretici secte scismaticique seculares et religiosi la[i]ci et ordinati hij omnes in †natiuitate domini vsque ad crepusculum ieiunant. Et tunc quiuis ponit mens[a]m suam cum potu et cibariis que durare possunt vsque ad diem Epiphanie, ita quod mensam cum mensalibus coopertam et positam cum cibariis †subpositis secundum quod qui[ui]s est facultatis stare permittit. Et in vigilia natiuitatis domini candelam et lampadem accendunt, quam vsque ad diem Epiphanie iuxta mens[a]m die ac nocte ardere permittunt; nam oleum et omnia cibaria ibidem in optimo foro sunt et reperiuntur. Et a vigilia natiuitatis domini vsque ad diem Epiphanie itaque cum vxoribus et paruulis de ipsa mensa itaque posita comedunt et †bibunt cum maximis gaudiis illos dies a natiuitate domini vsque ad diem Epiphanie domini deducunt.

Item in vigilia Epiphanie domini post solis occasum extunc quiuis amicus vadit ad domum amici vel cognati cum candela ardenti, et semper in introitu domus dicit, Bona dies sit vobis; et si aliquis †dicit, Bonum vesper vel Bona nox †sit, pro eo ipsum in iudicio pro maxima iniuria conuenirent et accusarent. Et itaque $^{+}$ totam noctem Epiphanie cum maxima [f. 60^{r}] leticia et solempnitate de domo ad domum eundo comedendo et bibendo †atque saltando† cum candelis ducunt insompnem. Et hoc faciunt in memoriam quod stella ardens que

† natiuitate] vigilia natiuitatis. † subpositis] superpositis. † bibunt] bibunt et. † dicit] diceret. † sit] sit vobis. † atque saltando] et itaque salutando.

shynyd from þe Natiuite to þe Epiphanye were led wiþ her cumpany into Bedlem & to hem semyd neuere nyght but euere day.

Also on the Epiphany day all Cristyn, boþe pilgrymes and sismatikes & heretikes, from ferre & ny cuntres comyng wiþ her bisshopis, abbotis, prestis, and [f. 264r] religious with crossis of siluer or gold & ensencers & candels gone to the ryuer callid Iurdan, fyve litil myle from Ierusalem. And þan eche secte stondyng in his speciall place, wiþ grete ioy & silence m<a>de among all þe peple, wiþ grete [reuerence] they ley her crosses on þe ground, redyng than in Latyn (of what langage þei be) þe gospell *Cum natus esset Ihesus in Bedleem*. And aftir þe gospell redde, euery secte with grete reuerence wurship her crosse and offryn her offringes aftir þat þei be of faculte in signe of þe thre Kynges which offrid tho her yeftis to God. And þan euery secte aftir oþir by ordre gone in procession to the Iurdan bank to þe place wher Ihesus was of Iohn baptisid, redyng þere euery secte in Latyn þe gospel in this manere *(secundum Iohannem): In illo tempore venit Ihesus a Galilea ad Iohannem vt baptizaretur ab eo in HOC Iordane IN ISTO LOCO &c.* And aftir the gospel red they blesse the watir &

8 reuerence] *om.* L.

in natiuitate domini apparuit vsque ad Epiphaniam et per illud tempus tres Reges et eorum comitatum in Bethleem duxit et precessit, quibus non er[a]t aliqua nox set cum inmensa claritate eis vna dies videbatur.

Iterum in die Epiphanie omnes christiani incole et peregrini scismatici et heretici de longinquis partibus cum eorum episcopis abbatibus presbiteris et religiosis et ordinatis cum crucibus argenteis thuribulis et candelis vadunt et perueniunt ad Iordanem, qui distat a Iherusalem ad quinque miliaria parua. Et extunc omnibus christianis scismaticis et hereticis iuxta Iordanem congregatis extunc queuis pars christianorum stat simul in loco speciali. Et tunc magno silencio facto in populo ponunt reuerenter cruces in terram. Et extunc queuis pars christianorum eciam quorumcumque ydiomatum sit vel linguarum legunt ibidem in latino illud euangelium: Cum natus esset Ihesus in Bethleem. Et lecto euangelio tunc queuis pars crucem suam cum maxima reuerencia et deuocione adorant et oblaciones offerunt reuerenter secundum quod quiuis est facultatis, in signum trium Regum qui tunc domino optulerunt munera. Extunc vna pars post aliam ad ripam Iordanis ad locum quo baptizatus fuit Ihesus ordinat[i]m procedunt. Et tunc queuis pars legit in latino euangelium in hunc modum secundum Iohannem: [f. 60v] In illo tempore †venit Ihesus a Galilea ad Iohannem †vt baptizaretur [ab eo in hoc Iordane] in isto loco etcetera. Et lecto euangelio benedicunt aquam et

† venit] venit huc. † vt] vt hic.

baptise the crosse therin, and þan þerin all sike are borne [nakid & bathid]. And þan þei bere of þat watir into meny diuers ferre cuntres which bydith al þe ȝeer clene without corrupcion, and þerof the sike drynke and of diuers infirmitees bene helid. And aftir þis fulfillid, euery secte goth pesibly home to his owne. And by the sowdon be ordeynid that tyme strengthe of armyd men, to kepe þat þer be no stryves or discordis.

And bytwene Iurdan & Ierusalem is a litil wildirnes which is callid Montoste, and in that wildirnes Iohn Baptist dwellid and prechid penaunce, and þere come Ihesus to hym [f. 264v] to be baptisid of hym. And in that desert fastid [Ihesus] .xl. dayes & .xl. nyghtis, and ther the devil temptid hym. And beside Iurdan, ayen þe place wher he was baptisid the space of þe draught of an arowblast, is a mynstre of þe ordre of Seynt Makare, of the which mynstre the monkis sey þei have Seynt Iohns arme. And Iurdan in his verrey cours is of .xij. paces of brede, and hit hath a clayy ground and hye bankis & depe pyllis, &, safe þere þat Ihesus was baptizid, no shalow forthes, and þere also the childrin of Israel went ouere wiþ dry foot whan they distroyed Iericho. But the Iordan sumtyme of [reyn watris] is so

1 nakid & bathid] *trs.* L. 10 Ihesus] they L. 17 reyn watris] watir reynes L.

crucem baptizant. Et tunc omnes claudi ceci et infirmi quorum maxima multitudo tunc ibidem conuenit et portantur nudi in Iordanem se mergunt †et bal[ne]antur. Extunc ex Iordane aquam† ad longinquas partes portant et mittunt que per totum annum manet incorupta, et ex ea infirmi bibunt †vel lauant quorum plurimi in honore dei sanitates consequntur. Et itaque peracto iuxta Iordanem ordinatim diuino officio extunc omnes partes christianorum ad propria pacifice recedunt. Et eciam est ibidem tunc magna custodia armatorum ex parte soldani, ne fiant ibi alique ri[x]e vel discordie seu conspiraciones.

Et inter Iordanem et Iherusalem est †quoddam paruum desertum quod† ibidem Montost vocatur; et in ipso deserto Iohannes baptista habitauit et penitenciam predicauit, et ibidem venit Ihesus ad Iohannem vt ipsum in Iordane baptizaret; et in hoc deserto Ihesus quadraginta diebus et noctibus ieiunauit, et ibidem eum diabolus temptauit. Et iuxta Iordanem contra locum quo baptizatus fuit Ihesus ad tractum baliste est monasterium ordinis sancti Macharij, cuius monachi brachium sancti Iohannis dicunt se habere. Quia Iordanis in vero et communi suo fluxu et via est circa xij passus lata. Et habet multum limosum fundum et ripas altas ac palludes nec habet aliqua vada nisi in loco in quo Ihesus est baptizatus; et ibidem [f. 61r] eciam filij Israel sicco pede transierunt quando Iericho destruxerunt. Set †Iordanus aliquando ex aquis pluuialibus de monte Libani et aliis montibus v[eni]entibus

† et balneantur ... aquam] balneantur et lauantur quorum quamplurimi ex fide sanantur et tunc omnes homines habent flasculas vel vasa in que recipiunt aquam benedictam de Jordane quam. † vel] vel se. † quoddam ... quod] quedam pars deserti que. † Iordanus] Iordanis.

myche woxyn and flowyn þat hit ouerpassith alle the cuntrees to þat mynstre so that þan hit myght bere shippis ladyn, and þerfor the mynstre is so ferre set þerfrom. And Iurdan bygynnith from the rote & fote of the mount of Liban of two ryuers of which þe tone is more þan þat oþir, which in two placis fallyn into the see of Galilee and of hem two into o flood gadrid is callid Iurdan. And þe cours of Iurdan is .xxiiij. myle of þis cuntre, and from the place wher Ihesus was baptisid hit fallith into þe Cursid See, and þan hit apperith no more. And hit is a question in tho cuntrees whi þat watir so blessid entrith into þe watir so cursid. And some seyn þat in his fallyng yn hit is swalowid yn of þe erthe. For some ...

... [f. 265r] savyng in the day of the Epiphanye. But hit is red dyuersly, aftir the cuntrees wher hit was diuersly made. For in Ierusalem and in his diocise hit is red thus: *Cum [natus] esset in Bedlem Ihesus in diebus Herodis HIC regis, ecce [magi ab oriente] venerunt HIC dicentes.* Also in Bedleem and in his diocise hit is seid þus: *Cum natus HIC esset Ihesus in*

10 *a lacuna of one folio follows* L. 13 natus] *om.* L. 14 magi ab oriente] *om.* L.

tantum inundat et crescit quod fines suos vsque ad istud monasterium excedit quod exportare posset naues honustas; et ideo monasterium a Iordane tantum est translatum. Et oritur †Iordanus a radice monti[s] Libani ex duobus riuis, quorum vnus †est maior altero†; qui duobus locis in mare Galilee incidunt et aperte per illud mare transeunt, et eis in vno fluuio congregatis extunc Iordanis vocatur. Et durat fluxus Iordanis ad viginti quatuor miliaria istius patrie, et a loco in quo baptizatus fuit Ihesus incidit †ad mare maledictum et vltra non apparet. Et questio est in partibus †istis quare aqua tam benedicta intrat in aquam tam maledictam. Et dicunt quidam quod in suo introitu et [in]fluxu a terra absorbetur. Nam aliquando Iordanis tantum crescit et inundat quod esset impossibile †ipsum mare intraret† quod fines suos non excederet et †intraret ... [f. 62r]

Item omnes episcopi abbates presbiteri christianorum et hereticorum cuiuscumque ritus et condicionis vel nacionis existunt in omnibus partibus orientis omni die post missam legunt illud euangelium Cum natus esset Ihesus in Bethleem etcetera, †et sicut in partibus istis post missam legitur euangelium In principio erat verbum, †sic legitur in eorum litteris et linguis et non in latino nisi in die Epiphanie. Set tamen legitur diuersimode secundum quod ibidem illud euangelium peractum est. Nam in Iherusalem et sua diocesi legitur [f. 62v] sic: Cum natus esset †in Bethleem Ihesus† in diebus Herodis hic regis, ecce magi ab oriente venerunt †hic dicentes etcetera. Item in Bethleem et sua diocesi legitur sic: Cum natus [hic] esset Ihesus in

† Iordanus] Iordanis. † est maior altero] Jor et alter Dan vocatur. † ad] in.
† istis] illis. † ipsum mare intrare] si ipsum mare intraret. † intraret] inundaret.
† et] *om.* † sic] sed. † in Bethleem Ihesus] Ihesus in Bethleem. † hic] huc.

diebus Herodis TUNC HIC IUDEE regis. Also the Nubians, Indes, and Soldynes rede hit þus: *Cum natus esset Ihesus in Bedlem Iude in diebus Herodis regis, ecce NOSTRI REGES venerunt de oriente DE REGNIS SUIS IN PARTIBUS NOSTRIS Ierosolimam dicentes*. Also oþir Cristin and heretikes þurgh whos londis þes thre Kynges in her goyng out went yn special worship which þei wold have in her londis and oþere places whereuere they lyve they rede þis gospell in this manere: *Cum natus esset Ihesus in Bedlem Iude in diebus Herodis regis, ecce magi REGES GLORIOSI CUM MAGNA AMBICIONE ab oriente venerunt ET PER NOS TRANSIERUNT*. And so al Cristyn in her masse rede þis gospell as hit [wa]s done and made among hem.

Also al þat be of the lawe of Machomete and oþir Tartarins and T[urk]is have sumwhat thes thre Kynges in reuerence specialy. For in all þe parties of the Cristyn and chirches which þei have distroyed and left desolate they kytte and defoule all the noses & þe eyen of al þe ymages gravyn or peyntid inasmyche as they may, but [f. 265v] the ymages of the thre Kynges they leve hole & vndefoulid.

Also the cursid Iewes have sumwhat thes thre Kynges in reuerence and memorie, but derkely, as they expowne & vndirstonde all scriptures &

11 was] is L. 12 Turkis] Tartis L.

diebus Herodis tunc hic + †Iudee regis. Item Nubiani Indi et Sold[i]ni legunt sic: Cum natus esset Ihesus in Bethleem Iude in diebus Herodis regis, ecce nostri Reges venerunt de oriente de regnis suis in partibus nostris Ierosolimam dicentes etcetera. Item alij christiani heretici per quorum terras et loca hij tres Reges in †exitu + transierunt in specialem honorem quem exinde habere volunt in eorum terris et aliis locis vbicumque degunt legunt illud euangelium in hunc modum: Cum natus esset Ihesus in Betheleem Iude in diebus Herodis regis, ecce magi Reges gloriosi cum magna ambicione ab oriente venerunt et per nos transierunt. Et sic omnes christiani in missa et post missam legunt illud euangelium in presenti sicut in eorum terris et partibus est peractum.

Item Saraceni qui sunt de lege Machometi et alij Tartari et Thurci eciam ipsos tres gloriosos Reges habent in aliquali reuerencia speciali. Nam in omnibus partibus et terris eorum in ecclesiis christianorum per eos destructis et desertis omnium ymaginum in [hiis] scultarum vel pictarum cum cultellis oculos eruunt et nasos †obsidunt et deturpant in quantum possunt, set ymagines ipsorum trium Regum semper integras et illesas stare permittunt. †Set vt ad propositum redeatur†.

Item Iudei perfidi habent hos tres Reges gloriosos in [f. 63r] reuerencia et memoria, set obscure sub velamine, prout omnes scripturas et

† Iudee] et Iudee. † exitu] exitu et reditu. † obsidunt] abscindunt. † Set ... redeatur] *om.*

prophecies. And seth þat the thre Kyngis in Ierusalem her citee [with that seld] seyn shynyng sterre leder of Iewis soght þat kyng borne and fond hym not þere, þerfor in memory and in signe of þes Kynges and sterre from þat tyme a sterre of siluer o[r] brasse yotyn in manere of a laumpe in her festis of Epiphany in the night into this day be wont to hange ouere her bordis; which sterre is callid Messias, as þogh he were not ȝet borne. And whan he shal come and be borne, þan he shal alone in al þe world hold empire ovir al þe world and þe Cristyn holde vndur foot, and shal the Iewes above all oþir peple & nacions exhalte and enhaunce, and al londis and kyngdomis to hem, in which meke and trewe peple now lyve dyvidid, shal subiecte. Wherfor in the bokis of the Iewis conuertid to þe Cristyn [f]eith is conteynid that þe same aungell which þe childrin of Israel in the goyng out of Egipt led and went byfor in a fyry cloude, the same aungel with that seld seyn sterre & fyr[y] led thes thre Kynges and went byfor, and his voys also out of that sterre was herd which to þo thre Kynges and to al þe peple shewid and denouncid þe kyng of Iewis þan to be born and hem comaundid þan to worchipyng þerof. Wherfor the [f. 266[r]] seniours

1 with that seld] *om.* L. 4 or] of L. 12 feith] seith L. 14 fyry] fyre L.

prophecias intelligunt et exponunt. Nam ex quo ipsi tres Reges in Iherusalem eorum ciuitate †regia (alias† regali) cum rara radiante flammea stella duce Iudeorum regem natum quesierunt nec inuenerunt, vnde in huiusmodi †signi Regum et stelle memoriam ab illo tempore stellam ex argento vel [e]re fusam in modum †lampadis in eorum festiuitatibus de vespere et de nocte supra mensas eorum in presentem diem pendere consueuerunt. †Qu[e] Messias vocatur, quasi† adhuc non sit natus. Set dum ille aduenerit et nascetur extunc solus in vniuerso mundo mille annis imperabit, christianos suppeditabit, et Iudeos super eos et omnes gentes et populos exaltabit, et ipsis omnes terras et vniuersa regna in quibus nunc humiles †subdegunt dispersi ad voluntatem eorum subiciet et subiugabit. Vnde in libris Iudeorum in oriente ad fidem christianam conuersorum contra hoc †in caluerunt† Iudeorum exposiciones †continetur, videlicet quod ipse angelus qui filios Israel in egressione de Egipto [in] columpna ignea duxit et prece[ss]it et omnes eorum vias ill[umin]auit, ipse idem angelus et hos tres Reges cum stella rara et ignea duxit et antecessit, et ipsius eciam vox ex stella si[t] audita qui ipsis Regibus et omnibus tunc Iudeorum regem natum anunciauit et ipsum ad inquirendum et adorandum [+] mandauit. Vnde ab illo tempore Iudeorum seniores

† regia alias] *om.* † signi] signi et. † lampadis] lampadis pluribus luminibus accensam et irradiantem et totam domum eorum illuminantem precipue. † Que ... quasi] nam in eorum libro secreto qui Talmoth vocatur continetur quod Iudeorum rex qui Messias vocatur. † subdegunt] sunt et degunt. † in caluerunt] in Thalmot. † continetur] continentur.

of the Iewis, vndirstondyng the scriptures and knowyng the fulfillyng of the prophecies of that sterre, ordeynid that all that come aftir shold have a sterre brennyng in her housis in her festis principall in memory of the thre Kynges, secretly and vndur hidyng, as is seyd byfor. And in alle parties of the Orient fro þan into þis tyme they did grave and peynte in her sinagoges a sterre, as ȝet may be found in meny of her sinagogis into this day.

Also the Percens, thogh þei be without feith, ȝet with Cristynmen þei go into cherches, as they are enfourmid and taught of her auncestres. And they seyn that aftir tyme that þe bodies of þe thre Kynges from þe parties of þe Orient were translatid, from þat tyme that sterre in þo parties neiþer þe londis of þe Nestoriences was neuere seth seyn.

Nestoryns beth neighbours to þe Persens, which, as is seyd byfor, be of the kyngdom of Tarce and of the ile of Egrisculle in which regnyd Iaspar, the thrid Kyng, in Ethiope, which offrid to our Lord mirre. And in the world be no wors heretikes, for with [her] here[sye] in þe Orient werin

15 her heresye] heretikes L.

scripturas scientes †et huius† stelle prophetate perfeccionem et complecionem et ipsorum Regum memoriam sub velamine et secrete (vt supradictum est) [f. 63v] in eorum precipuis festis in domibus eorum habere stellam accensam posteris eorum instituerunt, et in omnibus partibus orientis ab illo tempore vsque in presentem diem in eorum synagogis stellam pingere †et sculpere† fecerunt, prout in partibus cismarinis adhuc in pluribus synagogis reperitur. Et eciam sciendum est quod Iudei habent quendam secretum librum qui †Calmut in hebraico vocatur, in quo omnes prophe[ci]e et euangelia sunt scripta et omnium scripturarum †litteris in nouo testamento† speciales articuli et super hiis et contra hos varie et diuerse ac peruerse continentur opiniones et quamplurima fabulosa †in illis scripturis† exponunt et declar[an]t.

Item Persi, licet sint absque aliqua fide vel lege, tamen cum christianis in ecclesiis eorum †intrant, secundum quod a parentibus et aliis sunt instructi; tamen dicunt quod, postquam corpora trium Regum de partibus eorum de oriente ad occidentem fuerunt translata, quod extunc stella maris in partibus eorum et regnis Nestorinorum postmodum non sit visa. ... [f. 64r]

Nestorini Persarum vicini (de quibus est supradictum) sunt homines de regno Tharsis et insule Egrosille nati, in quibus eciam regnauit Iaspar tercius rex Ethiops, qui domino mirram optulit. Et in mundo non sunt peiores heretici, et eorum heresi in oriente

† et huius] in huiusmodi. † et sculpere] vel sculpere. † Calmut] Thalmoth. † litteris in nouo testamento] veteris et noui testamenti. † in illis scripturis] que nec in biblia nec in alijs scripturis inueniuntur cum quibus omnes prophecias euangelia et scripturas equiuoce ad eorum voluntatem. † intrant] orant.

about .xl. kyngdomes infecte & corrupt. And þes among all oþir errours bene circumcidid. And these fro þe trewe feith & from Prestre Iohn, her lord, and from þe fey of Thomas, patriarke of hem and of Ynde, rebellid and errid and longe tyme myght not be revokid with no doctours ne holy prechours by no signes or vertues. Wherfor þe ȝeer of our Lord a .MlCClxviij. God sette þe [f. 266v] rude and pore peple which were but as shipardis in the londis of Nestoriens aȝens hem. Which callid hem Tartarines, and þei chose into her captayn a smytth. Which þan distroyed fast þe londis of þes Nestoriens and with[out] mercie, as God wold have hit, yong and olde þei slowe and toke her londis, cites, and castels, in which into this day dwell þe Tartarynes. And þei toke Camball, and in .xxx. dayes þei ouercome þe towne of Balauch in which was Colipha, lord of þe Sarazins, the successour of Machomete in her law, as our pope is successour of Seynt Petir; and Calipham þan slow at Rome, and aftirward þei had neuere into þis day none suche. And also they ouercome and wanne the cite of Thauris. And þes thre citees bene the beste and ricchest citees of all þe sowdanis lordship. For of þe strengthe and of þe ricches of Cambaleth may no man speke. And Baldach is a citee which was callid of

9 without] with L.

circa quadraginta regna sunt infecta et fuerunt corrupta. Et hij inter alios suos errores vt Iudei circumciduntur. Et hij a fide catholica et domino presbitero Iohanne eorum domino et a fide Thome Indorum et ipsorum patriarche se potenter alienabant appostatabant et rebellabant, et per longa tempora ab aliquibus doctoribus et sanctis patribus et predicatoribus virtutibus et signis ab eorum heresi et nequicia nunquam potuerunt reuocari. Vnde anno domini millesimo ducentesimo sexagesimo octauo deus homines rudes et viles qui in horum Nestorinorum terris pastores erant contra hos Nestorinos incitauit. Qui se Tartaros vocauerunt, et sibi fabrum in cap[ita]neum elegerunt et prefecerunt. Qui [t]unc potenter eruperunt et omnia terras et regna eorum [f. 64v] Nestorinorum destruxerunt et ipsos iuuenes et senes (prout deo placuit) absque aliqua misericordia interfecerunt et deleuerunt, et omnes eorum ciuitates et villas castra et regna et terras ceperunt, in quibus nunc Tartari habitant et regnant in presentem diem. Et †[Cambal] ceperunt, et in triginta diebus oppugnauerunt †Balauch, in qua fuit sarracenorum calipha (successor Ma[chomot]i in eorum lege, sicut papa successor sancti Petri, et itaque per omnia ei obediuerunt), et ipsum calipham †Rome occiderunt; et postmodum sarraceni calipham non habuerunt nec habent in presentem diem. Et eciam oppugnauerunt Thauris. Et hee tres ciuitates [sunt] meliores et diciores quam totum dominium soldani. Nam de fortitudine ciuitatis Cambaleth et diuiciis nullus plene potest enarrare; et Baldach est ciuitas que ab

† Cambal] Cambalech. † Balauch] Baldach. † Rome] fame.

olde tyme Babiloyne, in which was the Tour of Babell; but from the place wher Babyloyne stood for watris, wormes, and perilous bestis stont now þat citee þens half a myle. And that citee Thauris was callid of olde tyme Susas, in which regnyd Assuerus, and in þat citee in the temple is a drye tree of which meny merveiles be tolde þurgh al þe world; which strongly is kept wiþ soudiours & squyers, and shet and closid wiþ diuers lokkis, wallis, & iryns. For of old tyme in all þe parties of þe Orient was þe custom þat what kyng or lord or peple [f. 267^{r}] were of such strengthe that myght his swerde or sheld hange with strengthe myghtily on þat tree, to þat kyng, lord, oþir peple as to her verrey kyng or lorde in all thinges a .C. & .xxv. provynces from Ynde into Ethiope shold obeye. And ȝef eny kyng, lord, or peple toke and ouercome þat towne and henge not his helme or swerde on þat tre, þei shold not þan obey to hym. And þat cite all men þere defende into þe tyme that they [be] with strengþe put out þerof, for to the wynnyng of all a londe is soght no citee but Thauris ne bysegid. And now the lord of Tartarie in that cuntre is callid þe Grete Cane of Tartarie, and þer is not a gretter lord ne riccher in the world into this day, for God sometyme all londis, regnys, and provinces and peplis with whom he was

14 be] *om.* L.

antiquo †Babilonia vocabatur, in qua fuit turris Babell, set est a loco quo Babilonia quondam stetit propter paludes et vermes et bestias periculosas ad dimidium miliare translata; et illa ciuitas Thauris ab antiquo vocabatur Susis, in qua regnauit Ass[u]erus. Et in ipsa ciuitate in templo Tartarorum est arbor arida de qua plurima narrantur in vniuerso mundo. Que vltra modum cum armigeris et stipendiariis custoditur et †ceris et aliis diuersis muris et ferris †et quam multipliciter est serata et inclusa. Nam ab antiquo in omnibus partibus orientis fuit et est consuetudinis quod siquis rex vel dominus vel populus tam potens efficitur quod scutum vel clipeum ad illam arborem potenter penderet et [f. 65^{r}] violenter, illi regi vel domino ac populo centum viginti quinque prouincie ab India vsque ad Ethiopiam absque omni contradiccione aliquali vt vero eorum regi vel domino in omnibus et per omnia obedirent; set si aliquis rex vel dominus aut populus ipsam ciuitatem bene caperet et oppugnaret et in illam arborem scutum vel clipeum suum non penderet, non possunt extunc ipsi obedire. Et ipsam ciuitatem omnes ibidem maxime defendunt quousque ab ipsa violenter depellantur; nam ad optinendam totam terram aliqua ciuitas nisi Thauris non queritur vel circumvallatur. Et nunc dominus Tartarorum in illis partibus magnus canis imperator †Carthagie vocatur in presentem diem, et non est nunc maior vel dicior dominus in mundo. Nam deus †vicinis temporibus sibi omnes terras regna et prouincias et gentes quibus

† Babilonia] Babilonia magna. † ceris] seris. † et] *om.* † Carthagie] Cathagie. † vicinis] breuibus.

offendid and wratthid put in subieccion to hym. For þat emperour hath now vndur hym and regnith in alle þe londis, provinces, and kyngdomes in which Nabogodonosor, <D>arius, Baltazar, Arfaxath, Assuerus, and the Romayns of oold tyme regnid yn. Wherfor the emperour of Tartarie favorid myche and ʒet fauourith in þ[o] londis and kyngdomes + þe Cristyn, and þe Cristyn feith, which was by the vntrewe heretikes and Nestorines done awey & defoulid, is now by Frere Austyns, menours, Prechours, & Carmelites of newe reflorisshid. For riche marchauntis of Lumbardie and of meny oþir diuers cuntres, for they lyve and dwelle in þo londis myche and mych come thidir + , drawe mych thidir þese ordres, and with her help & of oþir marchauntis [f. 267v] foundyn hem housis & cloystres and largely yeve hem aftir þat they love hem. And þo marchauntis drawe ʒong childrin taght of diuers langages, which þei ʒeve into þes ordres, and they teche þe childrin Latyn and expoune hem bokis in which are conteynid alle the confusions of þe Iewes & heretikes and her opynions, and techyn hem by hert, as scolers be taught here by rote in scolis her rewlis o[r] her donet. And from diuerse ferre cuntres bene such apte childrin sette to þo ordres

4 favorid] r *perhaps altered from* y L. 5 þo] þe L; kyngdomes] kyngdomes of L.
10 thidir(1)] thidir and L. 16 or] of L.

[ir]atus fuit tradidit propter peccata eorum et subiecit. Nam ipse imperator sub se habet et regnat in omnibus terris et prouinciis et regnis in quibus Nabugodonosor Darius Balthasar Arfaxat Assewerus et Roma[ni] ab antiquo in oriente regnabant. Vnde ipse imperator Tartarorum postmodum in omnibus multum fauebat et fauet in terris et regnis suis †christianos, et fides christiana, que in omnibus predictis terris et regnis per infideles et hereticos et Nestorinos fuit [aboli]ta et oblita, nunc per fratres minores augustinenses et predicatores et †alios carmelitas de nouo incipit reflorere. Nam mercatores de Lumbardia et ab aliis partibus ditissimi, †quia in ipsis partibus degunt et frequenter [f. 65v] perueniunt, trahunt hos ordines ad illas [partes], et eis cum auxilio †eorum et† aliorum mercatorum et fidelium c[lau]stra fundant et omnia necessaria largiter aministrant, secundum quod quiuis aliquem ordinem diligit. Et ipsi mercatores in diuersis prouinciis †trahunt iuu[e]nes + pueros diuersis linguis eruditos, quos dant ordinibus; qui tunc ab eis non possunt se alienare et apostatare. Et illos pueros tunc fratres docent latinum et exponunt eis libros in quibus continentur omnes confusiones Iudeorum et hereticorum et omnium eorum opinionum et errorum. Et tales libros et eorum exposicionem docent ipsos pueros cordetenus, sicut scolares docent in scolis regulas cordetenus vel donatum. Et tales pueri †et apti in diuersis legibus† eruditi dantur et portantur et mittuntur ibidem + ordinibus de longinquis partibus

† christianos] christianis. † alios] alios doctores ac. † quia] qui. † eorum et] *om.*
† trahunt] emunt. † et ... legibus] apti et diuersis lingwis.

for the loue of God, and þei may not þan out of þe ordris, for to þe ordres þei be boundyn by ȝok of bondage, and þerby þe frere mendinantz have diuers worþi doctours in tho cuntres to the emperour & meny othir kynges and meny oþir peple wel bylovid. And the Emperour of Tartarie which regnid þe ȝeer of our Lord a .M[l].CCC.lxxj. was a man of short stature, houmble and deuoute, worshipyng the God ymmortall. He [ma]de and yaf his dome in all his londis and kyngdomes that euery man myght vse what manere lawe and feith or ryte as hym lyst, while þat he worshipid none ydolis but the immortal God. And þo Frere menours meny diuers men of diuers rites, errours, and heresies have drawe to þe feith. And þe same freris enducid and counceylid þe emperour that he hath do the Bible be translatid into many diuers langagis & writings, and al þat God wroght by þe thre Kynges in whos kyngdomes he now regnith + lete [f. 268[r]] rede þerof byfor hym at metis and sopers, and þerof thonkid God þat he so predestenyed hym that he shold so regne aboue all þe kynges of all othir kyngdomes. And euermore aftir mete and byfor he was wont to sey graces and *benedicite* in his owne langage. And he had iiij sones. The eldest hight Melchior, þe second hight Baltazar, the thrid Iaspar, the fourþe David; and ordeynid foreuere þat his sones shold be callid so — and he was the thrid emperour of Tartarie — of certeyn causes, as hit shal be told aftir.

2 mendinantz] *or* mendiuantz L. 6 made] stode L. 13 regnith] regnith and L.

amore dei. Et illi tunc ab ordinibus non possunt fugere nec apostatare, quia ordinibus iugo seruitutis sunt astricti. Et per talem modum fratres mendicantes in partibus illis quamplurimos egregios doctores habent et predicatores ipsi imperatori et quamplurimis regibus et aliis hominibus dilectos. Et ille imperator Tartarorum qui regnauit anno domini millesimo trecentesimo †septuagesimo primo fuit homo statura breuis et multum humilis et deuotus, adorans deum immortalem. Hic fecit et dedit edictum in omnibus terris et regnis suis quod quiuis homo posset vti quacumque lege fide vel ritu ipse vellet, dummodo ydola non adoraret set deum immortalem. V[nde] ipsi fratres de ordine mendicancium quamplurimos diuersorum errorum et rituum homines ad fidem catholicam attraxerunt. [f. 66[r]] Et ijdem fratres ipsum imperatorem induxerunt quod bibliam in diuersas linguas et litteras transferre fecit, et omnia que deus per ipsos Reges in quorum regnis ipse regnauit fuit operatus quam semper in prandiis et in cenis legere fecit, et deo gracias egit quod ipsum predestinauit quod ipse super omnia regna aliorum regum regnaret. Et semper ante prandium benedicite et post prandium gracias in lingua sua legere consueuit. Et habuit quatuor filios: primogenitus Melchior vocabatur, secundus Baltazar, tercius Iaspar, et quartus Dauid vocabatur; et constituit imperpetuum itaqu[e] filios suos nominari — et ille fuit tercius imperator Tartarorum — ex causis prout inferius audietur. Set ad propositum redeatur.

† septuagesimo] xl.

And whan the peple of Tartary was multiplied and alle kyngdomis, londis, and provincis of þes vntrewe heretikes, and specially of þe Nestoryns, as hit was ordeynid of God, þei had take and distroyed and hem without mercy had sleyn, than thes Nestoryns bysoght helpe of Prestre Iohn, byhetyng hem to conuerte hem to the rytes of his lawes and to h[er] oold feith vndur his tribute. Which thing whan Prestre Iohn wold have done, þan the thre Kyngis warnyd hym in his slepe, forbedyng þat he shold in no wyse yeve helpe or counceile to hem; for hit was diffynid afor God that they shold vttirly be perisshid and distroyed, for God nold no lenger suffre ne susteyne her obstinate wikkidnes. Neuerþeles þes Nestorines ouercome the counceillours of Prestre Iohn wiþ ȝeftis þat þei shold sey to Prestre Iohn þat he shold recche of no sweuenes. And þei excitid [f. 268[v]] and counseylid hym that he shold yeve hem helpe, so þat he sent Dauid his sone with an houge oost to helpyng of hem; whom the Tartarines slowe aftir, and þe Nestoryns also and all þe oost, and meny londis [and] kyngdomes from Prestre Iohn they toke from. But Prestre Iohn, repentyng, bysoght þe help of God and of þe thre Kyngis. Which by night wiþ a passyng oost apperidyn and comaundedyn to þe Emperour of Tartarie þat he shold leve from þe persecucion of [+] Prestre Iohn and of his londys, comaundyng hym hyly þat he shold trete and make bytwene hem sikir and

5 her] his L. 15 and(4)] *om.* L. 19 of(1)] of the L.

Cum itaque populus Tartarorum †creuisset et omnia regna terras et prouincias infideli[um] et specialiter istorum Nestorinorum (prout a deo fuit diffinitum) itaque cepissent et destruxissent et ipsos sine misericordia interfecisse[n]t et funditus deleuissent, †et tunc† isti Nestorini de presbitero Iohanne auxilium implorabant et se ad fidem pristinam et ad suum †ritum sub tributo se conuersuros spoponderunt. Quod cum presbiter Iohannes facere voluisset, extunc tres Reges beati ipsum in sompnis monuerunt et ne Nestorinis auxilium vel consilium ferret inhibuerunt; nam apud deum esset diffinitum quod deberent deleri et †periri et funditus exterminari, nam deus eorum nequiciam diucius nollet sustinere obstinatam. Tamen Nestorini consiliarios presbiteri Iohannis muneribus circumuenerunt quod presbitero Iohanni dixerunt [quod] sompnia non deberet curare, set ipsum in eorum auxilium [f. 66[v]] mulcerunt et incitauerunt quod Dauid suum primogenitum cum valido excercitu in auxilium misit Nestorinis. Quem Tartari cum Nestorinis et omni excer[ci]tu suo interfecerunt, et quamplurimas terras et regna presbitero Iohanni abstulerunt. Et quamplurima alia sibi abstulissent; set presbiter Iohannes, penitencia ductus, auxilium dei et trium Regum beatorum inuocauit et implorauit. Qui [+] de nocte cum validissimo excercitu imperatori Tartarorum in sompnis apparuerunt horribiliter et preceperunt vt a persecucione presbiteri Iohannis et suarum terrarum statim desisteret et cum ipso

† creuisset] erupisset. † et tunc] extunc. † ritum] dominium. † periri] perire.

ferme pees, frendship, and trews for euermore duryng; but þe londis which he had reft from Prestre Iohn byfor for his inobedience he sholde holde, þat hit myght be to her successours yn ensaumple and memorie. Wherfor the Emperour of Tartarie, ferid wiþ [t]his vision and heste, alþog[h] he were þat tyme wiþ[out] lawe a gentile, he sent þan messagers and legatis to Prestre Iohn for tretyng of a finall pees & frendship, so þat þan evir aftir þe eldest son of þat one shold have þe doghtir of þat oþir and þat such frendship and pees shold dure for euermore. And whan þe emperour of thes thre Kynges was in his slepe þus appering to hym enfourmyd and of her [f. 269r] kyngdomes, condicions, lyf, and dedis taght, he þere ordeynid & made by constitucion þat from þens forward euermore his eldest son and al his oþir sones shold be callid with the names of þes thre Kyngis.

And so þes Nestorynes were distroyed from her londis & put out of her kyngdomes. But they be now yet here and þere in þo parties and in oþir londis [lyvyng disparplid], as Iewis b[e] lyvyng disparplid in diuers londis, and byfor all oþir specialy þei ȝeve tribute. But þei have and hold ȝet vndur hem vndur speciall tribute a stronge and a famous yle which is callid Egriscull, of which Iaspar the thrid Kyng was kyng in Ethiope, which

4 this] his L; alþogh] al þoght L. 5 wiþout] wiþ L. 15 lyvyng disparplid] *trs.* L; be lyvyng] by lyvyng *or* bylyvyng L.

pacem et firmas amicicias et treugas iniret et faceret inter ipsos perpetue duraturas horribiliter preceperunt; set terras presbitero Iohanni propter eius inobedienciam ablatas optineret in memoriam vt suis posteris et aliis transirent in exemplum. [Vnde] ipse imperator Tartarorum, hac visione et ius[s]u perteritus, licet esse[t] absque lege tunc gentilis, †tunc + misit nuncios et legatos ad presbiterum Iohannem et perpetuam pacem et firmam amiciciam secum fecit et iniuit, ita videlicet quod imperpetuum primogenitus vnius filiam alterius recipere †deberet, et talis pax et amicicia †imperpetuum + duraret†. Et cum imperator de tribus Regibus qui sibi horribiliter in sompnis apparuerunt fuisset instructus et de eorum regnis condicionibus et vita et eorum gestis fuisset informatus, extunc constituit quod semper su[u]s primogenitus et alij filij suorum successorum horum trium Regum nominibus imperpetuum deberent nominari. Et sic isti Nestorini fuerunt deleti et de regnis et terris eorum [f. 67r] expulsi. Set nunc hinc inde in ipsis partibus et aliis partibus sicut in istis partibus Iudei vndique degunt dispersi, et in eorum propriis terris et quibuscumque locis degunt semper pre aliis hominibus specialiter dant tributum. Set optinuerunt et habent adhuc sub se sub speciali tributo fortissimam et famosissimam insulam que Egrosilla vocatur, [de] qua [Iaspar tercius Rex] Ethiops, qui

† tunc] tamen statim. † deberet] deberet in conthoralem. † imperpetuum duraret] et contractus est in presentem diem.

offrid to God mirre. And in that yle lieth þe body of Seynt Thomas þe Apostle, restyng þere without eny worshipyng, and þat body from þe Nestorynes twies hath be reft and to hem aȝen by lawful causes restorid aȝen as oft. And into þis yle, inasmych as in hem is, þei suffre none but he be of her rite, or ellis of þe officers of þe emperours, to passe or come ynto her londe, and al her marchaundise fro þat yle into anoþir yle they lete carie to selle, and into þe same yle oþir marchaundise is broght to selle and bye.

And in al þe parties of þe Orient is no marchaunt, pilgryme, [or] Cristyn þat can sey that he hath be in þat yle & seyn the body of Seynt Thomas. For hit is ȝet as a prophecie in þo cuntrees that þe body [f. 269v] of Seynt Thomas shal folowe the bodies of the thre Kynges & be translatid to Coloyne and there dwelle and abyde for euermore. And how and in what manere þat shold be do, opinly they prophecie and seye that ther shal ȝet come a tyme whan hit likith to God þat þer shal come an archebisshop of Coloyne which God shal chese þerto, which shal be wys and myghty and shal ordeyne þe couple of matrimoigne bytwene the son & the doghtir of þe Emperour of Tartarie and þe Emperour of Rome which God þerto shal chese and predestine, and in that trete and frendship-makyng shal be ȝoldyn to þe Cristynmen the Holy Londe, and al thing shal þan turne and restore

9 or] *om.* L.

domino mirram optulit, rex Insule vocabatur; et in ipsa insula corpus beati Thome apostoli absque aliquo honore quiescit. Et illud corpus Nestorinis bis est ablatum et ipsis ex legitimis causis totidem restitutum. Et ad hanc insulam Nestorini, in quantum in eis est et vertere possunt, nullum omnino hominem nisi sit de ritu eorum vel officiatos imperatoris Tartarorum transire vel peruenire permittunt. Et omnia eorum mercimonia ad vendendum ex hac insula ad aliam deportantur, et ad eandem insulam alia mercimonia de aliis partibus ipsis ad emendum deportantur. Et in omnibus partibus orientis non est homo christianus catholicus vel peregrinus aut mercator visus qui dixisset se in ipsa insula fuisse et corpus beati Thome vidisse. Nam commune vaticinium est in omnibus partibus illis quod adhuc corpus beati Thome apostoli tres Reges debeat sequi et Colonie transferri et ibidem imperpetuum permanere. Et quomodo et qualiter et per quem modum hoc fieri debeat et perfici publice vaticinantur et dicunt, videlicet quod adhuc veniet tempus quando hoc deo perfici placuerit quod erit et veniet adhuc archiepiscopus coloniensis quem deus ad hoc †eligerit tam prudens et potens quod ordinabit copulam [f. 67v] matrimonialem inter filium et filiam imperatoris Romanorum et imperatoris Tartarorum quos deus ad hoc el[e]gerit et †predestinauit; et cum ips[o] contractu et amicicia reddetur christianis terra sancta, et omnia ibidem reuertentur et restituentur in bonum et

† eligerit] elegerit. † predestinauit] predestinauerit.

into the olde state. And with þes the body of Seynt Thomas to the bodies of þe thre Kynges shal be translatid to Coloyne. And þogh þe Nestoryns make neuere so grete kepyng and wacche for the body of Seynt Thomas, ȝet þei do [to hit] no reuerence, as for the fame and for they be so [distroyed, and more shul be ȝet] distroyed and broght to noght.

Also the feste of Seynt Thomas þe Apostle afor al oþir festes in the parties of the Oryent is had, but of diuers miracles which be red of hym in þis cuntrees and oþir cuntres is not red þere, for his body now restith among þe worst heretikes. And hit is red that þe body of Seynt Thomas in a chayer of gold ȝevith to þe worthy Goddis sacrament and from the vnworthy withdrawith hit, & of al þis is not herd ne red; but sometyme, [f. 270ʳ] whan his body restid in oþir places among Cristyn folk, þan all þes & meny mo oþir miracles were red of hym and seyn.

Also in all þe parties of the Orient of the thre Kynges meny diuers miracles be seyd which be not seyn in Coloigne. For hit is red þere that the sterre which af[o]r þe dissece of þo Kyngis apperid aboue þe mount of Vaus ouer the cherche of Seuwa, into þe tyme of þe carying of þe bodies

4 to hit] *trs.* L. 5 distroyed and more shul be ȝet] ȝet distroyed and more shul be L. 16 afor] aftir L.

statum pristinum. Et cum hiis et in hiis corpus beati Thome apostoli ad corpora trium Regum Colonie debeat transferri. Et †si talem ac tantam custodiam Nestorini corpori beati Thome †ponant, non adhibent reuerenciam sicut† propter famam ex inuidia, cum itaque sint destructi et adhuc plus debeant adnichillari et dehonestari. + ...

Item festum sancti Thome ap[ostol]i pre aliis apostolorum †festis habetur in omnibus partibus orientis. Set de quampluribus miraculis que in partibus istis de eodem leguntur et dicuntur, de hiis in omnibus illis nil + †legitur + quia eius corpus [f. 68ʳ] absque aliqua reuerencia inter pessimos hereticos quiescit. Item legitur quod corpus beati Thome ibidem in cathedra aurea dignis eucaristiam tradat et indignis [re]trahat. Et de hiis omnibus que de beato Thoma in hiis partibus leguntur et dicuntur penitus nunc nil videtur; set quondam cum corpus eius in aliis locis inter homines catholicos quiescebat, hec omnia et quamplurima alia miracula veraciter videbantur.

Item in omnibus partibus orientis quamplurima mirabilia de tribus Regibus dicuntur que in Colonia non †videbantur; videlicet dicitur et legitur ibidem quod ipsa stella que ante ipsorum Regum decessum super ciuitatem Seuwa et montem Vaus apparuit quousque

† si] *om.* † ponant ... sicut] non adhibent ex reuerencia sed. † festis] festis celeberrimum. † legitur] videtur vel reperitur nam legitur in istis quod in ciuitate qua corpus beati Thome quiescit ibidem vltra annum non possunt viuere heretici vel Iudei de hiis ibidem modo nil scitur. † videbantur] videntur.

of þes .iij. Kyngges aftir her deth to Coloyne aboue þe cite and ouer þat hill chaungid no place, but aftir þe translatyng of þo bodies to Coloyn, þan þat sterre, afor all oþir fairest & moost shynyng, ouer Coloyn is gone and left vnmeble, [and] may be seyn so into þis day.

Also þe Indes seyn þat afor the bodies of þo thre Kynges entoumbyd in Coloyne is a grete sterre of gold in þe manere as was seyn appering in the Cristemasse night to tho thre Kynges (as is red in her bokis); of whos light al þe chirch, as hit were of meny candels light byfor þo bodies, is lightyng and shynyng. Also the Indis seyn [and] hit is red in her bokis that the right armes of þo thre Kynges be yn Coloyne wondur richely and worshipfully more þan þe oþir armes yclosid in gold, and in þe right honde of þat o kyng is gold, and in þe honde of þat oþir is encense, and in the honde of þe thrid is mirre. And whan þo armes to princes or pilgrimes be shewid, þan þe bones of þo armes with an instrument [f. 270^{v}] of syluer and with a cloþe a sendell be wypid, and þe more þo bones be wypid and rubbid, þe more yn manere of swote *aromata* thurgh all þe chirche mirre with swete sauour is felid. Also the Yndes seyn [and] hit is red in her bokis that whan eny tribulacion or tempeste þurgh deserte of synne fall to the londe or chirche or citee of Coloyne, þan þes armis of þe thre Kynges of þe thre prestis þerto ordeynid, crounyd with crounes of gold, and a sterre of gold

4 and] *om.* L   9 and(2)] þat L.   15 be wypid] *one word* L.   17 and] þat L.

ipsorum trium Regum corpora Colonie d[e]ferebantur super ciuitatem et montem locum non mutauit, set postquam eorum corpora fuerunt Colonie translata extunc ipsa stella, ceteris stellis pulcrior et splendidior, super Coloniam transit et inmobilis permansit [e]t videatur in presentem diem. Item dicunt Indi et [in] eorum libris legitur quod in Colonia ante honestissimum ipsorum trium Regum loculum sit stella magna aurea in modum prout ipsis tribus Regibus in nocte natiuitatis domini apparuit formata, ex cuius splendore †quasi candelarum antepositarum tota ecclesia intus refulgeat et illuminetur. Item dicunt Indi et in ipsorum libris legitur quod in Colonia dextra brachia ipsorum trium Regum sunt multum venerabiliter et ditissime aliis brachiis aureis inclusa: in vnius Regis brachij manu sit aurum et in secundi Regis brachij manu sit thus et in tercij Regis brachij [f. 68^{v}] manu sit mirra. Et cum ipsa brachia principibus et peregrinis ex reuerencia demonstrantur, extunc ipsa ossa sacra cum instrumento argenteo fricantur et sindone terguntur; et quanto plus fricantur, tanto plus in modum aromatum †concernitur per totam ecclesiam †mir[r]a odoris fragrancia in ipsis ossibus sa[cr]is senciatur. Item dicunt Indi et legitur in ipsorum libris quod quandocumque aliqua tribulacio peccatis exigentibus terre vel ecclesie vel ciuitati coloniensi instat vel immineat, extunc ipsa brachia predicta a tribus presbiteris coronis aureis coronatis cum stella aurea

† quasi] *om.*   † concernitur] cum teruntur.   † mirra] mira.

made þerfor is bore byfor þe sacrament þurgh þe citee of Coloyne. And whan þei come to a chirche which þei chese þerto, þan þes prestis [so] crownid on aftir anoþir offre to þe sacrament leyd þan on þe autir ȝeftes and reliques hangyng on þe armys, in manere of the iij Kyngis; & þan þurgh þe grete contricion & deuocion of þe multitude of þe peple comyng þan thidir God from hem turnith al her tribulacion and dissese. Also the Yndes seyn þat þe sepulcre of þo thre Kynges in the citee of Seuwa, in which ferst aftir deth they were leyd and aftir take þens, ȝet levith þere hole and ȝet from ferre diuers londis and nacions devoutly is visitid, and God by her merites þere wurchith many vertues. And þei sey þat ou[i]r þat + sepulcre ȝet is the sterre which + is left from þat tyme that the thre Kynggis were þere biried, and God by her merites [f. 271r] to many c[omyng] from meny diuers londis to that sepulcre for worshipyng of tho thre Kyngis worcheth meny vertues and mervailis into this day.

Also the Yndes seyn which gone oft to Ierusalem and oþir diuers cuntres bycause of deuocion and for marchaundise þat they have in the citee of Seuwa reliques of Balaam and Iosaphath and oþir worshipful reliques of

2 so] þei L. 10 ouir þat sepulcre] our sepulcre *with a caret sign between* our *and* sepulcre *and* þat þe *interlineated* L. 11 which] which was of old tyme into now L. 13 comyng] cuntres L.

ad hec facta ante sacramentum dominicum per ciuitatem portantur coloniens[em]; et cum perueneri[n]t ad aliquam ecclesiam quam ad hoc elegerint, extunc ipsi presbiteri †coronati ipsa trium Regum brachia alternatim vnus post alium ad dominicum sacramentum in altari positum et in modum trium Regum offerunt dominico sacramento munera qu[e] in ipsis brachiis sunt annexa; et quod tanti populi concursus et confluxus et contricio et deuocio ab omnibus populis eueniat oriatur et accrescat quod deus quamcumque tribulacionem et angustiam iminentem auertat. Item dicunt Indi quod sepulcrum ipsorum trium Regum in ciuitate Seuwa, in quo primo defuncti fuerunt positi et postmodum excepti, adhuc ibidem integrum remansit, et adhuc a longinquis partibus a diuersis nacionibus et hominibus deuote visitatur, et deus per merita ipsorum trium Regum ibidem multas virtutes operatur. Et dicunt quod super idem sepulcrum adhuc sit [f. 69r] stella aurea que ab illo tempore quando ipsi tres Reges primo fuerunt sepulti adhuc remansit, et deus per merita ipsorum trium Regum ad sepulcrum eorum venientibus et ipsos venerantibus multa mira et virtutes operetur in presentem diem.

Item dicunt Indi qui frequenter in Iherusalem et ad alias c[ertas] partes causa deuocionis et mercimoniorum vel delectacionis perueniunt quod adhuc in ipsa ciuitate Seuwa habeant reliquias †Balaam et Iosaphath et aliorum plurimorum sanctorum de semine regali reliquias venerandas.

† coronati] coronati ferunt. † Balaam] Barlam.

oþir seyntes. Also the Yndes have wiþ hem penyes which þei have boght of pilgrimes, & also [r]inges, which have touchid þe reliques of the thre Kyngis in Coloyne, which wiþ deuocion þei worship mych and ofttyme with reuerence kysse, and þei afferme that meny sike by þe feith and deuocion þerof recouere her hele. And meny merveiles of the thre Kynges & of the bodies of .xj. M^{l} virgines in þo cuntres of the Est be red, more þan in þes cuntres. [Wher]for the Yndis which oft gone to Ierusalem and to meny oþir cuntres for diuers causes desire mych to come passyng Coloyne, if þei myght suffre colde and þe state of þe cuntre; and meny of hem dyen in þe wey and meny turne aȝen. For the Indis whan þei are passid out of her contre of Inde may suffre no colde, but anone þei cloþe hem in skynnis down to þe helis longe, which be made of noble bestis, reed of kynde and mych rough. And þei in Auguste be with vs moste heet of þe sonne, ȝet hit semith hem þat þei may not suffre so grete colde. For the nerre the este toward [f. 271^{v}] þe sonne arisyng, more be þe men þere febler & lasse, and good archers and bolde. But whan þei come to Ierusalem & to oþir cuntres about, al þat þei may enquere of princes, lordis, kyngis, londis [and kyngdomes] of þes cuntres of þis half, and

2 ringes] þinges L. 7 Wherfor] For L. 18 and kyngdomes] *om.* L.

Item Indi qui ad Iherusalem et ad alias partes frequenter perueniunt habent et portant penes se denarios et †anulos quos a peregrinis cismarinis emerunt qui reliquias sanctorum trium Regum in Colonia tetigerunt, quos cum deuocionibus multum venerantur et frequenter osculantur; et asserunt quod per fidem et deuocionem per [ips]os quamplurimi infirmi sanitatem †consequentur... . [f. 69^{v}] ... Et quamplurima et alia mirabilia de reliquiis trium Reg[u]m et vndecim millium virginum in omnibus partibus orientis dicuntur et leguntur, plus quam in istis partibus — de quibus per singula longum esset enarrare. Vnde quamplurimi Indi qui frequenter Iherusalem et alias c[ertas] partes propter diuersas causas perueniunt multum anxie et ardenter vlterius Coloniam transire desiderant, si frigus et statum patrie possent tollerare; quorum eciam quamplurimi in itinere moriuntur et quamplurimi reuertuntur. Nam Indi postquam partes Indie et terram eorum sunt egressi nullum omnino frigus pati possunt, set statim induunt pellicia vsque ad talos longa, que sunt facta ex pellibus nobilissimorum animalium naturaliter rubeis et multum hirsutis. Et licet sit in augusto feruentisimo solis ardore, tamen eis videtur quod tantum frigus in alienis partibus non †possent tollerare. Quia quanto plus versus ortum solis, tanto sunt homines debiliores et minores; set sunt optimi sagittarij et in omnibus multum astuti. Set cum Iherusalem et ad alia[s] circa partes perueniunt (scilicet Indi), omnia que de regibus et principibus terris et regnis istarum parcium cismarinarum et

† anulos] anulos aureos. † consequentur] consequuntur. † possent] possunt.

specialy of þe thre Kyngis [and] of Coloyne and of her peple, þei wil aske and receyve vndur þe lettre & sele of some kyng or prince to shewe or sende to Prestre Iohn or to Patriark Thomas.

For in al þe parties of Ynde and of þe Orient all peple, nacions, & langages have more in wurship, reuerence, & special honour þes thre Kynges þan in þes cuntres, and worthily of all londis, nacions, and langages þes thre Kynges *tanquam primicie gencium* of al virgines be moost specialy to honoure and to be glorified. For þes [be þe] werkmen in the inchoacion of þe Newe Testament in þe last tymes of þe world by þe Fadir of hevyn sent into his vineȝerd, which in þe erly mornyng, atte þe prime houre, at þe tierce, at þe sixte, & none, & mydday houre treuly trauailid in the vyne tre and wiþout grucching a[n] evyn perpetuel mede have receyvid.

In the mornyng þei trauailid in Ierusalem and Bethlem, thes thre Kynges, in the vyne among þe Iewes, castyng out the hard stones of þe inexcusable Iewis mysbyleue and envye.

Atte prime the thre Kyngis in flesshe among þe peple clensid wele the vyne ocupied with diuers thistles and wedis of ydolatrie and diuers errours wiþ [f. 272r] the help of þe holy Thomas, and newe plantis and vynes

1 and(1)] *om.* L.   8 be þe] *om.* L.   12 an] at L.

specialiter de tribus Regibus et Colonia et eius clero et populo poss[u]nt inquirere et inuestigare sub alicuius episcopi vel principis sigillo †litteram scriptam† petunt et recipiunt, vt presbitero Iohanni et patriarche Thome cercius †possunt mittere et demonstrare. Nam in omnibus partibus Indie [f. 70r] et orientis omnes populi et naciones et lingue hos tres Reges gloriosos multum plus quam in hiis partibus habent in reuerencia speciali et honore.

Et merito ab omnibus populis tri[bu]bus et linguis hij tres Reges gloriosi primicie gencium et ex †gentibus virginum specialissime sunt hon[o]randi et glorificandi. Nam hij sunt operarij qui [in] inchoacione noui testamenti et vocacione gencium in nouissimis mundi temporibus per celestem patremfamilias in suam vineam missi, qui mane hora prima tercia sexta nona ac vndecima in ipsa vinea fidelissime laborauerunt et absque murmure mercedem equalem perpetuam receperunt. +

Mane videlicet in Iherusalem et Bethleem hij tres Reges gloriosi inter Iudeos ex ipsa vinea durissimos et inexcusabiles iudaice perfidie et inuidie lapides longe foras miserunt et eiecerunt.

Hora prima hij tres Reges gloriosi in carne viuentes inter gentes ipsam vineam diuersis tribulis cardis et spinis diuersorum errorum et ydolatrie occupatam vna cum beato Thoma apostolo mundauerunt et nouas fidei catholice palmites et vites

† litteram scriptam] et littera scripta.   † possunt] possint.   † gentibus] gentibus primicie.

of [+] trewe feith emplantid and foundyd þerin.

Atte tierce þes thre Kynges aftir her dethe, gadrid aȝen togidir by Eleyne, matiers of diuers impedimentes of heresie and ydolatrie hardnyd þei have newe refourmyd by plantis of the feith — for in the vyne þe plantis of the feith þan bygan to drie and perisshe — and with vertues and diuers signes have wette and wiþ diuers miracles refresshid, þat þei now have broght forþe newe grapis and froyt of trewe feith.

Atte the vndurtyde þes thre Kynges, as in þe myddis of þe world translatid into Constantinople in Grece, have purified wiþ vertues and signes þe vyne, þat the froyte of þe feith might more braunche and extende þe knowlech of hem by þe feith into all þe endis of þe world, and all peplis, nacions, and langages, fulfillid of þe grapis and froytis of þe vyne, myght prayse the name of God from the risyng of þe sunne into þe doungoyng, which byfor was hid but as only in Ynde.

Atte the our of none thes glorious Kynges wroght in the vyne of God of Sabaoth, by the see fro þe Est into þe West, from Constantinople translatid into Milayne, put out and flemyd many foxe whelpes envenemyd wiþ diuers errours of heresies out of the vyne, which strengthid hem to distroy

1 of] of newe L.

in ea mirifice plantauerunt.

Hora tercia hij tres Reges defuncti, per venerabilem Helenam denuo congregati et collecti, huius vinee maceri[a]s ex diuersis impedimentis heresis et ydolatrie †d[ura]tas eciam de nouo reposuerunt †ad palmites fidei — [†quia in ipsa vinea iam †palmites fidei†] perire et arescere ceperunt — virtutibus et signis irrigauerunt et diuersis miraculis refecerunt, [f. 70^{v}] quod denuo fidei catholice vuas fructusque p[ro]duxerunt.

Hora sexta hij tres Reges, quasi in medio mundi in Grecia et Constantinopolim translati, ipsam eciam vineam iterum virtutibus et signis putauerunt et purificauerunt, vt plus fidei fructus faceret †in eius propagines [in] omnes fines terre per fidem et noticiam eorum se †extenderet, et omnis populus et tribus et lingue et naciones de eorum fructibus ac vinee vuis et botris saciati et inebriati nomen domini, quod prius solummodo in †I[ndi]a latitabat, ab ortu solis vsque ad occasum †collaudauerunt.

Hora nona hij tres Reges †vineam domini Sabaoth sunt operati tam in ipsa vinea plus operand[um]† per mare transeuntes de oriente in occidentem (videlicet de Constantinopolim in Mediolanum) translati, ex ipsa vinea diuers[a]rum heresum et errorum hereticorum vulpeculas,

† duratas] dirutas. † ad] et. † quia] que. † palmites fidei] marcescere. † in] et.
† extenderet] extenderent. † India] Iudea. † collaudauerunt] collaudarent.
† vineam ... operandum] vinee domini Sabaoth operarij gloriosi causa in ipsa vinea plus operandi.

the vyne by diuers errours and venymes of heresye, by declaracion, significacion, & exposicion [f. 272v] and interpretacion of her ȝeftis which þei offrid to God.

Also the .xj. hour, about goyng doun of þe sonne, þes glorious Kynges from Milayne to Coloigne, receyving an evyn eternal mede to hem of þe hye Fadir of hevyn, chosin þere a perpetuel place of restyng, ne neuere aftir seth left to worship þe vyne and to tylie the vyne of God of Sabaoth wiþ vertues, merites, and signes.

Hit was neuere herd in scripture of þe Newe Testament eny halowe fro the risyng of þe sonne into the dounfallyng so reuerently, gloriously, or merveillously as þes .iij. glorious Kynges to so worthy places be translatid, and at þe laste to þe citee and cherche of Coloyne, of almyghty God þerto specialy predestinate, chosyn, and ordeynid. For thogh fro þe risyng of þe sonne to the dounfallyng be meny chirches, citees, & places grete and also more + which God in his deite and also humanyte by hemself and also by meny oþir of his seyntis in her lyf and also in her deth and aftir her deþe hath specialy honourid and glorified and wiþ meny diuers prerogatif< . >s halowid and wiþ meny diuers vertues, merveiles, signes, and worshipful

15 more] more in L.

que ipsam vineam diuersis erroribus et heresi demollire nitebantur, per declaracionem et significacionem exposicionem et interpretacionem eorum muner[um]que domino optulerunt (vt supradictum est) expulerunt et effugarunt. +

Vndecima vero hora circa solis occasum hij tres Reges, gloriosi operarij, de Mediolano in Coloniam †sunt translati eterna mercede equaliter ab eis a celesti patrefamilias recepta perpetu[um] quiescendi locum ibidem elegerunt; nec †cum postmodum predictam vineam domini Sabaoth virtutibus meritis et signis ibidem in presentem diem colere desierunt.

Nusquam enim [f. 71r] in tocius noui testamenti scripturis reperitur aliquem vel aliquos sanctos ab ortu solis vsque ad eius occasum tam reuerenter gloriose et mirabiliter sicut hos tres Reges gloriosos ad loca tam insignia fore translatos, et nouissime ad ecclesiam et ciuitatem †[Coloniam] ab omnipotenti deo ad hoc specialiter †predestinatos electos et deputatos†. Nam quamuis ab ortu solis vsque ad occasum sint quamplurime ecclesie et ciuitates et loca magna ac maiora et maxima que deus sua deitate et + humanitate per se et per alios quamplurimos suos sanctos in vita et morte et post mortem specialiter honorauit et glorificauit et quamplurimis prerogatiuis honorauit et consecrauit et diuersis virtutibus et signis et

† sunt] *om.* † cum] tamen. † Coloniam] absque dubio. † predestinatos electos et deputatos] predestinatas electas et deputatas.

reliqs declarid, ȝet in al þes chirches & places or citees is no cherche decorate with so faire a collage of chanons, which to serue God in propre persone durably be boundyn, [f. 273r] as the chirche of Coloyne, or eny citee as the citee of Coloyne. And that of þe prouidence of God we may vndurstonde specialy to be do, þat he wold in þat cherche ordeyne so noble mynistres and in that citee so noble peple predestine in whiche he wold ley þes glorious Kynges so noble as *primicias gencium* and of virgines þere to dwelle foreuere.

Be glad þerfor, noble college, þat God with so singuler priuilege of love and with so principal prerogatifs of worship and ȝeftis of kynde lovid þe and richid byfor al oþere colleges, and ordeynid so noble mynistris in þe, and forchese the his speciall tresour, þe thre Kynges, *primicias gencium*, and her fundement afor all oþir places & cherches merveilously hath honourid & more diligently commendid. Wherfor in thonkyng God of his worshipis [and] praysynges to þe of hym specialy yovyn and benefices so large leve þou neuere, ne be wery, ne to serve hem be thow shamyd, þat þou be not, as þe Nestorynes, had in dispite of God & al his trewe peple,

15 and(1)] *om.* L.

reliquiis venerandis illustrauit et †declarauit, tamen inter has ecclesias et ciuitates et omnia alia loca non est aliqua ecclesia tam nobili canonicorum collegio, qui deo in propriis personis ad seruiendum sunt astricti, sicut ecclesia coloniensis ornata, vel aliqua ciuitas †vt coloniensis decorata; quod ex diuina prouidencia sciamus specialiter fore factum quod omnipotens deus in ipsa ecclesia tam nobiles suos ministros ordinaret et [in] hac ciuitate tam honestissimum populum predestinaret in quas tam nobilissimos tres Reges suas primicias gencium et virginum perpetue manendo collocaret.

Letare, nobile collegium, quod te deus tam singulari priuilegio amoris et precipuis prerogatiuis honoris et nature donis pre cunctis collegiis preamauit et ditauit, et te in suos nobiles ministros preelegit et ordinauit, et tibi specialissimum suum [f. 71v] thesaurum, tres Reges, primicias gencium et virginum et †eorum fundamentum ab ortu solis pre aliis locis et ecclesiis egregiis et insignibus mirabilius destinauit et predestinauit et diligencius commendauit! Vnde de hiis semper deo gracias agere et in eius et suarum pr[imi]ciarum laudibus et seruiciis tibi specialiter iniunctis ex hiis et commissis de tantis beneficiis consecutis nunquam cesses vel fatigeris nec ipsis seruire verecunderis, ne, vt Nestorini, deo et suis pr[imi]ciis et hominibus despecti

† declarauit] decorauit. † vt] cum tam honestissimo populo et alijs dei ministris sicut ciuitas. † eorum] earum.

visitid wiþ the wratthe of God and reprovid, and of so special prerogatiues with which afor al oþir þou precellist be pryvid as þe Nestorynes, and be cast from al thy worship and in the laste dome with thes on þe left honde be reprovid; but that þow may with þe Nubyans, lovid and [f. 273^{v}] chosyn to God and to his, with which in all the world byfor all oþir collegis [þou art] exaltid and of all peple singulerly worshipid and in the dome with þe thre noble Kynges, *primicijs gencium* and of maydenis, on Goddis right honde with ioy and eternale glorie be praysid.

And noght without forsight þat cite which was callid of olde tyme Agrippina $^{+}$ now of worshiping of God is callid by name Coloyne. For in all þe parties of þe Orient in alle cherchis, chapels, oratories, and placis in whiche the praysing of þes thre glorious Kynges [is]writyn in diuers lettres or langages, among alle oþir of her praysinges in ryme or in prose in Latyn be writyn þes verses and wordis as they folowyn here:

Ab Helena crux inuenta;
Post hijs regnis est intenta
Congregandis regibus.

5 þou art] bene L. 10 Agrippina] Agrippina and L. 13 is writyn] ywrityn L.

ira et furore domini aliquando visiteris arguaris vel corripiaris †vel extenueris†, et tam specialissimis prerogatiuis quibus ex hiis cunctis precellis ex ingratitudine sicut ipsi Nestorini priueris et ab omnibus honoribus abiciaris, et in extremo iudicio cum sinistris reproberis; set cum Nubianis gloriosis deo et suis primiciis et hominibus dilectis et electis cum quibus in vniuerso mundo ex hiis pre aliis collegiis extolleris et ab omnibus populis singulariter venereris †et in iudicio cum nobilissimis tribus Regibus, et primiciis gencium et virginum, a dexteris cum gloria †collauderis. Nec absque presagio eciam illa ciuitas gloriosa que ab antiquo Agrippina vocabatur nunc sortita est nomen quod a colendo deum Colonia nuncupatur. Nam in omnibus partibus orientis, in omnibus ecclesiis oratoriis et capellis et locis in quibus istorum trium Regum gloriosorum [laus diuersis litteris et linguis est scripta, inter alia que de ipsorum] laudibus ritmatice vel prosayce in latino sunt scripta prout subsequitur scriptum reperitur: [f. 72^{r}]

Ab Helena crux inuenta;
Post hiis regnis est intenta
Congregandis Regibus.

† vel extenueris] et extermineris. † et] *om.* † collauderis] colloceris.

Inde reges peregrini
Ornant vrbem Constantini
Allatis corporibus.

Tandem inde sunt translati
Cuidam pulcre ciuitati
Cui nomen Ambrosia.

Ter inuentos, ter translatos,
Nutu Dei sibi datos
Colit hos Colonia.

Ortus dedit Occidenti [f. 274r]
Quod tres Reges, ter inuenti,
Excolunt Coloniam.

Nusquam locum mutaturi
Nec, vt olim, reuersuri
Sunt per viam aliam.

Inde Reges peregrini
Ornant vrbem Constantini
   Allatis corporibus.
Tandem inde sunt translati
Cuidam pulcr[e] ciuitati
   Cui nomen Ambrosia.
Ter inuentos, ter translatos,
Nutu dei sibi datos
   Colit hos Colonia.
Ortus dedit occidenti
Quod tres Reges, ter inuenti,
   Excolunt Coloniam.
Nu[s]quam locum mutaturi
Nec, vt olim, reuersuri
   Sunt per viam †aliam. +

† aliam] aliam Colunt Reges propter regem Summi regis seruant legem Coloni Colonie.

And witith þat the names of thes thre Kyngges be thes, as writith [þe] Maystir in H[is]tories. The[s] be her names in Hebrew: Appellus, Amerus, and Damascus. In Latyn thes be her namys: Iaspar, Mel<c>hior, and Baltazar. In Greke thes be her names: Galgalath, Magalath, Serachym. And thes Kynges be not callid *magi* of evil doyng but of wytte. For by seynt Austyn *magi* in Caldee is as mych to sey as *philosophi* in Greke, *sapientes* in Latyn ('wyse' in Englisshe). Also aftir Remige is þer diuerse opinion of this woord *magi*. Some seyn that þei were Caldees: the Caldees worship a sterre for her god. Some seyn þei were Percens. Some sey þei were of þe ferrest parties of þe world. Othir seyn þei were cosyns to Balam, which is moost to byleve.

Wherfor Crisostome seith [þat he fonde in some bokis] þat þer was a peple in the parties of the Orient †which was not right wys or† noblenesse. þei fonde in the bokys of Balaham [f. 274^{v}] — for they were perauntre of his kynrede — th<a .. h .. > had prophecied *Orietur in diebus stella ex Iacob &c.* Vndirstondyng as to þe lettre þat the sterre shold appere in the birthe of Cryst, meny of þe peple lete ordeyne to serche and awayte to se þe shewyng of þat sterre, þat þei myght þerby knowe and vndirstonde Crist

1 þe Maystir in Histories] a maystir in his stories L. 2 Thes] The L.
12 þat he fonde in some bokis] in some bokis þat he fonde L. 13 which ... or] *see note.*

Nota quod nomina trium †[regum] magorum sunt h[e]c, vt scribit magister in [Historia Scolastica]: hebrayce, †Appel[lu]s Amerus Damascus; grece, Galgalat[h] Magalat S[e]rathim; latine, Iaspar Balthazar Melchior.

Nota quod isti magi dicuntur non a maleficio set sapiencie studio; secundum enim beatum Augustinum magi in Caldeo idem quod philosophi in greco et sapien[te]s in latino. Item secundum Remigium varia est de magis opinio: qui[dam] dicunt ipsos fuisse Caldeos (Caldei enim stellam pro deo colunt), quidam dicunt ipsos fuisse Persas, quidam dicunt ipsos de vltimis finibus fuisse. Alij dicunt ipsos nepotes fuisse Balaam, [f. 72^{v}] quod magis credendum est; Balaam enim inter cetera que prophetauerat dixit, Orietur stella ex Iacob.

Vnde [C]risostomus narrat se inuenisse in quibusdam libris quod erat quedam gens in partibus orientis in qua fuit multa sapiencia et nobilitas. Isti, inuenientes in libris Balaam (quia forte erant de stirpe eius) quod prophetauerat Orietur stella ex Iacob [etcetera], intelligentes ad litteram christo nascente apparere huiusmodi stellam, fuerunt †multi curiosi inuestigare et videre ortum illius stelle, vt per ipsum cognoscerent christum natum.

† regum] *om.* † Appellus] Appellius. † multi] multum.

to be borne. And for to have bettre knowleche and serching, þei ordeynid that þere shold be ordeynid .xij. wise astronomers, the beste among hem, so that aftir the dethe of one anoþir shold be substitute in his place duryng þat tyme, so þat þere shold be euere .xij. which shold euere concidre and wayte aftir þe risyng and shewyng of the sterre. And as þei myght do beste, they lete make in the hyest hille in the Oryent, wher was þe purest and clennest ayre, a faire paleys with all copie of all store of vitaille and alle necessaries to þe lyvelode, and þe[r] sholde stonde þes .xij. men with silence, orison, wakyng, & abstinens, abyding & deuoutly praying for the risyng of þat sterre. And þan neighyng and comyng ny the tyme of þe natiuite of Crist, and hem beyng in the Orient, in the mydnyght oure of þe night apperid aboue hem in þe eyre a bright shynyng sterre and a faire, in the coppe and h<e>ithe of which sterre was an ymage of a litil child bering wiþ hym ...

8 þer] þes L. 14 *ends imperfectly* L.

Et ad [+] melius inuestigandum ordinauerunt quod eligerentur duodecim de melioribus †[astrologis] inter eos, ita quod vno decedente alius subrogaretur, ita quod semper essent duodecim qui solicite considerarent ortum illius stelle. Et vt hoc melius facerent, in quodam altissimo monte in oriente, vbi semper erat aer purissimus, construi fecerunt pulcherimum palacium cum copia omnium rerum necessariarum ad victum. Et ibi stabant duodecim viri cum silencio oracione vigilia et abstincencia, expectantes et deuote deprecantes ortum istius stelle. Adueniente autem tempore natiuitatis [christi] et ipsis in †oriente persistentibus, in ipsa hora noctis media apparuit super eos in aere stella prefulgida et pulcherima, in cuius summitate erat ymago pueri parui secum ferens ymaginem crucis ...

† astrologis] familiis *or* famulis. † oriente] oracione.

COMMENTARY

49/1 ff.: The first pages blend matter from the apocryphal gospel of Pseudo-Matthew (*PsM*) with passages from chapter 6 of *HTR,* beginning with the story of Mary's vision from *PsM*. The two sources are distinguished in the parallel Latin text by the use of contrasting fonts, *PsM* in Universal, *HTR* as in the main text. The opening words could be based on either source, though only *HTR* cites the gospel directly:

> Cvm autem vt deus peccatoribus misereri voluit et venisset plenitudo temporis in quo deus filium suum vnigenitum mittere voluit in mundum de Maria virgine nasciturum, in illo tempore Octauianus Augustus frena romani imperij et monarchiam per vniuersum rexit mundum; et anno imperij eius xlijo, prout Lucas narrat, 'Exijt edictum ab eodem Cesare Augusto vt describeretur ...' (Hm. 219/14 ff., citing Luke ii.1–14).

How far the text continued with *PsM* material is impossible to tell owing to damage to the lower part of f. 228 in the Lambeth manuscript. The English and Latin more or less correspond up to 50/1 'into a cave vndur erthe', whereupon *PsM* continues:

> (... in speluncam subterraneam) in qua lux non fuit unquam sed semper tenebrae, quia lumen diei penitus non habebat. Ad ingressum vero Mariae coepit tota spelunca splendorem habere, et quasi sol ibi esset ita tota fulgorem lucis ostendere; et quasi esset ibi hora diei sexta, ita speluncam lux divina illustravit; nec in die nec in nocte lux ibi divina defuit quamdiu ibi Maria fuit. Et ibi peperit masculum, quem circumdederunt angeli ...

This seems to have small connection with what survives of the English (though *Et ibi peperit masculum* ... has definite echoes in 51/7–8 ff.). However some of the lost matter will be accounted for by the lead-in to the sentence at the beginning of f. 228^{v} 'and straungers ...', which comes from *HTR*.

The same problem arises on the verso. Here *HTR* is the source of the surviving matter in f. 228^{v} and, it would seem, the first words of f. 229^{r}, but it is unclear exactly how the transition was effected, as the passages on either side are separated in the original by a passage previously translated (50/4–9, Hm. 222/n9 ff.). The reference to 'Ierusalem' (51/4) may derive from a passage of *HTR* referring to the fate of the house of Jesse, father of King David, in a general destruction of the city and its environs (Hm. 221/n34 ff.).

HTR describes the nativity as taking place in the ruins of the house in which David was born, where an inn (*cf.*, *Et huiusmodi domus*) once stood, though the connection does not seem to have been brought out in the translation. These ruins later became popular in visual representations of the nativity (see Freeman 1955: 72–3). Other motifs which appear in *HTR* are a courtyard (*area*) in the ruins where bread was sold, a cave (*spelunca*) used for storage, and a hut (*tugurrium*) standing before the cave to which animals were tethered. The notion of gods born in caves is ancient but the location of Christ's nativity in a cave is apocryphal; in *PsM* (but not explicitly in *HTR*) it becomes 'a cave vndur erthe' (50/1; *cf.*, 50/13 'above þat cave'). The bread market perhaps derives from the supposed etymology of Bethlehem as 'house of bread'.

49/6 in white: The variant reading *veste candida* of the *PsM* witnesses AB is closer to the English than *veste splendida* of the printed text.

49/11 of þe sede ... peplis: *cf.*, Genesis xii.3.

51/7 without peyne: The motif appears both in *HTR* (Hm. 222/13–n21 *Et in ipsa spelunca eadem nocte deus pro nobis in tanta paupertate de Maria virgine absque dolore partus prout decuit fuit homo natus)* and in a variant reading to *PsM* (B *Et ibi peperit masculum sine dolore)*. The source of 'as aftre mydnyght byfor dawnyng as yn an oryson lying' is unaccounted for.

51/10–12 And than Ioseph ... which she had born: This is closer to the variant reading of AB *Iam enim nativitas domini advenerat, et Ioseph perrexerat quaerere obstetrices. Qui cum invenisset, reversus est ad speluncam et invenit cum Maria infantem quem genuerat.*

51/16 to come visite the: AB add *ut te visitent* after *cauta esto.*

51/17 they: AB read *eas* for *unam ex eis.*

51/18 & Salome left stondyng without: AB add *Salome non ingressa* after *Cumque ingressa esset Zelomi.*

52/10 and Salome withdrow her honde from Marie: *Cf.*, A *Dum autem manum suam a palpitatione retraheret*, E *statim ut manum dexteram suam ab aspectione eius abstraxit.*

52/10–11 her hondis bothe: The Latin has the singular (*aruit manus eius*) both here and at line 19.

52/13 Y have curyd: In the Latin the midwife pleads that she took no material reward for her services.

53/7–9 an houge sterre ... world: Nothing in the gospel account suggests that the Star of Bethlehem was conspicuously large or bright, but the motif appears from an early date, for example in the probably mid-second century *Book of James* (v. 21, James 1924: 47) and in Origen (*c.* 185–*c.* 254) *Contra Celsum* 1: 58 (see Hughes 1979: 127).

53/9 And the prophetis which were þat tyme in Ierusalem: So AB *Et prophetae qui erant in Ierusalem*, but the original reference seems to be to earlier prophets (*qui fuerant in Ierusalem*), though which ones exactly are meant is unclear.

53/12–14 without þe cite ... the crecche: Not in the Latin.

53/16–17 Abacuk ... Isaye: In fact the first prophecy is from Isaiah (i.3), the second from Habakkuk (iii.2, in the Old Latin version *In medio duorum animalium cognosceris*).

54/1–4: The syntax is faulty but no obvious explanation or emendation suggests itself. The spelling 'chrecche' (for 'crecche' or 'cracche') is anomalous; possibly the scribe started to write 'cherche' (as at 103/4, 121/12 etc.), but corrected himself after the second letter.

54/8–9 And in meny places ... knowyn: This is all the translation reproduces of an extended topographical description of the Holy Land at the end of chapter 6 of *HTR* (Hm. 222/21–223/15); the subsequent chapter concerning Herod (Hm. 223/n22–224/n5) is also omitted.

54/10–55/3 And whan ... sonnys: This complicated sentence had already suffered some corruption in the translator's exemplar; however the Latin shows that 54/13 'sete' is intended to refer to the 'xij astronomers' and 'abydyn' to the 'sterre'. The astronomers appear in chapter 5 of *HTR* (see Introduction 6). Balaam's prophecy is discussed in chapter 2 of *HTR*, the ultimate source being Numbers xxii–xxiv. In some traditions (e.g. Remigius) the Magi are described as descendants of Balaam (see 155/10–11).

55/4–5 And that sterre ... othir sterris: It is not certain what the translator's exemplar read, but the English does not reproduce the original reference to paintings of the star 'in churches in these parts'.

55/9 ff.: The voice in the star is an attempt to solve a problem inherent in the gospel account, namely how the Magi knew that they were to come to Jerusalem to worship the king of the Jews after they had seen his star in the East (*cf.*, 67/6 ff.); according to modern interpretation the message may have been couched in astrological terms (see Hughes 1979: 2). The utterance of the star combines phrases from Matthew's gospel with the prophecy of Balaam (Numbers xxiv.17, cited in *HTR* in the form *Orietur stella ex Jacob et exsurget homo de Israel et dominabitur omnium gencium*).

55/14–15 of which ... Newe Testament: The sense of the Latin is rather that as God in the Old Testament caused an ass to speak to Balaam, so in the New Testament he caused the star prophecied by Balaam to deliver a message to mankind.

56/16 housholdis beddyng: In the manuscript 'beddyng' is linked to 'ornementis' over the page by hyphens, suggesting the scribe thought of 'beddyng ornementis' as a single concept, though the corresponding *lectisternijs et vtensilibus* does not support this. I have retained the manuscript reading 'housholdis', which can be taken as a plural (rare, but for examples see *MED* s.v. hous-hold *n.* 1a.(b); 1b.; 2.(b); 2.(c), of which only the first two — 'retinue, court'; 'home' — are possible in the present context), or as a genitive, equivalent to 'of housholde' (as in 57/4 'store of housholde' — MED s.v. hous-hold *n.* 1b.). But perhaps the original reading was 'housholde beddyng' (for which *MED* s.v. bedding *ger.* 1.(a), (*c.* 1440) **Pet.Chanc.* offers an exact parallel), 'housholde' subsequently being taken as a coordinate noun and attracted into the plural under the influence of the preceding nouns.

57/5 but as þei trusse such cariage: 'unless they carry such equipment'.

57/16 xxv: The Latin has '125'. The allusion is to the opening words of the book of Esther (where, however, the figure appears as 127).

58/2–3 and an appil of gold: This (like 69/13–14 'wiþ the goldyn appil') is an addition in the English anticipating the account at 71/14 ff., which may imply that the scribe had copied the text previously.

58/9–10 byȝend þat see: This, like 'on this syde of the Reed See' at lines 6–7, is probably a misinterpretation, as the author normally uses *cismarinus* and *vltramarinus* in reference to the Mediterranean (e.g. at 117/7).

59/8 Babyloigne: This is not ancient Babylon, but the medieval city (*Babilonia noua*) adjoining Cairo; see 80/20–81/4.

60/5 Tarce: The name occurs elsewhere in ME — see *MED* s.v. Tars(e *n*. 'Tharsia, a kingdom said to border on China ... ' — but in our work it is associated with the biblical Tarshish (itself a concept of many layers; see Young 1939 s.v. Tarshish, Tharshish 4) and perhaps also with Tarsus (see 75/1 ff.n).

60/8 and with some ... Egriscula: The translation reproduces what is evidently a gloss in the Latin reporting variant spellings. The name (originally perhaps 'Egrisoulla') has received no convincing explanation.

60/17–18 Reges Tharsis ... adducent: Psalms lxxi(lxxii).9–10.

61/1 subget: Perhaps 'under the control, rule, or influence of; subordinate' — *OED* s.v. subject *a*. 2; *MED* s.v. subget *adj*. 3.(b) — or 'appended, subjoined' — *MED* s.v. subget *adj*. 6.(c), one example only, (*c*. 1384) *WBible*(1). The translator's exemplar evidently had G's reading *subicientur* (?'shall be added on') rather than the generally received *subticentur* (?'are downplayed'). But the whole passage is confused in the Latin, which may account for the abridgement at line 5. The author is evidently offering an explanation of the dual titles of the Kings: they were rulers of greater kingdoms, but were known by the titles of the lands the gifts came from. The question of this dual nomenclature is complex, but one set of titles (Arabia, Sheba, Tarshish) has biblical precedents, the other (Nubia, Godolia, Egrisoulla) is of obscure origins. Other passages in *HTR* attest to the author's habit of blending two disparate traditions from his sources (e.g. 114/9 ff.n).

61/11–12 with the goers ... the stonders stode: This is a literal translation of the idiomatic Latin meaning that the star moved when the travellers moved and stopped when they stopped.

61/13 were not shette: *Cf.*, Isaiah lx.11.

61/17 with passyng spede: This is not in the Latin, but is implied by 62/9 ff.

62/9 merches: *paludes* 'marshes'; *cf.*, line 6 'marches': *finibus* 'borders'. *Sed erant ... planas* is an allusion to Isaiah xl.4 ('Every valley shall be exalted ... ').

62/13: The lost matter (Hm. 229/11–231/n11) includes a discussion of the Kings' miraculous journey in thirteen days to Jerusalem (i.e., from Christmas to Epiphany, 25 December to 6 January), a description of a chapel dedicated to the Three Kings at the Mount of Calvary, and an account of the cloud (*nebula densa et caligo tenebrosa*) which enveloped the Kings as they approached Jerusalem (an allusion to Isaiah lx.1–2 *Surge illuminare Ierusalem* ...).

63/1 a litil towne ... Galilee: There is no town named Galilee in Scripture; all references are to a district in northern Palestine, one of the four administrative divisions of Roman Palestine (*cf.*, lines 3–4). The present information derives from Ludolf 113, where the editor identifies the town with a tower called Viri Galilei (an allusion to Acts i.11). The confusion is also noted in Von Harff (Letts 1946: 215).

63/3 *Precedet vos in Galileam*: Mark xvi.7.

64/9–12 *Fortitudo ... ministrabunt tibi*: Isaiah lx.5–7 (Isaiah lx, on the coming of the gentiles to the New Jerusalem, contains numerous allusions pertinent to our author's theme).

64/16 as who seith litil or noght: *quasi nichil vel parum*. The phrase 'as who seith' apparently acts here as a mere intensive — *cf.*, *MED* s.v. seien *v.*(1) 1b. 'as who seieth trei-as' (vr. 'tryes') and examples s.v. as *conj.* 7, especially *c.* 1450 Spec.Chr.(2) 'What seynte es crouned wyth-outyn trauelos victorye? As who seythe noon'. The original version of the Latin explains that these rams store their body fat in their tails.

65/7 ff.: Herod the Great was appointed King of the Jews by the Romans in 40 B.C. and ruled from 37 B.C. to 4 B.C. He was ruler at the time of Christ's birth and for some time after (until the return of the Holy Family from Egypt). He came from an Edomite family, and as a secular king pursued an active policy of Hellenization — see *ODCC* s.v. Herod family; *Oxford Classical Dictionary* s.v. Herod(1).

65/10–11: The gospel (Matthew ii.1–11) is cited in full in the Latin. Having raised the question of why the Kings came first to Jerusalem rather than to Bethlehem, the author proceeds to explain why Herod was troubled and all Jerusalem with him (Matthew ii.3).

66/2 to confusion of þe Iewis: The theme is more extensively treated in the original (which may have suffered loss in the translator's exemplar, for example by eyeskip *quia Iherusalem ... Quia nimirum* or *Iudei et scribe ... Iudei prophecie*). The source is a homily (I.10.2) of Gregory the Great (*c.* 540–604), where the Jews are likened to Isaac who in his blindness failed to recognise his son Jacob (Genesis xxvii); but the essential word *ceci*, referring to the blindness of the Jews, to which line 3 'for they knew not hym ...' should have referred, had dropped out in the translator's exemplar.

67/3–4 all ... that they had herd and seyn: This is a garbled allusion to the visitation of the shepherds, Bethlehem being specifically mentioned in the original Latin. For all its dramatic force the meeting between the shepherds and the Magi has no scriptural basis — the protagonists appear in separate gospels — and probably reflects the influence of liturgical plays (Freeman 1955: 65; Muir 1995: 17, 106).

67/7 some bokys: *Cf.*, *quidam libri in oriente*. The Arabic Gospel of the Saviour's Infancy refers to an angel in the form of a star which guided the Magi on their journey both outward and homeward (Hughes 1979: 20–1). The identification of this angel with the one which appeared to the shepherds in the gospel would have been an easy step; Remigius's seventh Homily (*PL* 131: 902) lists among interpretations of the Star that *alii dicunt fuisse* [sc. *stellam*] *angelum ut ipse qui apparuit pastoribus apparuerit etiam magis*. The identification of the angel with the Pillar of Fire (Exodus xiii.21 etc.) is attributed by our author to 'Jewish converts [to Christianity] in the East'; for the author's claims to have based his account on eastern sources see Introduction 8.

67/13: The English omits a sermon of Fulgentius (?468–?533) comparing the shepherds and the Kings to the two walls of faith (Ephesians ii); see Hm. 235/n10–n13.

68/11 *et ... eum:* The justification for such emendations of scriptural citations is presented in Introduction 10.5.

68/12: The English omits a passage describing contemporary oriental practice in making offerings to royalty (Hm. 236/9–16).

68/13–17: This interpretation of the gifts, for which the original names Fulgentius as source, is of great antiquity (see Hughes 1979: 28) and was widely cited, but the author also notes a more prosaic interpretation (from St Bernard) whereby gold is explained as an expedient to alleviate Mary's poverty, incense as an antidote to the odours of the manger, and myrrh as a vermifuge (Hm. 239/n20; only the first part, reproduced at 72/13–15, survived in the translator's exemplar). At 91/16–92/1 we find a further explanation of the gifts as symbols of virginity, and at Hm. 276/n22 (omitted in the present work, *cf.*, 116/11n) an explanation of the efficacy of the symbolism of the gifts in combatting heresy.

69/5 sumwhat flesshy: *Cf.*, *carnosa et aliquantulum fusca* (*cf.*, 102/11–13) Freeman suggests the image of a swarthy Madonna with her plump baby derives from Italian paintings (1955: 64). Her traditional blue robe appears in the English as a 'mantel of plunket', evidently reflecting the corruption *blanco vel albo* (for *blaueo*) in the translator's Latin.

69/17–18 an Ethiope and blak: This may be the first explicit statement in Western literature that one of the Kings was black; as Kaplan 1985: 63 notes, the wording *de quo nullum dubium sit* (vr. *de quo nulli dubium*) implies that the author was quite convinced on this point, though he expected that it might be somewhat novel to his readers.

69/18–19 *Coram ... lingent:* Psalms lxxii.9; *venient ... tuorum* — Isaiah lx.14.

69/20–70/1 as in respecte ... mene: The Latin says they were quite small (*multum pusilli*) for men of their time. It was a common notion that people had decreased in stature since earlier ages (*cf.*, 102/11 'aftir the stature': *secundum staturam tunc temporis hominum*), but why were the Kings relatively small? Perhaps the author's comment is based on his impression of the relics in Cologne, or on seeing an icon in which they were depicted on a smaller scale. At any rate the strongly visual quality of the description of the nativity is noteworthy.

70/8 more in quantite: 'greater in size' (*maiora*).

70/8–14: The account of the sound of the sunrise is paralleled in *BC* 12, though the editors are unable to trace the source of the legend.

70/15: The context suggests that 'Ynde' (*ad partes regni Indie*) is an error for 'Judea', a common confusion in the Latin witnesses (the reverse confusion occurs at 71/1 'Ynde', where T and G both transmit *Iudea*, but the translator or his exemplar guessed the true reading).

71/1–4: The story of the Queen of Sheba's visit to King Solomon (1 Kings x, 2 Chronicles ix) was early interpreted as a prefiguration of the visit of the gentile Magi to Christ (see Kaplan 1985: 9 ff., 37 ff.). The story of the removal of the sacred vessels to Babylon (strictly speaking solely the work of the Chaldeans under Nebuchadnezzar, not the Persians) is told in 2 Chronicles xxxvi.18 and 2 Kings xxv.13–17.

71/8–9 þe wallis of þe cave: In the original the 'wallis' (*parietes*) are the ruined walls of the inn that stood in the foreground of the cave (see 49/2 ff.n).

72/4 ff.: The source of the story of the golden apple is unknown. However in a Latin *Iter ad Paradisum*, a popular account of Alexander's journey to the earthly paradise deriving from pre-A.D. 500 Jewish sources, Alexander was given a stone that would outweigh any amount of gold put in the balance; at the same time if but a little dust were scattered upon it the lightest feather would outweigh it (Cary 1956: 18–21). This allusion to the King's ambition and cupidity on the one hand and his mortality on the other gives the stone a significance similar in general terms to that of the apple in our work. The adaptation of the motif to Christian exegesis would have been a separate development (perhaps a contribution of the Jewish converts cited as sources by the author; see 67/7n).

72/12–13 so ... the world: The grammar is faulty but so is the Latin, and what exact significance the author attached to the apple is unrecoverable. After this sentence the translation omits a discussion of the golden apple as an attribute of royalty and, after the next sentence, of the burning of incense as an act betokening obedience and submission (Hm. 239/n18, 239/n20–240/n8).

73/3: The translation omits the ensuing interpretation of the destruction of the golden apple (Hm. 240/12–n33).

73/11 merveillously mekely: The Latin suggests that the first adverb is to be taken with 'ledyng', the second with 'declarid and expownyd'.

74/1 Duk Olofernes: In the apocryphal book of Judith, Nebuchadnezzar, 'king of the Assyrians', sends the 'chief captain of his army' Holofernes on a punitive expedition against 'all the west country' (at line 2 'Ynde' is a mistake for 'Judea'; *cf.*, 70/15n).

74/4–5 by the hering of her passage: The original sense is 'because of old legends' ('went' meaning 'imagined').

74/9 as kynges worshipfully were receyvid: The Latin originally said 'they behaved with kindness and beneficence, as befitted kings'.

74/10–11 of the Iewys was neuere seth foryeten: *Cf.*, *a Iudeis ... postmodum nunquam potuit aboleri* 'could never after be erased by the Jews'. The reference to the countries and provinces of the Jews is not in the original Latin.

75/1 ff.: The story of the assistance offered the Kings by the *Tharsenses* (people of Tharshish, or Tarsus), only hinted at in the translation, and Herod's consequent vengeance is found in the fifth century commentator Arnobius the Younger (Freeman 1955: 66b) as well as in Comestor 1526: 187b and Nicholas of Lyra (Muir 1995: 229); its ultimate basis is Psalms xlvii.8(xlviii.7) *in spiritu vehementi conteres naves Tharsis*. In *HTR* Herod accuses the *Tharsenses* of allowing the Kings to escape across the (unidentified) river Siler.

75/3 herof: I.e., of the Kings.

75/13: The translation omits an account of the origin of the term *magi*, which the author is at pains to dissociate from any connection with the working of magic (*cf.*, 155/5–7n).

75/14–76/2: The sentence lacks a main verb (*cf.*, 76/17–77/3 'and of ... for hem').

76/2–4 For if ... aduersite: The sense originally intended seems to be that if any (human) artifice (*ars*) had been available to them previously, it would not have been lacking on their return journey.

76/4–5 þat byfor his natyuite in Ynde was vnknowyn: The translation is plausible, but the original sense is that knowledge of God had hitherto been confined to the land of the Jews (another case of confusion between *India* and *Iudea*).

77/14 þan eny othir: *omnibus hominibus*, more plausibly 'towards everyone'.

78/5 counceilid: *celabant* 'concealed', though the scribe may have taken the word as 'counselled' (see the spellings in *MED* svv. 'concelen' *v.*, 'counseilen' *v.*).

79/3 seruauntis: *gentiles*, an unexpected translation; however, Latham lists 'people, followers' as a sense of *gens, gentes*.

79/9 aunte: *Cf.*, *annicula*. If this is an exact translation it is an antedating of OED s.v. aunt 2. 'old woman', 'gossip'; but possibly the translator's exemplar read *amit(ul)a*. For the prophecies of Simeon and Anna, see Luke ii.25–38; for the flight to Egypt, Matthew ii.13–15.

80/1 ff.: The translation rearranges the original matter at various points (for the significance of which see Introduction 10.3).

81/4 more than xij sithe the toun of Parys: *maior quam septem ville parisienses*. The confusion between twelve and seven is an easy slip in Roman numerals and could have arisen either in the Latin or the English.

81/5–6 noght a stonys cast thens: *Cf.*, *qui non est ad iactum lapidis magnus* 'not as much as a stone's throw large'.

81/16 clense (L close): Either reading fits the context, but if 'close' corresponds to *irrigat* it is a very rough equivalent (?*cf.*, *MED* s.v. closen *v.* 4a.(b) 'put a wall or ditch around'), whereas 'clense', reinforced by 'pyke' (*MED* s.v. piken *v.*(1) 3.(b) 'to cleanse from dirt and impurities by picking'), corresponds exactly to *mundat*. Another possibility is that both variants are corruptions of 'arose' (*OED* s.v. arrouse *v.* 'bedew, sprinkle, moisten, water', first in Caxton), but the translation at 150/6 uses 'wette' for *irrigauerunt*. See further at Introduction 10.2.

82/2 the kyttyngis-of and the twyggis: *Cf.*, *scissure*, which sound more like incisions in the body of the vine, from which the balm distills through the cotton into the containers.

82/17 brasyll: 'brazil' (a reddish dye). This is an inspired guess on the translator's part, as the original has *braxina* (?= *brasina* 'malt'), whereas the corresponding passage in Ludolf describes the balm as being of 'a reddish colour, with some mixture of black' (69).

84/5–13 And þis ... dyed: On the significance of this duplicated matter (and that at 85/16–27 and 88/5–6) see Introduction 10.3. The present passage is evidently not copied directly from 95/16 ff. since it includes the detail 'afor all þe peple' (*coram omni populo*) not found at 95/17–19.

84/14 ff.: The origins and development of the legend of the thirty golden pennies are documented in Hill 1905 (see also Ludolf 111/n1). In classical mythology Ninus was the eponymous founder of Nineveh. For Joseph and the Ishmaelites see Genesis xxxvii; the buying of corn in Egypt, Genesis xlii ff.; the embalming of Iacob, Genesis l.2.

86/11–12 wiþ the encens and mirra: The translator omitted to mention at line 3 that these gifts were bound together with the thirty pence.

86/18 that they be indifferent of his passion and deþe: The Latin says that they were all alike (*indifferenter*) responsible. See Mark xv.36, John xix.29 for the vinegar offered to Christ; John xix.39–40 for Nicodemus and the myrrh; Matthew xxvii.3–5 for Judas and the thirty pieces of silver; Matthew xxvii.6–10 for the field for the burial of strangers; Matthew xxviii.11–15 for the money given to the keepers of the sepulchre.

87/15–16: The suppression of the Jewish revolt of 66 A.D. was entrusted by Nero to Vespasian; on the latter's accession in 69 A.D. his eldest son Titus (ruled 79–81) brought the war to an end with the destruction of Jerusalem in 70 A.D. after a four-year siege.

88/4: The translation here omits a passage on feudal customs in the East (Hm. 251/n16).

88/8–9 ***Defuncto ... eius &c:*** Matthew ii.19 ff.

89/1–2 toke on hym aȝens his will þe office of prechyng: This detail derives from the opening of the apocryphal *Acts of Thomas* (James 1924: 365), an account of how Thomas brought the gospel to India and was martyred there. According to another tradition mentioned by Eusebius (*c.* 260–340) and others, St Thomas evangelised the Parthians (*ODCC* s.v. Thomas, St., Apostle; Letts 1946: 162/n3).

89/3: The faulty sentence structure and the discontinuity in the narrative point to a lacuna. The first part of the sentence is explaining Thomas's suitability for the office of apostle of the lands of the Three Kings (the original includes a citation from Gregory and a note of the activities of other apostles; see Hm. 252/n8 ff.), whereas the second part (Hm. 252/n17 ff.) is discussing some of the achievements of his ministry. This textual lacuna, however, is followed at line 7 by a physical lacuna, in which further particulars of Thomas's ministry would have been recounted, including his meeting with the Kings and their baptism (Hm. 253/4–255/n21).

89/9 her: The Latin suggests that this refers to the worshippers, not the Kings.

89/11 Sculla: The original spelling in the Latin is Seuwa. Medieval travel accounts, notably Marco Polo, refer to a city of similar name as the burial place of the Magi (see MV 81–90), and in *BC* 9–10 Prester John is described as living in a city *Sowa*.

90/11 by ... merveilles (MS merveillous) worchyng: *varia mirabilia operatus*. The manuscript reading is certainly possible, but the stylistic parallel 89/4–5 'by diuers langours ... helyng ... and meny othir miracles worchyng' favours the emendation; *cf.*, 129/5–7 'in etyng drynkyng ... and al þing doyng'. Another possibility is 'merveille-worchyng', the manuscript reading having arisen through misinterpretation of the first part of the compound as an adjective (OED s.v. marvel *a.*) and its replacement by a synonymous form.

90/14 and wondur rogh: The original Latin states that their faces are not hairy. For the dog-faced men in whose land St Thomas was martyred compare *BC* 12. Originally *cynocephalus* referred to an ape with a dog-like head found in Africa, but Isidore used the term to refer to a kind of wild man (*Orig.* 11.3.15, 12.2.32), whence the medieval legend of the race of dog-faced men (see further Christern 1963: 136, who suggests the text in *HTR* implies that this physical characteristic was a punishment for the martyrdom of the saint, and Letts 1946: 167/n1).

91/4 so: *adhuc*, i.e., in their retirement. As the text stands 'all her londis and kyngdomes' is presumably the subject of 'obeying and ... lovyng', but the Latin suggests these words were originally the object of 'gouernyd', some matter (to the effect 'all their subjects') having dropped out before 'noght althing'.

91/13 all þat landis: Parallels for 'þat' 'those' are very rare — *LALME* 4 s.v. THOSE NOR *yat* Yks — but the form was ostensibly a rare alternative for the scribe (108/15–16 'in þat cuntres', 116/13–14 'of þat londes & provinces'); *cf.*, 67/8 'tho aungel' (*sg.* or *pl.*?), but also Introduction, p. 16, n6.

92/11 as to her heed: *vt priori*, presumably taken as 'as to her prior, i.e., superior', though perhaps a more likely interpretation is 'as (they had) to the previous incumbent'.

93/13 ff.: There survive numerous copies of a letter (ed. Zarncke 1878) purporting to be addressed by Prester John to the rulers and prelates of Europe; these in turn made repeated attempts to establish communications with this elusive ruler.

94/4, 94/6 shal be clept, callid: *Cf.*, *deberet vocari*, *nominari* 'was to be called', this passage properly picking up the discussion at lines 92/18 ff., to which 93/12–94/3 'which ... enpeyntid' constitutes a parenthesis.

94/5 moost chosyn and lovid: I.e., *a domino*, the evangelist being identified with 'the disciple whom Jesus loved' (John xiii.23 ff., xxi.20 ff.). The description of him as 'priest' is unparalleled in Middle English outside the present context; see *MED* s.v. prest *n.*(3) 4.(c).

94/7–8 afor whom ... not a more: *Cf.*, Luke vii.28.

95/3 hath made: *fecerunt*. The tense is in fact historic, the fall of Acre ('Acon') in 1291 marking the end of crusader rule in Palestine.

95/4–5 meny of þe princes of hem ... londis: The Latin suggests rather that many other princes have wedded wives of this family. The seat of the papacy ('the courte of Rome': *curia romana*) was at Avignon from 1309–77. The composition of *HTR* presumably falls within this period, which makes the date 1351 one of the rare pieces of internal evidence in support of the traditional authorship; John of Hildesheim was resident at Avignon c1350–2 and may possibly have collected material for his account of the Three Kings from the princes of Vaus at that time (see Introduction 8).

95/11 ff.: The information on the dates of the Kings' deaths and their ages is found in the manuscript *Florarium Sanctorum*; *cf.*, *Acta SS Boll.* I, 8, 323, 664 (Harris 1954: civ). According to this tradition the Kings differed in age by only a few years, whereas the more familiar tradition portrays one as old, one middle aged, and one young. The miracle recounted at 96/9–13 appears in other accounts of the legend; see Harris 1959: 25, 27.

96/17 ouere þo Kynges: The Latin suggests something to the effect 'After the death of the Kings God' originally stood in place of these words, the rest of the sentence corresponding to the Latin once 'hym' is altered to 'hem'. There is no sentence break before 'ouere þo Kynges' in the manuscript, but '... þe same citee' corresponds to the end of the previous sentence in the Latin.

98/3 þe childrin of blessid men: This odd phrase results from a literal translation of the corrupt *beatorum nati*; the original Latin has 'the people born in the kingdoms of the three blessed Kings'.

98/11 ff.: Constantine the Great after his victory at the Milvian Bridge in 312 extended toleration and favour to the Christian faith; a tradition that he was baptised at the Lateran and cleansed from physical leprosy by Pope Sylvester goes back to the fifth century. For the tradition that his mother Helena was a Jew before her conversion see Harris 1954: cxvi. St Ambrose (*c.* 340–97) was the first to connect the 'invention' (i.e., finding) of the Cross with St Helena, a legend recounted in the apocryphal *De Invencione Crucis Dominicae* (*ODCC* s.v. Invention of the Cross). The date 1234 is of course quite fanciful (the original Latin reads 234).

99/12–13 a faire chirche ... places forseid: The original Church of the Holy Sepulchre was built *c.* 335 and destroyed by the Persians in 614. The Constantine basilica covered the Holy Sepulchre and left the rock of Calvary outside, but the Crusader church with which the author's sources would have been familiar embraced under one roof the Sepulchre and Calvary (*ODCC* s.v. Holy Sepulchre).

101/3 ff.: The historical achievements of Charlemagne attracted legendary accretions (see Cobby 1988: 12–14), and the exploits here ascribed to the king are largely fictitious. 'Zacharie the patriarke' is perhaps a conflation of two figures, a patriarch Zachary of Jerusalem, captured by the Persians in 614 and released in 628, and St Zacharias the pope, who had cordial relations with the Frankish kingdom, though at a period anterior to Charles's accession — *ODCC* s.v. Zacharias, St.; Smith and Wade 1877 s.v. Zacharias(4). The phrase at line 8 'by askyng and graunting of Eleyne' is not in the Latin; the translator evidently imagined that Charles obtained the relics from Helena herself, a chronological impossibility.

103/1 sclattyd: *Cf.*, *testudinata* 'vaulted'.

103/1–2 out of þis cherche: The Latin says the cave is reached from inside the church, and contains another altar.

103/3–4 And a litil fro þe autur in a walle (MS vale) is þe crecche (MS cherche): Perhaps the scribe first mistook 'crecche' for 'cherche', as elsewhere, and then substituted the seemingly more appropriate 'vale' for 'wall' (there are parallels for 'vale' as a spelling for 'wall' — *OED* s.v. wall *sb.*1 — but it was evidently not the scribe's form, *cf.*, 71/9, 139/7 'wallis').

103/7–8 Seynt Poule and Eustas nobles and lordis of Rome: St Paula (347–404), a Roman lady of noble birth, and her daughter Julia Eustochium (370–*c.* 419) followed St Jerome in 385 to Palestine in pursuit of a life of devotion, Paula settling in Bethlehem from 386 (*ODCC* s.vv. Paula, St.; Eustochium, St. Julia). However it is not clear whether the translator (or the scribe) appreciated that these were female names (a confusion already apparent in the Latin tradition, *cf.*, vrs. *nobiles urbis romane ... sepulti* G, *qui* T).

104/10 dyvidid and odiouse: Since *odiose divisi* is correctly translated as 'odyously devidid' at 97/13, 98/12 etc., I conjecture that the exemplar here read *odiosi* (*et*) *divisi*.

104/17 þe double cherche: I.e., the church described at 100/1 ff.

105/9 a table ... Eleyne: The Latin adds that it was composed by Jerome.

106/3 ff.: Nazareth was the village which was home to Mary and Joseph and where Christ lived till the beginning of his ministry. Its more important sanctuaries include the

Church of the Annunciation, believed to be built over the house of Mary, the Church of the Nutrition (or St Joseph's), and St Mary's well (*ODCC* s.v. Nazareth). For the Annunciation see Luke i.26–38; the apocryphal *Book of James* tells how the angel first greeted Mary when she went to draw water (xi.1, James 1924: 43). For the information in this passage compare Ludolf 124–6.

106/10–11 by which þe aungel stode and knelid: *Cf.*, *circa quam angelus stetit et reclinauit*. The translator has made the best of the curious wording of his exemplar; the Latin originally said 'against' (not 'around') 'which the angel stood and lent'.

107/3 grett wiþ: This is ostensibly 'greeted by' (*OED* s.v. with *prep.* 40), *cf.*, 106/10, 107/6, but as 'grett' is a variant spelling of 'great' (*MED* s.v. gret *adj.* & *adv.* & *n.*) the suggestion of 'pregnant by the angel' is perhaps also present (*OED* s.v. with *prep.* 37.d); for the notion (recorded in the *Book of James*) that Mary conceived at the words of the angel see Warner 1990: 37. The same formulation appears in the opening line of *The Devils' Parliament*: 'Whan Marye was gret with Gabryel'; for discussion see C. W. Marx, ed., *The Devils' Parliament and The Harrowing of Hell and Destruction of Jerusalem*, Middle English Texts, 25 (1993), p. 95.

107/10, 107/13 seyd, bygunne (MS seyn, be bygunne): The context is past ('in þe tyme whan hit was Cristyn'). Line 10 *Ave Maria* is followed in the Latin by words to the effect 'and this chapel is called Ave Maria'; the loss could have arisen by eyeskip in either version, but if it was already present in the Latin, the wording of the translation is very clumsy.

107/12 of Nazareth: The Latin is ambiguous, but more probably means 'to Nazareth'.

107/15: After this sentence the original Latin includes a description of the degraded contemporary state of the church and chapel (Hm. 269/n21–19).

107/18 mons Thabor: Tabor is an isolated mountain in the middle of Galilee traditionally identified as the site of the Transfiguration (the gospels — Matthew xvii.1–13, Mark ix.2–13, Luke ix.28–36 — speak only of 'an high mountain'); see *ODCC* s.v. Transfiguration; Young 1939 s.v. Tabor.

108/5–6 on (MS of) þe day of: The preposition 'of' normally introduces phrases referring to a period, not a point of time — *MED* s.v. of *prep.* 5. The date indicated is 6 August. Pope Sixtus (Xistus) II together with his deacons Felicissimus and Agapitus suffered martyrdom in 258 under the second edict of the Emperor Valerian; Sixtus was one of the most highly venerated of early martyrs (*ODCC* s.v. Sixtus II, St.; Christern 1963: 141).

108/15 wurshipyn: This apparently means 'deck out', 'adorn', i.e., their church (*multum ornant ecclesias suas*).

108/18 a wey: *via*, which could also mean 'the way', i.e., 'the distance'.

109/6 Blansagarda: 'Blanche Garde'. The matter concerning the 'castell', along with previous details about Mt Tabor, the monastery, and the festival of the Transfiguration is paralleled in Ludolf; however, according to the editor Ludolf's information about Blanche Garde is faulty, the fortress being located on Tell-es-Safieh, not far from Ascalon (Ludolf 126/n2). The 'nobles of Blanchegarde' appear again, together with the equally mysterious 'Lord of Vaus', in Ludolf's catalogue of the erstwhile noble inhabitants of the city of Acre, but no further details are supplied there (51–2).

111/8 potentis: As it stands this is either the plural noun (not elsewhere attested before Shakespeare — *OED* s.v. potent *a.*[1] and *sb.*[2] 3.B.2) or the corresponding adjective (only one citation in *MED* s.v. potent *adj.*, a1500(?c1425) *Spec. Sacer.*) with plural ending; but it may be a mistake for the commonly attested 'potestatis' (*MED* s.v. potestat(e *n.* 1.(a) 'A ruler, lord; an individual possessing power or authority, a superior') or even a garbled Latin gloss (e.g. *potentes*). In historical terms St Helena's dealings with the Nestorians are an anachronism, since Nestorian Christianity did not emerge as a distinct sect until the fifth century. The tradition that the relics were formerly in Constantinople appears in *BC* 18, and the exchange of St Thomas's relics for those of the third King in *BC* 14.

112/10 cumpase: If synonymous with *turne*, this is an unrecorded nuance — *cf.*, *MED* s.v. compassen *v.* 5.(b) 'to go or travel around in (an area)'. **Verbygene:** The Latin adjective *verbigenus* means 'word-begotten'; many of the Greek fathers following the terminology of the OT and St Paul use 'wisdom' (*sophia*) as a synonym for the Incarnate Word or Logos (*ODCC* s.v. Wisdom).

112/18 þe verrey croune of God: The crown of thorns, first mentioned as a relic in the fifth century, was acquired from Emperor Baldwin II in 1239 by Louis IX, who built Sainte-Chapelle in Paris to house it and other relics (*ODCC* svv. Louis IX, St.; Crown of Thorns).

113/3 payment: The Latin suggests some text to the effect 'that crown; and that crown' has dropped out here.

113/7–8 of which ... here: See Introduction 10.4 for the significance of this reference to Mandeville.

113/14 wiþ: Some text has clearly been lost here; the sense of the Latin is that God would deliver them through the merits of the Kings.

114/1 þe persecucion of þe swerd: In fact though Emperor Julian (332–63) used a wide variety of means to promote his policy of degrading Christianity and promoting paganism, he stopped short of open persecution (*ODCC* s.v. Julian the Apostate).

114/4 ff.: The beginning of the Great Schism cannot be exactly dated, but in 451, against the objections of the Pope, patriarchial powers were formally conferred on the bishop of Constantinople and a gradual estrangement ensued between the Catholic West and Orthodox East; the final breach is usually assigned to 1054 (*ODCC* s.vv. Constantinople; The Great Schism).

114/9 ff.: The author evidently faced conflicting traditions in his sources. Of all the Greek emperors it was perhaps Maurice or Mauritius (582–603) and Manuel (1143–80) whose names would have been most likely to survive in the local traditions of northern Italy, Maurice for his energetic measures to restore Byzantine authority there in the face of the Lombard advance, and Manuel for his Westernised habits and his far reaching diplomatic manoeuvres, including his support of the Lombard cities in their struggle against the Emperor Frederick (Manuel was also the addressee of the 'letter' from Prester John; see 93/13 ff.n, Zarncke 1878: 909); however the appearance of either in connection with St Eustorgius (bishop of Milan 315–31) is quite anachronistic.

The documentary sources for the prior translations of the Kings are examined in Hm. xvii–xxi, where they are deemed no older than the last translation, i.e., they arose after the (historical) discovery of the bodies in Milan (Mediolane) and their subsequent translation to Cologne by Rainald of Dassel, Chancellor and later Archbishop of Cologne; *cf.*, Harris 1954: xvi–xvii and 1959: 28.

Eustorgius ('Eustorche') was a predecessor of St Ambrose but the latter, though he mentions Eustorgius, knows nothing of the translation of the Three Kings. The story connecting Eustorgius with the relics probably arose from the discovery of the bodies in his church, where he lay buried (Hm. xx). The church of St Eustorgius belonged to the Dominicans ('Frere Prechours') from 1220, in other words subsequently to the translation of the relics to Cologne (Hm. xxi).

114/15–16 a Greke of berþ (MS bery): *nacione Grecum* — 'of berþ', rather than 'by berþ', is the normal form in ME (*MED* s.v. birth(e *n.* 4a; *OED* s.v. birth *sb.*1 7). Another possible emendation is 'born'.

114/17–115/3 And turnyng ayen to þe kyng ... thre Kynges: There is no mention in the original Latin of a king; the translation reflects an anomalous passage in the exemplar.

115/9 M[l]Cliiij: *Cf.*, 1164 in the Latin; in fact the destruction of Milan took place two years earlier. The German Emperor Frederick I 'Barbarossa' (*c.* 1123–90) was occupied with Italian affairs during much of his reign and led expeditions against the cities of Lombardy in 1154, 1158, and 1162. In the third campaign he succeeded in capturing and destroying Milan after a long siege.

In June 1164, as a reward for the services which he and the people of Cologne had rendered on the Emperor's campaign, Rainald of Dassel obtained from Frederick the bodies of the Three Kings, together with other relics, discovered in 1158 in the church of St Eustorgius outside Milan and subsequently hidden within the town. Travelling via Burgundy to avoid his enemies, he arrived in Cologne with the relics on July 23, the present anniversary of the translation. Rainald instituted a festival in honour of the Kings on the Epiphany, and his successor, Philipp of Heinsberg, founded the shrine in which the bodies are still deposited. It was to the translation of the relics, and thus ultimately to Rainald of Dassel (significantly perhaps, a former provost of Hildesheim, as well as a figure of some importance in the history of letters) that the beginnings of the growth of Cologne as a centre of pilgrimage can be attributed.

This much of the story is historical, but many of the details seem to have been supplied by our author. The tradition that Rainald got the bodies clandestinely from a noble Milanese before asking the Emperour for them cannot be traced earlier than the thirteenth century (Hm. xvii–xix).

115/15, 115/16 Asso(ne): Azzo della Torre (Latin *de Turri*, in the exemplar corrupted to *decurij*); the family was one of the most powerful in Milan in the thirteenth century. According to another tradition it was the sister of a nobleman of the town, Gualvagno Visconte, Count of Angleria, who betrayed the bodies to Rainald in order to save her brother (Hm. xix).

116/1–6 kyng ... emperour ... kyng ... kyngis ... kyng: The confusion may go back to the anomalous passage **114/17–115/3** in which a king as well as an emperor is referred to.

116/11: The translation here omits a passage (Hm. 276/n22) from the theologian Rabanus Maurus (776 or 784–856) on the effect the symbolism of the gifts had in combatting heresy once the relics of the Kings were brought to Milan (*cf.*, 150/15–151/3).

116/12 þe reliqes of: This is not in the Latin here or at line 19.

117/12 Indes: *Indi*, but the context proves the latter to be a mistake for *Latini*.

117/16 syng (MS seyn) her gospell: The scribe missed the point, that they chant (*cantant*) the gospel reading.

117/17 Nubianes: This is probably the people of northern Ethiopia (Abyssinia), introduced to Christianity in the fourth century (see *ERE* s.v. Abyssinia; *ODCC* s.v. Ethiopian or Abyssinian church).

118/2 þe childis birthe: This curious phrase springs from a corruption in the translator's exemplar; the original sense is that the Nubians follow the example of their King Melchior in the faith.

118/11 Soldynes: This is possibly the Soldains (Soldins, Soldinis, Soldis) mentioned by Hayton of Armenia (*Histoire des croisades, Docum. Armeniens*, II, 124, quoted in Harris 1955: cxix), though this identification is problematic (see MV 209).

118/17 as Baltazar her kyng which: The original sense, however, is 'as they [the Nubyans] do, for as B. (offered incense ... , so the faith in them ...)'; the translator was evidently rationalising losses in the Latin (ostensibly of *sicut*, as in G, as well as *sed* after *seruauerunt*).

119/6–120/3: After the deposition of bishop Nestorius ('Nestoryne') at the Council of Ephesus in 431, those Eastern bishops who refused to accept the subsequent decisions on doctrinal matters evolved a separate Nestorian church centred outside the Roman Empire in Persia, from where it spread as far as Ceylon, Turkestan, and China (see *ODCC* s.v. Nestorianism; *ERE* s.v. Syrian Christians 8. East Syrians or Nestorians). In the present account the Nestorians are presented as the perverse and heretical inhabitants of the land of the black King Jaspar, lowest in the descending triad of the contemporary inhabitants of the lands of the Three Kings, who met a deserved fate at 142/1 ff.

120/4 ff.: The Thomas or Malabar Christians of southern India are perhaps meant; Christianity is acknowledged to have existed in India since the fourth century, whatever the truth of the story of its introduction by St Thomas (see *ERE* s.v. India).

120/6 as we to our pope emperour or our kyng: The original Latin is fuller — 'as we do the pope, and they obey Prester John as we do our emperour or king'. Assuming the loss occurred by eyeskip in the Latin (as it does in G), 'pope' must be a secondary addition in the English based on the description of the patriarch's role at 92/15–17.

120/12 þe Holy Goost descendid ynto þe disciples: sc. *in igne* (Acts ii.1–4).

121/1 ff. Also her prestis ...: The English reads as if still referring to the Christians in Inde, but in the original the discussion has moved on to the Greeks. The easiest explanation is to assume a one-word peculiar error in the Latin (*eorum* for the original *Grecorum*).

121/1–3 and they byleue ... Fadir alone: This is a reference to the controversy of the Double Procession, one of the obstacles to reunion between Eastern and Western churches (see *ODCC* s.vv. Double Procession of the Holy Ghost; Filioque).

121/13 þat londe: The Latin adds 'around Jerusalem', and throughout the passage originally read 'Iudea' (Judea) in place of 'Ynde' (India). Several different bodies of Christians — Jacobite, Maronite, Nestorian, Malabarese, and others — are habitually referred to as Syrians; here the discussion of their name implies that they were to be found living in the area around Jerusalem, whereas the reference to St Barbara could indicate a connection with Egypt, since her relics were preserved there.

121/18 in Babyloigne wher þe soudons comunly lyen: The Latin originally read 'whose body [St Barbara's] lies at rest in the sultan's (city of) Babylon'. After the reference to the celebrations of St Barbara's eve (4 December), the Latin adds a sentence telling how at this season friends send each other seeds to plant in their gardens.

122/5 Armenes: Though the earliest nation to embrace Christianity officially, the Armenians repudiated the Council of Chalcedon (451), in consequence of which the Armenian church has since been reputed Monophysite (for this term see 125/7n). However by the time the present work was composed the Armenians of Lesser Armenia were united with Rome and many Western practices had been adopted from the Crusaders (*ODCC* s.v. Armenia, Christianity in).

122/10 be made and halowid Latynes: This was originally, 'are consecrated by bishops (who are) Latins'.

122/11–12 cappis on her hede: The reference is perhaps to distinctive caps that the Magi are sometimes depicted as wearing.

122/14 Georgyens: The origins of Christianity in Georgia extend back to the fourth century; however while the neighbouring Church of Armenia adopted Monophysitism Georgia remained Chalcedonian. There still exists a small independent church of Orthodox communion called the Church of Sinai which is ruled by the Archbishop of Mount Sinai, the abbot of the monastery on that mountain; the monastery, which goes back to 527, claims to have been built on the site where St Catherine's body was miraculously transported after her martyrdom, but this tradition was unknown to early pilgrims (*ODCC* svv. Georgia, Church of; Sinai; Sinai, Church of; Catherine, St., of Alexandria).

123/5 Seynt Anthone ... Seynt Makary: St Antony of Egypt was an ascete who came out of the desert in *c.* 305 to organise a loosely bound community of hermits. Under his influence St Macarius founded a colony of monks in the desert of Scetis which became a centre of Egyptian monasticism (*ODCC* s.vv. Antony, St., of Egypt; Macarius, St.).

123/6–7 and þei ... about hem: The original Latin makes their good behaviour to the sultan's neighbours a condition of their exemption from tribute, but the translator's version is one possible way to take the corrupt text in the exemplar.

123/13 the hill: This is Mt Ararat in Armenia (see *BC* 17/n2).

123/18 Henissem: Spelt 'Henissen' in the original, and 'Heymissen' in *BC*, where the editors suggest that the name derives from the Georgian province of Hamsen and cite a parallel account in Hayton; the legend may derive ultimately from accounts of the land of perpetual darkness mentioned by Marco Polo (*BC* 17/n3).

124/9 Eracle: The emperor Heraclius (ruled 610/11–41), remembered for his energetic defence of the Byzantine empire against its foes and in particular for his restoration of the Cross, removed by the Persians from Jerusalem in 614, to the Church of the Holy Sepulchre in 629.

125/7 Iacobytes: The Jacobites were Syrian Monophysites who rejected the teaching of the Council of Chalcedon (451) on the person of Christ (monophysitism being the doctrine that in the person of the incarnate Christ there was but a single, and that a divine, nature, as against the orthodox teaching of a double nature, divine and human, after the incarnation; *cf.*, 'they byleve no trinyte but vnyte'). They took their name from their founder, the Syrian monk Jacob Baradaeus (*c.* 500–78), and claimed that their liturgy was given to them by the Apostle James (see *ODCC* s.v. Jacobites).

125/14 Maronytes: The Maronites are a Christian community of Syrian origin who trace their existence back to St Maro, a friend of St Chrysostom (d. 407) — see *ODCC* s.v Maronites; *Encyclopedia of the early Church* 1992 s.vv. Maro, Maronites.

126/3 Copti: The Coptic, i.e., Egyptian, church, traditionally said to have been founded by St Mark, became formally Monophysite after the Council of Chalcedon and increasingly isolated from the rest of Christendom, Upper Egypt becoming a centre of monasticism (*ODCC* s.v. Coptic Church). The *Gospel of Nicodemus* is an apocryphal gospel, the Latin version of which (*Euangelium Nicodemi*) dates from the fifth century and the Coptic version from 361–3; the *book of talis* is named in the Latin as the 'Secrets of St Peter', referring perhaps to the *Apocalypsis Petri* or the apocryphal *Acts of St Peter* (late second century) or the *Pistis Sophia* (*ODCC* s.vv. Apocalyptic literature; Apocryphal New Testament. See also the references at *BC* 15/n2,3).

126/8 Ismini: This is in the Latin also spelt *Isini*. This sect has not been convincingly identified, but modern consensus (see Kaplan 1985: 60, 65) favours the notion that the name was once used as a form of 'Abyssinian' (see 117/17n), though variously applied. Symon Simeon, an Irish Minorite friar who visited Egypt in 1322, reported seeing there 'Danubian' captives whose faces bore long scars produced by burning, an act which they described as a form of baptism (Esposito 1960: 92, *cf.*, 18/n3); Yule 1915 1: 115/n2 and Letts 1946: 159 report similar practices among eastern Christians.

126/14 þer shal not leve a stone: The translation omits the ensuing story of the local resentment occasioned by the boast of these Christians.

126/17 Maromynes: *Maromini* (*Maronini*), an unidentified sect, the note on them in *HTR* corresponding to a sentence from *BC* combined with a reference in Ludolf (*BC* 16, 9/n6).

127/4 Nicholaite: The reference is to the Nicolaites or Nicolaitans, a sect of somewhat shadowy existence mentioned in Revelations ii.6 and ii.14 ff.; it has been argued that they had no real existence as a sect at all, the name being merely a term of abuse (*ODCC* s.v. Nicolaites; *ERE* s.v. Nicolaitans). The brief notice at *BC* 16 gives *Antiochien* as an alternative name of the sect. There may be some confusion between them and the Nestorians — see Hm. 303/n34–n40.

127/6 pray: *prorogaret,* a plausible conjecture on the part of the translator for an essentially meaningless corruption; in the original Latin the request is specifically sexual.

127/11 Origene: Origen (*c.* 185–*c.* 254) was an Alexandrian critic and theologian of great influence, exemplary life, and prodigious literary output, the latter including commentaries on the Old and New Testament homilies, and a doctrinal treatise *De Principiis*. However Origen's audacious theology was compromised by his so called disciples and misinterpreted in the light of later controversies; his condemnation for heresy led to the loss of the greater part of his work in the original language.

The origin of the present notice is something of a mystery. There is a short passage of comparable matter on the Nicholaites at *BC* 16 but nothing on Origen in *BC* or Ludolf. The notion that the unacceptable portions of Origen's writings were the result of interpolation by heretics is found in the fourth century writer Rufinus in his defence of the *De Principiis*. Possibly our author (or his source) drew on his information concerning Origen in order to reconstruct the beliefs of the Nicholaites; the notion of the salvation of demons, for example, was one of the doctrines attributed to Origen (*ODCC* s.vv. Origen, Origenism; *ERE* s.v. Origen).

127/13 ... her errours: The Latin adds further details of the mischief caused by the interpolation of heretical views into Origen's writings.

128/2 ... such was his lyf: The Latin elaborates on Origen's saintly life and the authority of his writings.

128/7 Mandapoli: *Mandopoli* (*Mandopolos*). Judged from the description of their habits (itinerant lifestyle, a peculiar language, tinkering — to which *BC* adds deception and stealing) these Christians seem to be the people known to us as Gypsies. The Gypsies (Roma) are a distinct race who migrated slowly from India, reaching Persia by the eleventh century but being positively identified in Europe first in the fourteenth century, and then in Eastern Europe. This might explain why our author does not refer to them by the now familiar name, but leaves unexplained the origin of the name Mandopoli (see further *ERE* s.v. Gypsies).

128/10 slepe: *Cf.*, *in domibus dormiunt*, suggesting that the translation originally included some such words as 'yn eny hous' (*cf.*, line 15).

128/12–13 þei wurche ... with her hondis: The original *cribra et huiusmodi* is a clear reference to the trade of tinkering.

128/16 a name special: This was originally, 'a special language'.

130/1 they: I.e., 'all the above-mentioned heretics and scismatics', in contrast to 'al oþere Cristyn' (*aliis catholicis*).

130/5 Arriane: These reference is to Arian Christians. Arius was a third-century Alexandrian priest whose teachings on the nature of Christ were condemned at the Councils of Antioch (324) and Nicaea (325) but found widespread support (*ODCC* and *ERE* s.vv. Arianism, Arius).

131/16 dauncyng: *saltando*, but the original Latin has the more prosaic 'and exchanging greetings in this way'.

132/3 ff.: The connection between Epiphany and the riverside rituals is that originally the Feast of Epiphany was a celebration both of Christ's incarnation and baptism. With the coming into existence of Christmas in the fourth century, Epiphany in the West became associated instead with the manifestation of Christ to the Gentiles in the person of the Magi.

132/15 *secundum Iohannem:* The gospel cited is in fact closer to Matthew iii.13 or Mark i.9 than the account of Jesus's baptism in John i.

132/16–17 in HOC Iordane IN ISTO LOCO: The modifications of the canonical wording here and at 134/14–135/10 (signalled by editorial capitalisation) reflect the different local perspectives of the various sects on the gospel story.

133/8 Montoste: *Montost*, apparently a 'ghost' name deriving from a corruption in the author's source of the adjective *montoso*, referring to 'a hilly wilderness' (see Ludolf 114/n2).

134/1 cuntrees: presumably 'surrounding area', *cf.*, *MED* s.v. contre(e *n.* 4.(a) 'The area surrounding a walled city or other stronghold; countryside, environs', *c.* 1325(*c.* 1300) *Glo. Chron.A* 10518 'Hii smite out of hor castles ... & robbede þe contreies'.

134/4 þe tone is more þan þat oþir: The original Latin is quite different: 'one is called Jor and the other Dan' (the supposed etymology of the name Jordan).

134/10: In the lacuna the author continues his discussion of the natural history of the Jordan (the sunken cities, the Dead Sea apples, the serpents called 'tyri') and describes the rites performed by eastern Christians living too far away to be able to visit the Jordan on Epiphany. The English resumes in the course of a discussion of the wording of the gospel as it is read by different local Christians.

135/18 ff.: The passage on the Jews is corrupt even in the original Latin. The words *nam ex quo*, corresponding to 'And seth þat', introduce a hanging subordinate clause. The confusion about a 'sterre ... callid Messias' also arises from corruption in the Latin. But in the case of (136/2) 'sterre leder of Iewis soght þat kyng borne' (*stella duce Iudeorum regem natum quesierunt*) the translator's word-for-word technique has led him into a blunder, unless 'of Iewis' was intended to be taken not with 'leder' but with 'þat kyng'. Moreover rather than (136/10) 'in which meke and trewe peple now lyve dyvidid' the original is more plausibly translated 'where they [the Jews] now live humbly and scattered'. The contextually inappropriate words 'of Epiphany' at 136/5 do not appear in the Latin.

137/7 thogh þei be without feith: This statement cannot be taken at face value. Persia was Islamised after the fall of the Sassinid dynasty in 635, though the native religion, Zoroastrianism, survived sporadically. Christian communities existed in Persia from the third century and declared themselves autonomous in 404 (Christern 1963: 140).

137/10 that sterre: The Latin has 'the star of the sea'. After this sentence the translation omits a discussion of the problem of the curvature of the earth (Hm. 297/7–n25).

138/5 ff.: On the rise of the Mongols or Tartars (properly Tatars) see Power 1926. Genghis Khan seized Peking ('Cambaleth', 'Camball') in 1214, and Baghdad ('Baldach', 'Balauch') was sacked and the caliph put to death by starvation in 1258 (for which the date at line 6 is perhaps a slip; at line 14 the implausible 'at Rome' reflects the corruption of *fame* to *Rome* in the Latin). In spite of the threat they posed to Europe it became possible for the West to see the Mongols as potential allies against the Muslims (*cf.*, 144/13 ff.). Certain sections of the Mongol court were reported to be Christian, and Western diplomats and missionaries paid visits to the Great Khan ('Grete Cane'), notably John of Pian de Carpine in 1245–7 and William of Rubruck in 1251–4.

138/18–139/4 And Baldach ... Assuerus: The site of ancient Babylon ('Babiloyne') is in fact 50 miles south of Baghdad, and the Persian royal city of Susa ('Susas', biblical Shushan) was several hundred miles south of Tabriz ('Thauris'), the city in Northern Persia chosen as administrative capital by the Mongol Ilkhans. The palace of Ahasuerus ('Assuerus', probably to be identified with Xerxes I, ruled 485–65) in Shushan is the setting of the book of Esther.

139/4–5 a drye tree: For the Dry Tree and the prophecies connected with it see Letts 1953 1: 48–9 and n3, *BC* 60/n2.

139/9 swerde or sheld: *scutum vel clipeum*. Both Latin words are in fact synonyms for 'shield', but the translation here and 'helme or swerde' at lines 12–13 suggests that the translator was unclear about the meaning of either.

139/15 all a londe: *totam terram*, which could be rendered 'all that land', but the present phrase has a parallel in *MED* s.v. al *lim. adj. & n.* 2a.(c), *c.* 1390 *þe wyse mon* in 424: 'He ... may fulli conquerre Al a cuntre' [F *tut vn pays*].

139/16 of Tartarie (2): *Cf.*, *Carthagie*, i.e., *Cathagie* 'of Cathay'.

140/6–7 done away & defoulid: *abolita et oblita*, the second Latin participle evidently having been taken not as meaning 'forgotten' but as coming from the less obvious *oblinio* 'besmear, befoul'.

140/10 with her help: Who 'her' refers to is unclear; in any case the equivalent words do not appear in the original Latin.

140/12 ff.: John of Monte Corvino, the first papal legate to Peking, describes in a letter of 1305 how he bought 150 pagan boys between seven and eleven years of age, baptised them, taught them Greek and Latin, and trained a number of them as a choir, so that the Great Khan himself delighted to hear them chanting; he also translated the New Testament and the Psalter into the language and character most generally used among the Tartars (Yule 1915 3: 45–58). On Christian missionary activity in Persia in the late thirteenth and fourteenth centuries see Beazley 1906 3: 187–215. Despite promising beginnings this activity declined during the fourteenth century following the conversion of the Ilkhans of Persia to Islam in 1316, and the conquests of Tamerlane completed the process of exclusion (Power 1926: 124–53). Nevertheless our author, writing in the third quarter of the fourteenth century, presents an optimistic picture of the prospects of Christianity in the East — a combination, it would seem, of wishful thinking and reliance on out-of-date sources.

141/4 ff.: Owing to discrepancies in the dates it is not clear who is to be identified as this 'thrid emperour of Tartarie' who favoured Christianity (for one view see *BC* 60/n5). The personal statement of faith of one Mongol ruler, Mangu Khan, has been preserved by William of Rubruck: 'We Moal believe that there is only one God, by whom we live and by whom we die, and for whom we have an upright heart... . But as God gives us the different fingers of the hand, so he gives to men divers ways' (Power 1926: 129–30).

141/6–7 He made (MS stode) and yaf his dome: *Hic fecit et dedit edictum*. The manuscript reading seems impossible, but may have been suggested by expressions such as 'stod in' (or 'to') 'dom' — *MED* s.v. stonden *v.*(1) 7.(a); *fecit* suggests 'made' or 'did' as the original reading.

141/11, 141/13 hath do, now regnith: These are slips for historic past tenses.

142/5 byhetyng hem to conuerte hem ... : 'promising to convert ...', an imitation of the Latin accusative infinitive construction.

143/4 alþogh (MS al þought): *LALME* 4 s.v. 32 THOUGH records forms such as 'thoght', 'thought', 'thowt', but none of these with preceding 'al'.

143/9 in his slepe þus appering to hym: Despite the peculiar word order this phrase clearly refers to the Kings.

145/5 ... broght to noght: The translation omits further details on the Nestorians (Hm. 303/n34–304/n1).

145/6–13: The story of the miracle of the Eucharist of St Thomas occurs in other sources (see MV 151–6) and other versions (e.g. that in Mandeville — Letts 1953: 327). It derives ultimately from a text *De adventu patriarchae Indorum ad Urbem sub Calixto papa secundo*, an account of his country and the church of St Thomas by a Patriarch John of the Indians visiting the papal Curia in 1122.

145/8 is not red þere: The English is more abbreviated than the text in any surviving Latin witness, and I have postulated two corresponding eyeskip losses in the translator's exemplar. The lost matter reports a tradition that no heretic or Jew can live for over a year in the city where the relics of St Thomas lie.

146/5 þe Indes seyn: This is the first of a series of references to the 'books of the men of Inde' (see Introduction 8); curiously, the men of Inde are cited for information on the cult of the Three Kings at Cologne, a subject on which one might have thought the author himself better placed to comment than these alleged oriental informants.

146/11 more þan þe oþir armes yclosid in gold: This interpretation of *aliis brachiis aureis inclusa* can hardly be correct, whatever the 'other arms' may refer to (possibly gold clasps or casks).

146/16–17 mirre with swete sauour: The original *mira*, referring to a 'marvellous fragrance', has been confused with *mirra* 'myrrh' — a convincing example of a peculiar error in the translator's exemplar, as the confusion could not have arisen in the English.

147/10–13: It is hard to see what the scribe intended by his interlineal correction. Presumably 'was of old tyme into now' is an uncancelled false start, and 'to many cuntres' (*cf.*, *venientibus* 'to those coming') was perhaps a slip produced by the succeeding 'meny diuers londis'.

147/17 Balaam and Iosaphath: This was originally 'Barlaam and Joasaph' (or 'Josaphat'). These two figures, the first a prince and the second a hermit, were the subjects of a popular medieval legend glorifying Christian monasticism but ultimately of Buddhist origin (the second name is believed to derive from Bodhisattva, a title of the Buddha); see *ODCC* s.vv. Barlaam and Joasaph, Sts; Josaphat, St. That our text confuses the first with Balaam, and the second perhaps with the Old Testament king Jehoshaphat, is hardly surprising.

148/5 ... her hele: The translator evidently baulked at including the ensuing matter which describes the efficacy of dust from Cologne in silencing the croaking of frogs (Hm. 306/15–29).

148/6 the bodies of xj M^{l} virgines: The legend of St Ursula and her eleven thousand virgins was a favorite in the Middle Ages, especially after the twelfth-century discovery of a burial ground near the church of St Ursula in Cologne believed to contain the martyrs' relics; see *ODCC* s.v. Ursula, St.

148/8–9 to come passyng Coloyne: *vlterius Coloniam transire*, ie. 'to continue their pilgrimage on to Cologne'.

149/11 mydday houre: *Cf.*, (*hora*) *vndecima*, correctly translated 'the xj hour' at 151/4.

149/12 an (MS at) evyn: *equalem*. The manuscript reading is not inappropriate in the context (Matthew xx.8–10), but the emendation, which is supported by the Latin, has a little more point; *cf.*, 151/5.

150/3 matiers: *macerias*; the translator could hardly have recognised the original allusion to the repair of the 'stone walls' surrounding the vineyard once *duratas* ('hardnyd') had replaced the original *dirutas* 'crumbling, fallen down'.

152/1 declarid: *declarauit*. The Latin verb (which would normally mean 'stated', 'explained') is a corruption of the more appropriate *decorauit* 'adorned'; what the translator intended 'declarid' to mean in the present context is unclear.

153/10 of worshiping of God is callid by name Coloyne: *a colendo deum Colonia nuncupatur*. Though *colonia* 'colony' is etymologically connected with *colere* 'tend', 'worship', the author's derivation cannot be accepted literally. The settlement originally called Ara Ubiorum was made a Roman colony by the Emperor Claudius and renamed Colonia Agrippina (or Agrippinensis) after his wife Agrippina who was born there. The notion of a connection between the name of the city and the worship of the Christian deity is therefore fanciful.

153/15–154/15: The Latin sequence from which these verses derive is printed in Kehrein 1873 (without note of their incorporation in *HTR*). Most witnesses of *HTR* transmit seven three line stanzas, i.e., the three and a half sextets corresponding to 6, 7, and the first half of 8 in Kehrein, but the translator's exemplar evidently preserved only the first six; some witnesses include the full ten sextets.

155/1 ff.: The translator's exemplar contained the alternative ending, a series of notes which replaces the standard ending beginning *Gaude felix Colonia* (Hm. 311/16–312/18) and which is found only in witnesses of our subgroup (C G T CC D); its secondary nature is confirmed by discrepancies between its contents and the main text.

155/1–2 þe Maystir in Histories: I.e., Peter Comestor, whose commentary, the *Historia Scholastica*, became the standard work on biblical history for the Middle Ages; see *ODCC* s.v. Peter Comestor; *MED* s.v. maister *n.* 3.(c). The present passage is found on f. 187 in the 1526 edition of J. Crespin; it is also reproduced in Jacobus a Voragine's *Legenda Aurea*, though there is no evidence that the author of *HTR* used the latter.

155/5 magi: The term applied originally to a religious caste among the ancient Medes, but commonly came to refer to 'magicians', 'sorcerers', 'astrologers' (see Hughes 1979: 30 ff., Smith 1978: 71–4); St Augustine's more elevated definition is paralleled in Cicero *De divinatione* 1.23.46: *magos ... quod genus sapientium et doctorum habebatur in Persis*, as well as in the *Opus Imperfectum in Mattheum* (see 155/12n).

155/7 Remige: Remigius of Auxerre (*c.* 841–*c.* 908), a philosopher whose works include a commentary on Matthew's gospel (see *ODCC* s.v. Remigius of Auxerre).

155/12 Crisostome: I.e., the *Opus Imperfectum in Mattheum* attributed to John Chrysostomus (*c.* 347–407) — see Introduction 7 — though the present account differs from the version in *Opus Imperfectum* in a number of details.

155/13 which was not right wys or noblenesse: *Cf.*, *in qua fuit multa sapiencia et nobilitas*. There is no obvious explanation in the English for the corruption, and none of the surviving Latin witnesses has a negative reading; 'right wys' could be written as one word — *MED* s.v. right-wis(e *adj.* — but is even less satisfactory than the manuscript reading.

156/14: The translation ends imperfectly; judging from the Latin some 240 words of English (perhaps a little less than one page of the manuscript) have been lost. The Latin goes on to tell how the twelve astronomers told the news of what they had seen to the wise men (*sapientibus*) of that country, who chose three of their number to take gifts to the child and worship him as king and lord; they set out with the star to guide them and arrive on the thirteenth day. There follows an account (attributed to Germanus, *historiographus temporum Christi*, and Theophanus, *scriptor gestorum Christi*) of three miracles which moved the three Magi (*tribus magis*) to seek the child that had been born.

VARIANTS TO THE LATIN

The emended Latin text is an attempted reconstruction of the text in the translator's exemplar. Emendations (in square brackets), including omissions (indicated by plus signs), adjust the base text T in the direction of the translator's exemplar. Emendation most commonly involves the elimination of T's significant peculiar readings and omissions against the consensus of the other witnesses, of which G, CC, and O are the most relevant (see Introduction 11); occasionally the Vulgate is cited in scriptural citations, and D, but not O, in the last two pages); in such cases T's reading alone is reported, the other witnesses being assumed to agree with the lemma, but where G (e.g. p. 64 *intus*) or CC (e.g. p. 87 *semiiactum lapidis*) are also anomalous their readings are cited alongside T's (again, the remaining witnesses can be assumed to agree with the lemma). Occasionally G's readings or omissions have been imported into the text where the same reading is thought to have stood in the translator's exemplar; in such cases the lemma is followed by the sigil G, followed by the variants of T, CC, and O (e.g. at p. 56 the base and all other witnesses read *bouibus* or *bubus* 'oxen', but G has *bonis*, of which 56/15 *goodis* is clearly the translation, so *bonis* was presumably also the reading in the translator's exemplar). Much more rarely a reading of the contaminated C is adopted; otherwise the witness of C is not cited. Certain emendations assume that the translator's exemplar had peculiar readings of its own; in such cases the agreement of T G CC O against the base are reported (e.g. p. 121 *eorum*, *cf.*, 121/1 ff.n), or (as when the exemplar, or the translator, restored the more original reading independently by conjecture) of T G (e.g. p. 71 *Iudea*, see 70/15n) or T G CC (p. 136 *sit*) against the base.

The policy for emending the base text has been to eliminate T's peculiar readings on the least pretext; otherwise, to emend the Latin (rather than the English) where the Latin is the more plausible source of a discrepancy between the two versions, especially where there is support in G for an emendation, but to leave the discrepancy to stand if there is no grounds for emending one version in preference to the other.

The translator's exemplar contained the alternative ending (155/1ffn), found only in the secondary witnesses of our subgroup (C G T CC D; see Fig. 4). Here the witness of C becomes primary — elsewhere C shows a mixture of textual types, following at times the print P, at times our group — and agreement between C and G virtually guarantees the reading of the exemplar, as elsewhere does the agreement of G and T. The archetypal text of the alternative ending reported in the apparatus below the text has been reconstructed from the readings of the individual witnesses in preference to the text printed in Hm., which for this passage is based solely on the witness of C and CC.

Obeli (†) mark a different set of readings. These are the places where the translator's exemplar, unbeknown to him, was corrupt. The original readings, supplied out of general interest to the reader, appear below the parallel Latin text, not in the present section.

50 nullus] *om.* T. volebat] volebant T. est] *om.* T. cauerne] camere T.
51 vile] vtile T. diruti] directi T, dirupti G.
54 natum] *om.* T. eos] eas T. est] *om.* T. yemps] yemis T. idem] ibidem T.

prophetam] G, prophetatam T CC O.

55 Et] Et in T G. sicut alie stelle] G, *om.* T CC O. dominator] G, dominator eorum T CC O. adorandum] ad orandum T. rara] tam T.

56 separati] seperati T. adorandum] ad orandum T. bonis] G, bouibus T CC, bubus O.

57 incedentibus] incidentibus T. ipsis] ipsa T. et] G O, *om.* T CC. adorandum] ad orandum T.

58 peregrini et mercatores] *trs.* T. est] erit T. et licet fuerit alterius aqua coloris tamen] G, licet sit (erit T) alterius (vt alterius O) aque coloris et T CC O.

59 Nilum] alium T. situs] situata T.

60 comprimuntur] compr[*7 minims*]etur T.

61 subicientur] G, subticentur T CC O. Saba ac] Sabaat T. Egrisculle] Egrusculle T. stabat] *om.* T. omnia] omnium T.

62 vniuersis] vnuersis T. ignotas] *om.* T.

63 Egrisculle] Egrusculle T. per] *om.* T.

64 intus] vix T, infra G. venerit] G Vulgate, veniet T O, venit CC. est] *om.* T. Nabaioth] Nabioth T. crurium] crurum T. quod] *om.* T.

65 currunt per ventum et] et currunt per ventum G O, et currunt per aduentum et CC. tenentur] tuentur T. Iudee] Indie T. Regum] *om.* T. oriente] India T. adorandum] orandum T.

66 roborandam] reprobandam T. longe] *om.* T.

67 Israel] Iherusalem T. et] et cum T G CC O.

68 sepulturam] sepulcrum T.

69 pauperculo] paupercula T. infantuli] G, infantuli Ihesu T CC O. Godolie] Gadolie T.

70 adhibuit] adhibent T. nobiliora meliora] *trs.* T. vendunt] vend[*5 minims*]tur T. regni] regine T.

71 Macedo Philippi] G, *trs.* T CC O. India] Iudea T G. in tugurrio] intertigurrio T. nisi] *om.* T. optulit] *om.* T.

72 fuit] *om.* T. significauit] significat T. aliquod] aliquo T. fragilitate] facultate T.

73 eorum] eorum animalia et T. quieti et solacio se dederunt] quiete et solacio sederunt T.

74 Indiam] Iudeam T G CC O. acciderant] accederant T. sumpserant] sumpserunt T. exercitui] G O, exercitu T CC. peruenerunt] peruerunt T. ipsi] ipsi et ipsi T. homines] hom[*4 minims*]es T.

75 Tharsenses] Tharsensis T. seniores] *om.* T. diebus] dies T. et regiones transiuissent] in regione transmisissent T. suis et in] et T.

76 et] *om.* T. prosperis] asperis T. laboriosis] laboriosio T. India] Iudea T G CC O. ibidem] *om.* T.

77 obstupuerunt] obstipuerunt T. omnibus] omibus T. et] *om.* T. stellam] G O, *om.* T CC.

78 fama] fama et T. lactauit] lactitauit T. in] G O, *om.* T CC.

79 et omnibus] *om.* T. Moysi] Moisy T. infantuli] infantulo T. vsque] *om.* T.

80 partu] *The following passage* Iterum locus ... deportantur *is copied twice in* T; *the second version is printed here.*

81 loco] *om.* T.

82 recipit] recepit T.
83 balsami] balsamus T. habeat] habebat T. et perirent] *om.* T.
84 Iacob] Iacob Iacob T.
85 templum] G, templo T CC O.
86 quidam] quidem T. hominibus] ho[*8 minims*]bus T. denarios] denarios denarios T.
87 ori] ore T. peregrinorum] G, peregrinorum vnde ait euangelium et consilio inito emerunt ex hiis agrum figuli in sepulturam peregrinorum T CC O. est] *om.* T. semiiactum lapidis] semina aptus lapideus T, semiiactus lapidis CC. in] in in T. floreni] florenc' T CC. nunquam] nuquam T.
88 in] *om.* T. suam] *om.* T.
89 inuitus officium] *trs.* T. post] C, *om.* T G CC O. quem] G, quam T CC O. genti] gentibus T. veris] *om.* T. cum] *om.* T. miracula] G, *om.* T CC, mirabilia O. Sculla] G, Seuwa T O, Suwella CC.
90 baptizasset] baptizauit et T. consecrauit] consecrasset T. sanguinis] sanguinem T. irsutas valde] C, irsutas habent G, non irsutas habent T, non hirsutas CC O.
91 Sculla] G, Sewulla T, Suwella CC, Seuwa O. vero] quinto et T, namque G. episcopos presbiteros] *trs.* T. in] *om.* T. dictum] *om.* T.
92 eligerent] elegerunt T. Thome] *om.* T. vnius] videlicet T. Tunc] G, cum T CC, vnde O. Reges] G, Reges tunc T CC O. Antiochenum] Antiochium T.
93 consilio] auxilio T G. inuoluti] *om.* T.
94 benedicentem] benediccionem T, benedicicentem CC. ipsos] episcopos T. ordinatis] ordinatis et T G CC.
95 quinquagesimo primo] *om.* T. capite] *om.* T.
96 eandem] G, *om.* T CC O.
97 et incorrupta] *om.* T. extunc] extunc enim T. et] et in T.
98 reuocari] reuocari et T. repullulare] repulluare T. noluit] voluit T G. imperator] imparator T.
99 testamento] G, testamento et in T, testamento et CC O. confusionem] consuetudinem T. viderunt] G, viderunt et locum in quo Ihesus in cruce matrem discipulo commendauit T CC O. Marie Magdalene] *trs.* T. qua] *om.* T. ipsius] ipius T.
100 et] *om.* T, que O.
101 reperit et inuenit] G, *om.* T CC, hec omnia Helena tam recenter inuenit prout beata virgo ibidem oblita dimisit et reliquit O. alios] alio T. transisset] transsisset T. et] G, in T CC, et in O. quod] quam T.
102 plateis] plateas T, platea CC. partem] *om.* T. musaico] mirifico T.
103 lapideum] lapidium T. que] qui T. esset] esse T.
104 odiosi] odiose T G CC O. nullus] [*5 minims*]llus T. dominum] deum T.
105 penditur] G, pendebatur T CC O.
106 habet] *om.* T. valle] valde T. est] *om.* T, *interlineated* CC. fonte] forte T. ad] ab T.
107 dominicam annunciacionem] dominica annunciacionem G, dominica annunciacione T, de dominica annunciacione CC O. tegit] G, tetigit T CC O. et] *om.* T. cum] *om.* T.
108 montem] G, montem et T, montem eciam CC O. et muris] *om.* T. beati Benedicti] *trs.* T, sancti benedicti G, Benedicti O. Verbigene] virbigene T,

verbigine CC. distat] *om.* T. in] *om.* T.

109 ei] eis T. deum] G, dominum T CC O.

110 in] de? T. regnis] *om.* T. impleuit] G, implens T CC O. reliquias] reliquiis T. Indorum] Iudeorum T. diuinum] diuini T.

111 Nestorinos] Nestorines T. audietur] adietur T. suauitatem] suauitate T. et] de T.

112 omnibus] omibus T. que] G, *om.* T, reuerenter collocata et est sciendum quod ecclesia sancte Sophie in Constantinopolim CC O. se] *om.* T. Verbigene] verbigena G, verbigine T CC, verbigene O.

113 apostata] apostota T.

114 cribraretur] cribaretur T. in] *om.* T. Greciam] Greciani T. Armeniam] Armeniani T.

115 secum] secum secum T. nominauit] nominat T. ob] ab T. cepit] *om.* T. accessum] accessum et T. coloniensem] coloniensis T.

116 Et tunc] Extunc T. est] *om.* T. ornamentis] ornamentis et T.

117 pre] pro T. maioris] moris T. offerunt] offerrunt T. notandum est] notandum T. sciendum est] sciendum T. Mandapoli] G, Mandopoli T CC O.

118 nomine] *om.* T. Soldino] G, Soldinis T CC, Soldinus O. Nam] G, Nam sicut T CC O. seruauerunt] seruauerunt set T G CC O.

119 Egrisculle] Egrosilli T. Nestorinus] Nestorius T O. coram] coronatus T, eorum O. ipsis] ipsius T.

120 in ecclesiis eorum] G, regnis T, regnis in ecclesijs eorum CC O. sanctum] secundum T. in India] G, India T, Indi CC O. nos] G, nos domino pape et presbitero Iohanni obediunt vt nos T CC O. ad] *om.* T. Indorum] *om.* T. feruentissimo] frequentissimo T.

121 vna] C, vnum T G CC O. eorum] Grecorum T G CC O. scindunt] sindunt T. exquisiuerunt] exquesiuerunt T. presepe] prese T.

122 caulium] caulum T. episcopi] ipsi T. latini] G, latinis T CC O. in] *om.* T. incedunt] incidunt T.

123 Michee] G, Micee T CC, Methe O. Noe quieuit] Noee quieuit T. Noe adhuc] Noee adhuc T.

124 habitata] habita T. intrandi] G, intrandi vel exeundi T CC O. saraceni] sareceni T.

126 crucem] G O, *om.* T CC.

127 Origenis] Originis T. et] *om.* T. consentire] conscentire T.

128 et] in T. in] de T.

129 seu] T, sed G CC O. alterum] alteram T. tybiis] tubiis T.

130 eo] eos T. vocabantur] vocantur T. Ysmini] Ysini T. Mandapoli] G, Mandopoli T CC O. queuis] quouis T. sint] sunt T. faciant] faciunt T.

131 laici] laci T. mensam suam] mensem suam T. quiuis] quis T. mensam die] mensem die T. itaque] G, itaque per T CC O.

132 erat] erit T. ordinatim] ordinatum T. ab eo in hoc Iordane] in hoc Iordane ab eo T.

133 balneantur] baliciantur T. rixe] rite T. venientibus] vomentibus T.

134 montis] monti T. influxu] G O, fluxu T CC. hic] *om.* T.

135 hic] G, hic et T CC O. Soldini] Soldani T. exitu] G, exitu et reditu (redditu T) T CC O. hiis] *om.* T.

136 ere] here T. Que] G, qui T CC O. in] G, cum T CC O. precessit] precepit T. illuminauit] ill[7 *minims*]auit T. sit] sic T G CC. adorandum] G, adorandum et T, adorandum hortabatur et CC O.

137 prophecie] prophete T. declarant] declarabant T.

138 capitaneum] captineum T, capetaneum CC. tunc] nunc T. Cambal] G, *om.* T, Cambaleth CC, Cambalech O. Machomoti] G, Mago Methli T, mago mechli CC, Machometi O. sunt] *om.* T.

139 Assuerus] G, Assewerus T, Aswetus CC, Asswerus rex O.

140 iratus] natus T. Romani] Roma T. abolita] oblata T, obolita G. partes] *om.* T. claustra] castra T. iuuenes] iuuines T. pueros] C O, et pueros T G CC. ibidem] ibidem in T.

141 Vnde] vt T. itaque] ita quod T.

142 infidelium] infideliter T. interfecissent] interfecisset T. quod] G, *om.* T CC O. excercitu] excertu T. Qui] G, Qui cum T CC, Qui tunc O.

143 Vnde] *om.* T. iussu] iusu T. esset] esse T. tunc] G, tunc statim T, tamen statim CC O. imperpetuum] G, imperpetuum inter eos T, inter eos CC, et contractus est inter eos in presentem diem (*with following* duraret *omitted*) O. suus] suis T. de] in T. Iaspar tercius Rex] tercius Rex Iasper T.

144 elegerit] eligerit T. ipso] ipsa T.

145 dehonestari] dehonestari etcetera T. apostoli] aphi T. nil] nil videtur vel reperitur nam T G CC O. legitur] legitur in istis quod in ciuitate qua corpus beati Thome quiescit ibidem vltra annum non posunt venire (viuere G O) heretici vel Iudei de hiis ibidem modo nil scitur T G CC O. retrahat] trahat T.

146 deferebantur] differebantur T. et] vt T. in] *om.* T. mirra] mira T G CC O. sacris] satis T.

147 coloniensem] coloniensis T. peruenerint] peruenerit T. que] qui T. certas] G, circa T CC O.

148 ipsos] quos T. Regum] u *unclear* T. certas] G, circa T CC O. alias] alia T.

149 possunt] possent T. tribubus] tribus T. honorandi] honerandi T. in] *om.* T. receperunt] receperunt etcetera T.

150 macerias] maceries T. duratas] C, dirutas T G CC O. quia ... fidei] CC, *om.* T, quam ipsa vinea iam palmites fidei G, que in ipsa vinea iam marcescere O. produxerunt] perduxerunt T. in] G, et T CC, ad O. India] Iudea T G CC O. operandum] G CC, operand' T, operandi O. diuersarum] diuersorum T.

151 munerum que] muner[6 *minims*]que T. effugarunt] effugarunt etcetera T. perpetuum] perpetue T. Coloniam] G, absque dubio T CC O. et] et in T.

152 in] *om.* T. primiciarum] prouinciarum T. primiciis] pr[6 *minims*]ciis T.

153 laus ... ipsorum] *om.* T.

154 pulcre] pulcri T. Nusquam] C, Nunquam T G CC O. aliam] C, aliam Colunt Reges propter regem Summi regis seruant legem Coloni Colonie T G CC D.

155 regum] C G, *om.* T CC D. hec] hic T. Historia Scolastica] C G, scola historia T, *trs.* CC D. Appellus] C G, Appellius T CC D. Galgalath] C, Galgalat T G CC D. Serathim] Sarathim T. sapientes] C G, sapiens T CC D. quidam] quia T. Crisostomus] Grisostomus T. etcetera] *om.* T.

156 ad] C, ad hoc T G CC D. astrologis] C G, familiis CC, famulis D. christi] domini T.

GLOSSARY

The Glossary records obsolete senses and usages that are likely to cause difficulty, as well as items of lexicographical interest (antedatings, unusual forms or spellings, etc.). Senses elsewhere unrecorded or uncertain but suggested by the context or the Latin are preceded by a question mark. The Glossary is arranged alphabetically: *i* as a consonant (/dʒ/) follows *i/y* as a vowel, *u/v* as a consonant follows *u/v* as a vowel; *i/y* and *u/v* are not distinguished where they have the same phonetic value, nor are *th/þ* and *y/ȝ* (representing /j/), which are used apparently interchangeably by the scribe. Except to illustrate spellings or nuances, only two instances of each sense are noted. An asterisk indicates an emendation; § indicates an item of lexicographical interest; ? indicates uncertainty about grammatical status, applicability or validity of a meaning, or (before a line number) applicability of the meaning in that particular instance.

The standard grammatical abbreviations are used: *adj*. adjective; *adv*. adverb; *comp*. comparative; *conj*. conjunction; *dem*. demonstrative; *imp*. imperative; *inf.* infinitive; *intr*. intransitive; *n*. noun; *pa. t.* past tense; *phr*. phrase(s); *pl*. plural; *pp*. past participle; *ppl. adj*. participial adjective; *pr*. present tense; *pr. ppl*. present participle; *prep*. preposition; *refl*. reflexive; *super*. superlative; *syn*. synonymous with; *3 sg*. third person singular; *tr*. transitive; *v*. verb; *vbl. n*. verbal noun (gerund).

a *prep*. of 146/15(2)
acresyd *pa. t*. increased, grew 79/12
aduersaries *adj. pl*. hostile, opposing, *in phr*. **parties** ~ opposing group, enemies 98/6
afor *prep*. in precedence over, than 94/7, 145/6; *in phr*. ~ **God** in the sight of God, in God's judgement 142/8
aftir *prep*. according to 73/8, 155/7
aftir þat *conj*. according as 140/12
age *n*., *in phr*. **in** ~ advanced in years 65/9
althing *adv*. in any way 91/5
amplificacion *n*. increasing, enlargement 110/14 (§)
and *conj*. but 58/10, 77/5
aray *n*. garments 71/7
arayne *n*. spider 125/18
arblast, arowblast *n*. crossbow 124/3, 133/12
argentei *Latin* made of silver 87/11, 87/12
aromata *Latin* aromatic substances, spices 60/2*, 146/16
arraieth *pr. 3 sg*. clothes 117/3
arst *adv*. previously, before 53/8
as who seith *phr*. ?virtually, in effect 64/16n
assent *n*. will, desire 126/1
astony(e)d *pp*. dazed 71/11, 72/1
atwyn(ne) *adv*. apart 57/13, 81/2
aunte *n*. ?old woman 79/9n
auenture *n*., *in phr*. **in** ~ if in case 51/16

aye(e)n *adv.* back 73/20, 84/22; *in phr.* **answere ...** ~ 131/14; **restorid** ~ 144/3–4; **comyng** ~ return 80/10; *see also* **turn** *v. intr.*
ayen *prep.* against 109/4, 114/1; opposite 133/11
ayencomyng *vbl. n.* meeting; return, homecoming 76/17

bawme *n.* balm, balsam 81/5, 81/10; *in phr.* ~ **coct** balm extracted by boiling 83/12 (*syn.* **sodyn** ~ 83/12); **baumes** *pl.* 70/6
behight *see* **byhetyng** *pr. ppl.*
benefices *n. pl.* favours, gifts 152/15
bere ?*pa. t.* bore, took 106/15
by *prep.* through, down (*in phr.* ~ **the strete**) 68/3, 102/4; via 58/14(1), 101/6; according to 155/5
byfallid *v. intr.* ?*pa. t.* was fitting 96/10 (§)
bygunne* *pa. t. pl.* began 107/13
byhetyng *pr. ppl.* vowing, promising 142/5n; **behight** *pa. t.* 49/10
byleft *pa. t.* remained 77/20; *pp.* 107/4
byreft *pp.* taken away, stolen 111/11, 111/14
bysily *adv.* constantly, regularly 95/4
bolde *adj.* excellent, confident, ?astute, ?expert 130/17 148/16 (*syn.* **redy** *adj.*) (§)
bondis *n. pl.* cords 60/12
brasyll *n.* brazil (a reddish dye) 82/17n
brede *n.* breadth 64/16, 101/12
brennyngly ?*adj.* burning 55/6 (§)

Calde *n.* the Chaldean language, *in phr.* **lettris of** ~ the Chaldean alphabet 118/15
cariage *n.* baggage, equipment 57/5n, 61/10
chanons *n. pl.* canons 100/9, 103/14
chaunge *n.*, *in phr.* **for** ~ **of** in exchange for 111/9
chepe *n.*, *in phr.* **of good** ~ inexpensive 101/14
chere *n.* face, expression 71/19
chese ?*pa. t.* chose 90/3, 114/7*; **chose**, *in phr.* ~ **into** chose as 138/8 (§)
chrecche *see* **cracche** *n.*
cithre *n.* strong drink 128/1
clennest *adj. super.* clearest 156/7
clennest *adv. super.* most splendidly 56/10
clense* *pr. pl.* prune 81/16n
clepid, clept *pp.* called 68/3, 94/4
cler(e)nes(se) *n.* brightness 54/5, 55/1, 67/13
coct *ppl. adj.* boiled, extracted by boiling: *see* **bawme** *n.*
competent *adj.* appropriate, adequate 57/4
condyte *inf.* guide, conduct 126/16
conduyte *n.*, *in phr.* **safe** ~ safe conduct 115/16
confortid *pa. t.* refreshed, entertained 73/10; **comfortid** *pp.* strengthened (spiritually) 110/5
confoundyd *pp.* discredited, silenced 110/6
confusion *n.* confutation 73/12; **confusions** *pl.* 140/15
consecrate *pa. t.* consecrated 90/2 (§)
constitucion *n.* decree, ordinance, *in phr.* **made by** ~ decreed 143/11

conuenient *adj*. appropriate, adequate 57/4, befitting 76/17, suitable 92/5
conuersacion *n*. manner of life 77/16
conuersaunt *adj*. dwelling, associating 129/4
copie *n*. abundance 156/7
cop(pe) *n*. top, summit 123/15, 123/16, 156/13
cosyn *n*. kinsman/woman 131/13; **cosyns** *pl*. descendants 155/10
costoumable *adj*. usual, that to which one has grown accustomed 70/11
cote *n*. shed, shelter 51/1, 68/4
couchid *v. tr. ?pa. t.* laid 54/2; *pp*. 111/17, 113/10; **couchyng** *intr. pr. ppl.* lying 100/17
counceilid *pa. t.* concealed 78/5n
courte of Rome *phr*. the papal Curia 95/6–7*n, 104/13
cracche, crecche, chrecche *n*. manger 53/14*, 53/15, 54/1n, 69/4, 100/18, 103/4*n; **cracchis** *pl*. 54/3
craftily *adv*. by skill 59/12, 105/16
crose *n*. crozier 108/4
cumfort *n*. encouragement, assurance 99/5
cumpas, cumpace *n*., *in phr.* **in (a)** ~ in a circle, around 64/8, 90/18, 94/3
cumpase *inf.* ?turn 112/10n (§)
cuntre *n*. region, part of the world 54/2, 56/18; **cuntre(e)s** *pl*. 101/13, 111/19; surrounding land 134/1n (§)
curyd *pp*. tended, taken care of 52/13
curse *inf.* excommunicate 119/14
custome *n*. rite 104/12, 127/1 (§)

declaracion *n*. clarification 151/1
declarid *pp*. explained 65/12; related 106/2; *meaning uncertain* 152/1n
decorate *ppl. adj.* adorned 152/2
dede, did *pa. t.* caused, *in phr.* ~ **grave, halowe had ...** sculpted, consecrated 77/9, 99/15
dedified *pp*. dedicated, consecrated 108/8 (§)
defaute *n*. lack 74/14; *in phr.* **for ~ of** 70/14
defendid *pa. t.* prevented 109/5
defoule *inf.* besmirch 127/11; *pr. pl.* disfigure 135/15; **defoulid** *pp*. 140/7n; trampled 62/4, 78/11
deynte *adj*. rare, excellent 86/14
delitable *adj*. delightful 106/4
denouncyng *pr. ppl.* proclaiming 67/3, 100/5; **denouncid** *pa. t.* 136/16
departid *v. tr. pp.* separated (from each other) 56/6, 96/14; *intr. pa. t.* moved apart 96/11; **departyng** *pr. ppl.* separating 97/15
deserte *n*., *in phr.* **þurgh ~ of** (deservedly) by reason of 146/18
despyte, dispite *n*. contempt, scorn, *in phr.* **bene, had in** ~ (are) despised 79/2, 119/17; contemptuous defiance 120/3
detestable *adj*. ?detested 110/1 (§)
diffynid *pp*. determined, fixed 142/8
discreve *inf.* interpret 88/4; **discrevid** *pp*. recorded (in a census) 49/1, distinguished 54/9
disparplid *ppl. adj.* scattered, dispersed 143/15(1)*, 143/15(2)

disputison *n.* debate 62/5
dissese *n.* trouble 62/8; pain, suffering 84/11, 95/19; misfortune, hardship 147/6
dome *n.* judgement 127/14; *in phr.* **the (laste)** ~ 153/3, 153/6; decree 141/7n; **domys** *pl., in phr.* **in** ~ in court 122/2
donet *n.* Latin grammar 140/16
doumbe *adj.* deaf and dumb 70/12
dounfallyng *vbl. n.* setting (of the sun), west 151/10, 151/14 (§)
dowyng *vbl. n.* (giving of) dowry 102/4
dra(u)ght *n.* the distance a bow can shoot 124/3, 133/12
drowe *pa. t.* drew, pulled 107/9
duk *n.* title of a military commander 74/1n
durably *adv.* lastingly, eternally 152/3 (§)
durid *v. intr. pp.* continued 113/17; **duryng** *pr. ppl.* persisting 111/3

edified *pp.* built 105/8
eysel *n.* vinegar 87/2
eldremen *n. pl.* elders 75/1
emplantid *pa. t.* planted 150/1 (§)
enactyng *pr. ppl.* acting 94/15
encrese *pr. pl.* , *in phr.* ~ **to** ?grow closer to, ?increasingly join 122/9 (§)
enfourmyd *pp.* instructed 94/8, trained 137/8
enhabytid *pp.* established as inhabitants, dwelling 125/8, 126/3
enhaunce inf. exalt, elevate 136/9; **enhauncyd** *pa. t.* 110/1
enpeyntid *pp.* painted, depicted 94/3 (§)
enquere *inf.* learn 148/17
entere *inf.* inter 96/2; **enterid** *pa. t.* 96/6; *pp.* 120/9
entoumbyd *pp.* entombed 146/5 (§)
entoumbyng *n.* burial, ?tomb 95/15 (§)
envy(e) *n.* ill-will, hostility 75/14, 79/2; spite 98/5, 99/20
eris *n. pl.* ears (of grain) 60/10
evyn *adj.* equal 149/12, 151/5
evyn *adv.* exactly, constantly 61/10, 72/8
excitid *pa. t.* incited 142/12

faculte *n.* (pecuniary) means 117/4, 118/9
fame *n.* report (of a prophecy) 145/4
fast *adv.* much, vigorously 138/9
feble *adj.* of poor quality, worn 54/1
fey *n.* faith 97/3, 138/3
felt *pa. t.* detected, smelt (*with* **of**) 111/19 (§); **felid** *pp.* 102/9, 146/17
fere *n.* fire 120/10
ferid *pp.* alarmed 143/4, frightened (away) 103/12
figuracion *n.* prefiguration 55/15 (§)
fil(l) *pa. t.* fell 71/13, 104/1
flemyd *pa. t.* expelled 150/17
flood *n.* river 59/6, 123/19; **flodis** *pl.* 59/5
flowyn ?*pp.* risen 134/1 (§)
foldyn *ppl. adj.* rolled up 93/15

fond *pa. t.* procured, provided (with) 78/5
forchese *pa. t.* chose beforehand 152/12 (§)
forthes *n. pl.* fords 133/16
fourme *n.* likeness, image 77/8, 78/10
frendship-makyng *vbl. n.* alliance 144/19 (§)
fulfillid *pp.* filled, satiated 150/12
fully *adj.* big, plump 102/12

geete *n. pl.* goats 65/3
gentile *n.* heathen, ?a person without religion 143/5 (§)
gentilite *n.* paganism 98/14 (§)
go *pr. pl.* walk 102/10, 123/8
grasse *n.* plant, *in phr.* **thre levyd** ~ clover 81/13
Grege *n.* the Greek language 112/10 (§)
gret(te) *pa. t.* greeted 106/10, 107/6; **grett** *pp.* 107/3n
grucching *vbl. n.* murmuring, complaint 149/12

had *pa. t.* held, *in phr.* ~ **in dispyte** 152/17; *pp.* regarded, esteemed 145/7
half *n.* direction, part of the world, *in phr.* **on, of this** ~ 70/15, 148/18
halowe *n.* saint 151/9; **halowis** *pl.* 122/2
halowe *inf.* consecrate 99/15; **halowid** *pa. t.* 90/5; *pp.* 122/10
hardy *adj.* presumptuous 52/14
heir *n.* haircloth 127/17
hele *n.* good health 148/5; recovery 86/10, 106/16; safety 77/4
heliþ *pr. 3 sg.* covers 107/5; **helyd** *pa. t.* 107/8, 125/1; *pp.* 69/6, 103/1
helpyng *n.* relief 72/17
herbe *n.* the green part of a plant 60/13
herbergages *n. pl.* lodgings 104/6
herborowyng *vbl. n.* lodgings 73/18
herburgh *n.* lodgings 50/5; **herborow** 50/8, 62/10
herburgh *v. tr.* provide lodgings for 50/5; **herborowid** *intr. pa. t.* camped 64/8; *pp.* 104/9*
heste *n.* command 143/4
hidyng *vbl. n., in phr.* **vndur** ~ in a veiled fashion 137/4 (§)
hyed *pa. t.* hastened, rushed 63/15
hyingly *adv.* hastily 78/15
hyly *adv.* earnestly, strictly, ?fearsomely 142/20
hill(e) *n.* mountain 54/13, 107/17
hilly *adj.* mountainous 123/12
hilt *pp.* skinned 64/18
hyng *v. intr. pa. t.* hung 87/2, 107/9; *tr. pa. t. subj.* **henge** 139/12
holy *adv.* together ?95/9
holpe *pp.* helped, delivered 124/15
honest, honneste *adj.* befitting 67/17, irreproachable 77/16
honestly *adv.* richly 56/13
hopyng *pr. ppl.* thinking, suspecting 64/4
hostrie *n.* hostelry, lodgings 57/1
housyd *pp.* built upon (with a house) 50/14

housyng *n.* roofing, superstructure (of a building) 103/10 (§)

ydolatries *n. pl.* idolatrous things, idols 110/6
ylich *adv.* without distinction, in the same way, to the same extent 61/10
inchoacion *n.* beginning 149/9 (§)
into *prep.* as far as 57/17, 139/11

iewell *n.* precious object, treasure 115/1; **iewels** *pl.* 70/18, 85/26
Iewis ?*adj.* Jewish 98/16, 149/16 (§)

kepe *inf.* guard, ensure 133/6
kepyng *vbl. n.* guarding 145/3
kynd(e) *n.* nature 152/10, appearance 64/14; *in phr.* **of** ~ 148/13; **by** ~ 90/13; **of his owne** ~ naturally 83/6, 83/7; natural inclinations, instincts 73/8
knave child *n.* male child 52/4
knyghthood, -hode *n.* army, host, *in phr.* **heuynly** ~ angels 66/13, 100/6
kun *pr. pl.* know 105/5

large *adj.* broad 112/8; bountiful 152/16
largely *adv.* bountifully 90/5, 91/1
lawe *n.* faith, set of religious beliefs 99/5, 135/12; **lawes** *pl.* 142/5
lede *v. tr.* take (*in phr.* ~ **with hym**) 115/1; **led** *pa. t.* conveyed 98/7, 116/2; **lede** *intr. pr. pl.* go ?131/15
leftyd *pa. t.* raised 112/13
legacye *n.* diplomatic mission, *in phr.* **sent ... in** ~ sent as envoy 114/16
lese *n.* pasture land 124/4
lesyng *vbl. n.* loss 75/9
lettyd *pp.* blocked 100/14
lettris *n. pl.* texts 104/15
leve *inf.* remain 126/14; cease 68/16; **levith** *pr. 3 sg.* 147/8; **leve** *imp.* 152/16; **left** *pa. t.* 51/2, 151/7
levyd *see* **grasse** *n.*
lewde *adj.* lay 131/4
lybardis *n. pl.* leopards 65/4
lightyng *pr. ppl.* giving light, shining 146/8
lyng *pr. ppl.* lying 111/10; **lying**, *in phr.* **yn an oryson** ~ kneeling or prostrate in prayer 51/7
lytil *n., in phr.* **a** ~ **and a** ~ little by little 63/6
lyve *n., in phr.* **of** ~ alive 95/6
lyvelode *n.* the necessities of life, sustenance 78/6, 156/8
loghe *pa. t.* laughed 51/15

maydekyn *n.* maiden 50/6 (§)
manere *n.* religious practices, rites, *in phr.* **have hem ... aftir þe** ~ **of, ben in** ~ **of** follow the observances of 118/14, 123/5 (*syn.* **ryte** 125/11); **maners** *pl.* moral code ?129/5
manhede, -hode, -hood *n.* human condition 69/2, 73/8, 108/18
marches *n. pl.* borders 62/6n; **marchis** 107/17
marchyng *pr. ppl.* bordering, being neighbours 123/7
margarites *n. pl.* pearls 71/5

marices *n. pl.* marshes 57/11
medlyd *pa. t.* mixed 87/2
meyne *n.* retinue, host 65/7
mendinantz, menours *see* **Frere** *n. pl. in* Select Proper Names
merches *n. pl.* marshes 62/9n
metis *n. pl.* meals 141/14
metropolitan(e) *adj.* pertaining to a metropolitan bishop 108/15, 112/11 (§)
myche *adj.* large 64/7, 112/8
michilnes *n.* size 82/12
myrie *adj.* delightful, pleasant, charming 106/4
mysbyleue *n.* heathen beliefs, paganism 113/16
myscreaunt *n.* non-believer, ?convert (to Judaism) 66/1 (§)
modir berer *n.* mother who gives birth 52/5 (§)
monument *n.* tomb, sepulchre 99/10
mo(o)st *adj. super.* greatest (in number or importance) 95/1; (in size) largest 112/12, tallest 69/17, 84/9
more *adj. comp.* greater (in size or importance) 70/8n, 94/8, 151/15
motons *n. pl.* type of gold coins 87/13

name *n., in phr.* **in ~ of** for, as 93/15
namely *adv.* particularly 101/17
neiþer *conj.* nor 137/10
nempnyng *pr. ppl.* specifying 115/3
nere *pa. t.* were not 70/1
noblesse *n.* value, efficacy 83/6 (§)
none *n.* the ninth hour 149/11, 150/15

o *adj.* one 54/16, 56/7; a single 86/9; **on** a certain 92/13
obley *n.* sacramental wafer 121/7, 121/8
ocupie *inf.* use 106/18
opynions *n. pl.* divergent or false beliefs 97/10, 140/15
ordeyne *inf.* make ready 95/14; establish, appoint 100/9; **ordeynid** *pa. t.* 67/17; built, furnished 90/19; *pp.* dressed 56/10; formed, put together 73/1; assigned 104/11; stationed 133/5
oryso(u)n *n.* (act of) prayer 51/7, 91/18; *see also* **lyng** *pr. ppl.*
ornementis *n. pl.* equipment 56/16n, 61/6; furnishings 76/10; accessories 102/3
oþir *conj.* or 139/10
ouercome *pa. t.* won over 142/11
ouerlyvid *pa. t.* lived (beyond an event), continued in life 95/11
owne *adj.* (*n.*) (one's) own home, place, possessions 133/5

parcell *n.* part 87/2; **parcelles** *pl.* particles, small quantities 72/7
party(e) *n.* part 112/15; *in phr.* **for the more ~** mostly 59/13–14, 122/15; generally 57/1–2, 101/15; **yn ~** somewhat 102/12; **parties** *pl.* regions 55/12, 55/19; *see also* **aduersaries** *adj. pl.*
peyrid *pp.* damaged, lessened 118/3
pension *n.* payment, tax 104/3
peple *n.* gentiles, non-Jews 73/13, 91/15; pagans 77/10, 149/17 (§)
perauntre *adv.* as it happened 155/14

perfourme *inf.* complete 76/2; **perfourmyd** *pa. t.* 74/17, 75/8
pyke *pr. pl.* pick clean 81/16n
pilgrymage *n.* journey, wandering 84/16
pilgrymes *n. pl.* travellers 70/8, 80/16
pyllis *n. pl.* pools (in a stream) 133/15
pleynly *adv.* fully 110/8; fully recorded or explained, *in phr.* ~ **... founde** 80/2, 98/17
plunket *n.* (a fabric of) greyish-blue colour 69/6
potell *n.* (a vessel containing) half a gallon 82/7
potentis ?*adj. pl.* powerful 111/8n
power *n.*, *in phr.* **had no ~ to** were unable to 85/21; financial means, wealth 102/1, 131/7
precellist *pr. 2 sg.* surpass 153/2
prechid *pa. t.* declared publicly, recounted, spoke (about) 74/8, 75/2; *pp.* urged 56/12
Prechours *see* **Frere** *n. pl. in* Select Proper Names
presently *adv.* in physical presence, in that very place 66/4
princes* *n. pl.* leaders 86/17
prophane *ppl. adj.* profaned 125/16 (§)

quantite *n.* size 50/11; *in phr.* **more in** ~ greater in size 70/8n, 72/5
quere *n.* choir 103/3, 104/3

recche *inf.*, *in phr.* ~ **... of** care about 112/17; heed, pay attention to 142/12
recordyng *pr. ppl.* (*with* **of**) giving heed (to); pronouncing judgement (concerning); pondering (on); relating (about) 94/15
redy *adj.* capable, intelligent 70/14
redily *adv.* fully 66/9
reflorisshid *pp.* caused to flourish anew, flourishing 140/8 (§)
refte* *pa. t.* snatched (from danger), rescued 54/8; **reft** *pp.* taken away (by force) 143/2, 144/3
regne *n.* kingdom 99/13; **regnis** *pl.* 125/15, 139/18
relece *inf.* remit 127/8
remevyng *v. intr. pr. ppl.* moving, altering one's position 96/11
reprevid *pp.* condemned, rejected 126/5
resolucion *n.* dissolution, separation of the soul and body, *in phr.* ~ **of her lyf** their death 95/13
restore *inf.* revert, be restored 144/20 (§)
revokyd *pp.* recalled 88/7, 98/2
ryall *adj.* of a king, royal 68/14
right *n.* rite, ritual 104/12
rosers *n. pl.* rosebushes 81/10
ro(u)gh *adj.* hairy 90/14n; thick, long-haired 148/13

saveryng *v. intr. pr. ppl.* (of a smell) coming forth 111/18; **sauerid** *tr. pp.* scented 102/9 (§)
sclattyd *pp.* covered with slates or tiles 103/1n (§)
scutes *n. pl.* type of French gold coins 87/13
seld *adv.* seldom 70/15; *in phr.* ~ **sayn, seyn** rarely seen, extraordinary 55/13, 136/14
selde *adj.* rare 86/13
semyng *ppl. adj.* fitting, proper 109/12; **semyd** *pa. t.* was fitting 96/2

semith *pr. 3 sg.* is visible 123/16
sendell *n.* sendal (a rich silken material) 146/15
seniours *n. pl.* elders 75/4
sewid* *pa. t.* pursued 75/5; **sewyng** *pr. ppl.* following 96/7
shewid *pa. t.* explained, declared, made known 63/17, 66/6
significacion *n.* ?interpretation 151/2 (§)
sikir *adj.* certain, lasting 142/20
sismatikes ?*adj. pl.* scismatic 131/4 (§)
syte *n.* city 114/16
sithe *n. pl.* times 81/4
smaragdis *n. pl.* green stones, emeralds 59/11
solace *n.* help, support 73/13
sone *adv.* forthwith, *in phr.* ~ **sodenly** 64/1
sorid *ppl. adj.* pained, troubled 64/6 (§)
sorow(e) *n.* pain 52/6, 52/11
sowne *n.* sound, noise 70/11
specialite *n., in phr.* **in grete** ~ as a very special possession 82/9 (§)
speciall *n., in phr.* **in** ~ in detail, individually 90/16
squyers *n. pl.* attendants, retainers 139/6
stable *adj.* fixed, stationary 96/16
stabularie *n.* (female) stable keeper 105/6 (§)
stike *inf.* stick, fix 108/13
stillith *pr. 3 sg.* drips, trickles 83/6, 83/7
stont *pr. 3 sg.* stands 106/10*, 113/6; *in phr.* ~ **by** consists of 57/10
store *n.* what is stored, *in phr.* ~ **of housholde** household equipment 57/4, ~ **of vitaille** provisions 156/7
storid *pa. t.* provided 76/10
strakis *n. pl.* rays, beams 55/6, 55/8
streitly adv. ?with great concern, diligently, *in phr.* **had** ~ **in thoght** 109/12 (§)
stremys *n. pl.* rays, emanations 55/7
strengthe *n.* a body (of soldiers) 133/5; *in phr.* **wiþ** ~ by force 126/12–13, 139/9
strengthid *pa. t.* fortified 108/3; *in phr.* ~ **hem** strove 127/10, 150/18; *pp.* ?encamped 124/16
studye *n.* efforts, concern 110/15
subget *ppl. adj.* ?subordinate 61/1n
subleuacion *n.* alleviation 72/14 (§)
substitute *ppl. adj.* put in a position previously held by another 156/3
suffise *inf.* be capable 75/12; **suffisid** *pa. t.* 77/15
supperflue, **superfleu** *adj.* superfluous 49/5, 49/7
susteyne *inf.* tolerate, abide 142/10
sweuenes *n. pl.* dreams 142/12

taste *inf.* touch, test, examine 52/14
tempest(e) *n.* turmoil, upheaval, calamity 114/8; danger 146/18
þa *dem. adj. sg.* that 63/14
þat *dem. adj. pl.* those 91/13n, 108/15
þei *conj.* though 148/13
tho *dem. adj.* ?*sg.* that 67/8; *pl.* those 69/20, 70/12

tho *adv.* at that time 132/12
thre levyd *see* **grasse** *n.*
thrette *pa. t.* threatened (**of** against) 79/4 (§)
threwey, threway *n.* a place where three roads meet 63/10, 63/13
tylie *inf.* cultivate, till 151/7
tymbryng *n.* timber supports 103/10 (§)
togidir *adv.* each other 96/13
tokenys *n. pl.* signs demonstrating divine power and authority, miracles 98/13
towails *n. pl.* table cloths 131/7
translate *pp.* removed 71/4
translatyng *vbl. n.* translation (moving of relics) 146/2 (§)
treso(u)r *n.* treasure-chest 71/13; treasury 85/3, 85/9; **tresours** *pl.* 85/27
treuly *adv.* faithfully 149/11
troubly *adj.* cloudy, turbid 83/11
trusse *pr. pl.* load, pack; carry, take 57/5n
tunica inconsutilis *Latin phrase* Christ's robe 112/15
turn *v. intr.* revert 144/20 (§); **turne** *pr. pl., in phr.* ~ **aȝen** return 148/10; **turnyng** *pr. ppl.* 114/17
twyn *n., in phr.* **in** ~ apart 105/1

vnavisid *ppl. adj.* unannounced 64/5
vncouthe *adj.* unusual, strange 55/14
vndefoulid *ppl. adj.* not defaced, undamaged 135/17 (§)
vndryn *n.* the sixth hour, midday 68/2; = **vndurtyde** 150/8
vnknowyn *ppl. adj.* ignorant, unaware 56/7, 61/9
vnmevable, vnmeble *adj.* not moving 68/6, 96/16, 146/4
vnnethe *adv.* with difficulty, only just, barely 54/8, 74/18, 82/8, 87/9

varied *pa. t.* dissented, deviated 93/4
veiles *n. pl.* sails 112/9 (§)
vertu *n.* strength 61/12, 68/1; **vertues** *pl.* miracles 97/4, 115/8
vyne *n.* vineyard 149/15, 150/15
voyde *v. intr.* retreat, escape 124/12; *tr.* do away with, root out 75/14; **voydit** *pp.* 119/2

wacchyn *pr. pl.* keep vigil 108/14
wed *n.* pawn, pledge 113/3
went *pa. t.* believed 74/5
werrid *pa. t.* made war on 124/10
wher þat *conj.* wherever it may be that 130/15
whil(e) *conj.* when 60/11, 115/17
wildirnes *n. pl.* wildernesses 62/9
willy *adj.* eager 63/19
wynes *n. pl.* vineyards 93/17
wytte *n.* wisdom 155/5
woke *n.* week 129/12
wondirly *adv.* greatly, extremely 55/16, 61/16
wormys, wo(u)rmes *n. pl.* snake-like animals 70/7, 129/14, 139/2
worst *adj. superl.* very wicked 130/4 (§)

woxyn *ppl. adj.* risen, swollen 134/1
wratthith *pr. 3 sg.* becomes angry, displays anger 129/2; **wratthid** *pp.* moved to wrath 140/1
wroght *pa. t.* laboured 150/15
wurship, worship *n.* honour 77/2, 97/12; *in phr.* **in** *or* **þurgh (þe) ~ of** 76/9, 94/6, 108/8; importance, high standing 101/18
wurshipfully, worshipfully *adv.* with due honour 74/9, 96/6; commendably 95/8; impressively 146/10
wurship(yn) *pr. pl.* honour, venerate, do reverence to 130/2, 132/11; ?celebrate 121/17; ?adorn 108/15n; **wurshipyng** *pr. ppl.* 99/6; **wurshipid** *pa. t.* 112/14; *pp.* 92/8, 106/2
wurshipyng, worshipyng *vbl. n.* honour(ing), veneration 131/1, 144/2

yeldith *pr. 3 sg.* repays 129/2
yeve *inf.* give 78/8, 87/2; *pr. pl.* 143/16; **yeueth, ȝevith** *pr. 3 sg.* 59/16, 128/4; **yaf** *pa. t.* 86/19, 90/7; **yave** *pl.* 87/6; **yove** *pp.* 49/11, **yovyn** 55/14, 152/15, **yevyn** 113/12
ȝoldyn *pp.* restored, returned 144/19
yotyn *pp.* (metal) cast 136/4

SELECTIVE LIST OF PROPER NAMES

Aboas *mistake for* Abcas, i.e. Abkhaziya 123/11
Acon, Acres (1) the crusader city of Acre 95/3n, 109/3; (2) Aachen 101/9
Agapiti St Agapitus (d. 258) 108/6n
Alchaya, Alchaye Cairo 81/1, 81/3
Alisaundre (1) Alexandria 59/8; (2) Alexander the Great 70/18, 73/1n
Anthone St Antony of Egypt (?251–356) 123/5n
Arabie *mistake for* Arbea, i.e. Kiriath-arba 84/16 (Genesis xxiii.1)
Arabum Arabia 61/3, 62/16
Arfaxath Arphaxad ruler of the Medes 140/3 (Judith i.1)
Armenes Armenians 122/5n
Armeny the More Greater Armenia 123/12; *see also* **Ermeny**
Arriane Arians 130/5n
Asso*, Assone Azzo della Torre 115/15, 115/16n
Assuerus, Assweris (1) *probably* Xerxes I (ruled 485–65) 57/16, 139/4n; (2) father of **Darius** 140/3
Austyn St Augustine (354–430) 155/6

Babyloi(g)ne (1) Babylon in Egypt 59/8n, 81/3; (2) ancient Babylon 139/1n, 139/2
Bala(h)(a)m Balaam 54/12n, 55/15, 55/18 (Numbers xxii–xxiv); *mistake for* Barlam 147/17n
Balauch, Baldach Baghdad 138/12n, 138/18n
Baltazar Belshazzar (d. 539 BC) 140/3 (Daniel v, vii.1, viii.1)
Benet St Benedict (*c*. 480–*c*. 550) 108/4
Blansagarda, Blansagarde Blanche Garde 109/6, 109/7n

Calipham, Colipha the Caliph 138/12, 138/14
Cambaleth, Camball Peking 138/11n, 138/18
Charles Charlemagne (*c*. 742–814) 101/4n
Cirions, Siriani, Syrians Syrians 117/9*, 121/13n, 121/15, 130/8
Constantyn(e) Constantine the Great (d. 337) 78/19, 98/12n
Copti Copts 117/10, 126/3n
Crisostome St John Chrysostomus (*c*. 347–407) 155/12n
Cristien, Cristyn Christians 104/10, 118/7; **Cristinmen** 104/8
Cursid See Dead Sea 134/8

Darius* Darius son of **Assuerus** 140/3 (Daniel v–vi, ix.1, xi.1)
Dauid king (d. ?*c*. 970 BC) 50/12 (1 Samuel xvi.1–13), 54/7 (1 Samuel xvii.34–6); **Dauidis** *gen*. 50/12; *identified with* the Psalmist 60/17n

Ebron Hebron 84/16 (Genesis xxiii)
Egriscull(a), Egrisculle an unidentified island 60/8n, 84/8, 111/4
Eleyne St Helena, mother of **Constantyn(e)** (*c*. 255–*c*. 330) 78/18, 98/14n, 101/8n, 111/6n
Eracle Heraclius (575–641) 124/9n
Ermeny Armenia 114/10; *see also* **Armeny the More**
Erowde *see* **(H)ero(w)d(e)**

Ethiope (1) Ethiopia (a region of the East with dark-skinned inhabitants) 57/17, 137/14; (2) an inhabitant of Ethiopia 69/17n, 84/9; **Ethiopes** *pl.* 119/18
Eustas Julia Eustochium (370–*c.* 419) 103/7n
Eustorche Eustorgius (bishop of Milan 315–31) 114/15n

Felicissimi St Felicissimus (d. 258) 108/6n
Frederike Frederick I (*c.* 1123–90) 115/10n
Frere *n. pl.* friars, *in phr.* ~ **Austyns** Austin Friars (Augustines) 140/7; ~ **mendinantz** mendicant friars 141/2; ~ **menours** Friars minors (Franciscans) 140/7, *error for* mendicants 141/9; ~ **Prechours** Friars Preachers (Dominicans) 115/5 (*cf.*, 114/9 ff.n), 126/6
Frisons Frisians 118/8, 122/17

Galile(e) (1) a town 63/1n; (2) Galilee 63/3n, 107/16
George the Hyer Upper Georgia 122/14
Godoly(e) an unidentified kingdom 59/17, 61/3
Grecelond Greece 114/5
Grisailla *see* **Egriscull(a)**

Henissem an unidentified land 123/18n
(H)ero(w)d(e) Herod the Great (d. 4 BC) 65/8n, 66/1, 86/3
Hungries Hungarians 122/17

Ind(e) Inde (a vaguely defined area of the distant East) 54/13, 116/15, 120/4n; *mistake for* Judea 70/15n, 76/4n, 121/13n, 121/14, 121/17, 122/3; **Yndes** *pl.*, *in phr.* **thre** ~ 57/9–10; the people of Inde 96/16, 117/12n, 146/5n
Insule see **Egriscull(a)**
Ismini a heretical sect (?Abyssinians) 117/10, 126/8n

Iacob Jacob Baradeus (*c.* 500–78) 125/9n
Ierome St Jerome (*c.* 342–420) 103/7n, 103/8
Iosaphath Josaphat (Joasaph) 147/17n
Iulan þe Apostata Julian the Apostate (332–63) 113/15n

Kateryne St Catherine of Alexandria (early fourth century) 123/4n

Liban (mount of) *perhaps* Mt Hermon 134/4
Lowis St Louis IX (1214–70) 112/17n, 113/1

Machomete Mohammed (*c.* 570–629) 123/1, 124/9
(Þe) Maystir in Histories* Peter Comestor (d. 1179) 155/1–2n
Makary, Makare St Macarius of Egypt (*c.* 300–*c.* 390) 123/5n, 133/12
Mandapoli a heretical sect (*perhaps* Gypsies) 117/10, 128/7n
Manuel (E)manuel (1143–80) 114/14n
Marie Magdeleyn Mary Magdalene 99/11 (John xx.1–18)
(Þe thre) Maries the Three Maries 99/9 (Matthew xxvii.56, xxviii.1–2; Mark xvi; Luke xxiv.1–10)
Maro St Maro (d. before 423) 125/15n
Maromini, Maromynes an unidentified Christian sect 117/10, 126/17n
Maurice Mauritius or Maurice (582–603) 114/11n
Medee Media 58/8

Mediolane Milan 114/16n, 115/4n, 115/9n
Mediolanenses the people of Milan 114/12*, 114/17*
Michee Mecca 123/1
Montoste an unidentified wilderness 133/8n

Nabaoth Nebaioth 64/14 (Isaiah lx.7)
Nabogodonosor Nebuchadnezzar (*c.* 600 BC) 140/3 (Daniel i–iv)
Nestoryne Nestorius (d. *c.* 451) 119/9n
Nestoriences, Nestoriens, Nestoryn(e)s, Nostyrines Nestorians 111/8n, 119/8n, 119/11, 137/11, 138/7
Newbye, Nubye Nubia 58/1, 62/16, 69/13, 99/13
Nichodemus Nicodemus 87/3 (John xix.39–40); **þe gospel of Nichodeme** 126/6n
Nicholaite, Nicholaites Nicolaites *or* Nicolaitans 117/10, 127/4n, 127/10n
Nile river 59/5 (Genesis ii.10–14)
Nynus Ninus 84/19n

Occean the circumambient Ocean 59/2
Olyuete (mount of) the mount of Olives 62/18 (Acts i.12)
Oloferne(s) Olofernes 74/1n, 74/5
Origene(s) Origen (*c.* 185–*c.* 254) 127/11n, 127/17

Perce, Pers(e) Persia 54/13, 58/14; **Percens, Perces, Persens** Persians 71/3, 137/7n, 137/12; **hem of Pers** 114/10–11
Poule St Paula (347–404) 103/7n

Reynold Rainald of Dassel (d. 1167) 115/12n, 115/14n
Remige Remigius of Auxerre (*c.* 841–*c.* 908) 155/7n
Roboam Rehoboam 85/6 (1 Kings xiv.25–6, 2 Chronicles xii.9)

Saba Sheba 60/1, 61/4; **the qwene** ~ the queen of Sheba 71/2n, 85/5–6 (1 Kings x, 2 Chronicles ix)
Samuell prophet 50/13 (1 Samuel xvi.1–13)
Sculla, Seuwa an unidentified city 89/11n, 91/3, 145/17
Siluestre St Sylvester (bishop of Rome 314–55) 98/12n
Syna Sinai 59/9, 123/3n; **mons Synay** 58/4 (Exodus xix.1 ff., Deuteronomy xxxiii.2, Judges v.5)
Siriani, Syrians *see* **Cirions**
Sirye, Surye 58/4, 59/7, 70/15, 121/14n
Syxti St Sixtus (Xistus) II (d. 258) 108/6n
Soldyne an unidentified heresiarch 118/13
Susas Susa 139/4n

Tartary, **Tartarie** the land of the **Tartarin(e)s** 139/16n, 142/1
Tartarin(e)s Tartars (Tatars) 135/12, 138/8n
T(h)arce, Thars Tarshish 60/5n, 61/4, 61/5; **Tharcenses** the people of Tarshish (*or perhaps* Tarsus) 75/2n
Thare Terah (Genesis xi.26–32) 84/18
Thauris Tabriz 139/3n, 139/15
Thomas St Thomas 60/9, 89/1n, 145/9n (John xx.26–9)
Titus and Vaspasyan emperors Titus (39–81) and Vespasian (ruled 69–79) 87/15–16

BIBLIOGRAPHY

Allen, Rosamund, 'Some Sceptical Observations on the Editing of *The Awntyrs off Arthure*', in Pearsall 1985, pp. 5–25.

Ashton, John, ed., *The Voiage and Travayle of Sir John Maundeville* ... (London, 1887).

Beazley, C. R., *The Dawn of Modern Geography*, 3 vols (Oxford, 1906).

Behland, Max, ed., *Die Dreikönigslegende des Johannes von Hildesheim: Untersuchungen zur niederrheinischen Übersetzung der Trierer Handschrift 1183/485 mit Textedition und vollständigem Wortformenverzeichnis* (Munich, 1968).

Book of Cologne, see Röhricht and Meisner.

Book of James or Protevangelium, in James 1924, pp. 38–49.

Brie, Friedrich W. D., ed., *The Brut or The Chronicles of England*, 2 vols, EETS OS 131 and 136 (1906, 1908).

Brown, Carleton, and Rossell Hope Robbins, *Index of Middle English Verse* (New York, 1943).

Bülbring, Karl D., 'Über die Handschrift Nr. 491 der Lambeth-Bibliothek', *Archiv für das Studium der neueren Sprachen und Literaturen*, 86 (1891), 383–92.

Bulst-Thiele, Marie Luise, 'Ludolf von Sudheim', in *Verfasserlexikon*, ed. by Wolfgang Stammler, 2nd edn, 7 volumes published to date (Berlin, 1978—).

Cary, George, *The Medieval Alexander*, revised edn (Cambridge, 1956).

Chambers, R. W., 'The Manuscripts of *Piers Plowman* in the Huntington Library, and their Value for Fixing the Text of the Poem', *Huntington Library Bulletin*, 8 (1935), 1–27.

Christern, Elisabeth, 'Goethe, Sulpiz Boisserée und die Legende von den Heiligen Drei Königen', *Kölner Domblatt*, 14/15 (1958), 162–72.

——, *Johannes von Hildesheim: die Legende von den Heiligen Drei Königen* (Munich, 1963).

——, 'Johannes von Hildesheim, Florentius von Wevelinghoven und die Legende von den Heiligen Drei Königen', *Jahrbuch des Kölnischen Geschichtsvereins*, 24/25 (1959/60), 39–52.

Cicero, *De Senectute, De Amicitia, De Divinatione*, ed. & tr. by William Armistead Falconer, Loeb Classical Library, 154 (London, 1923).

Cobby, Anne Elizabeth, 'Introduction', in *The Pilgrimage of Charlemagne*, ed. and tr. by Glyn S. Burgess, Garland Library of Medieval Literature, A47 (New York, 1988).

Comestor, Peter, *Historia Scholastica* (Lyons, 1526).

Doyle, A. I., 'The Manuscripts', in *Middle English Alliterative Poetry and its Literary Background: seven essays*, ed. by David Lawton (Cambridge, 1982), pp. 88–100.

Dutschke, C. W., *Guide to Medieval and Renaissance Manuscripts in the Huntington Library*, 2 vols (San Marino, California, 1989).

Elissagaray, Marianne, ed., *La légende des Rois Mages* (Paris, [1965]).

Encyclopaedia of Religion and Ethics, ed. by James Hastings, 13 vols (New York, 1908).

Encyclopedia of the Early Church, ed. by Angelo Di Berardino, 2 vols (Cambridge, 1992).

Esposito, Mario, ed., *Itinerarium Symonis Semeonis ab Hybernia ad Terram Sanctam*, Scriptores Latini Hiberniae, 4 (Dublin, 1960).

Freeman, Margaret B., *The Story of the Three Kings* (New York, 1955).

Greetham, D. C., 'Challenges of Theory and Practice in the Editing of Hoccleve's *Regement of Princes*', in Pearsall 1985, pp. 60–86.

Gregory the Great, *XL Homiliarum in Evangelia Libri II* (Augustae Vindelicorum, 1761).

Hands, Rachel, *English Hawking and Hunting in 'The Boke of St. Albans'* (Oxford, 1975).

Hanna, Ralph, *The Awntyrs off Arthure at the Terne Wathelyn: an edition based on Bodleian Library MS. Douce 324* (Manchester, 1974).

——, 'Problems of "Best Text" Editing and the Hengwrt Manuscript of *The Canterbury Tales*', in Pearsall 1985, pp. 87–94.

——, 'The Scribe of Huntington HM 114', *Studies in Bibliography*, 42 (1989), 120–33.

Harris, Sylvia C., 'An Early New High German Translation of the *Historia Trium Regum* by Johannes de Hildesheim Edited from Pap. Man. No. 15, Stadt- und Stiftsarchiv, Aschaffenburg' (unpublished M.A., University of London, 1954).

——, 'German Translations of the "Historia Trium Regum" by Johannes de Hildesheim', *Modern Language Review*, 53 (1958), 364–73.

——, 'The *Historia Trium Regum* and the Mediaeval Legend of the Magi in Germany', *Medium Aevum,* 28 (1959), 23–30.

Hendricks, Rudolf, ed., 'A Register of the Letters and Papers of John of Hildesheim, O. Carm. (d. 1375)', *Carmelus*, 4 (1957), 116–235.

Hill, G. F., 'The Thirty Pieces of Silver', *Archaeologia*, 59 (1905), 235–54.

Historia Trium Regum, see John of Hildesheim.

Horstmann, C., ed., *The Three Kings of Cologne: an early English translation of the 'Historia Trium Regum' by John of Hildesheim*, EETS OS 85 (1886).

Hughes, David, *The Star of Bethlehem Mystery* (London, 1979).

Index of Middle English Verse (Supplement), see Brown, Carleton, and Robbins, R. H.

Index of Printed Middle English Prose, see Lewis, Robert E.

Isidore, *Isidori Hispalensis Episcopi Etymologiarum sive Originum Libri XX*, ed. by W. M. Lindsay, 2 vols (Oxford, 1911).

James, Montague Rhodes, ed., *The Apocryphal New Testament* (Oxford, 1924).

——, and Claude Jenkins, *A Descriptive Catalogue of the Manuscripts in the Library of Lambeth Palace: the medieval manuscripts* (Cambridge, 1932).

John of Hildesheim, *Historia Trium Regum*, in Horstmann 1886, pp. 206–312.

Kane, George, and E. Talbot Donaldson, eds, *Piers Plowman: the B version* (London, 1975).

Kaplan, Paul H. D., *The Rise of the Black Magus in Western Art*, Studies in the Fine Arts: Iconography, 9 (Ann Arbor, 1985).

Kehrein, Joseph, *Lateinische Sequenzen des Mittelalters* (1873; rpt, Hildesheim, 1969).

Kehrer, H., *Die Heiligen Drei Könige in Literatur und Kunst* (Leipzig, 1908/9; rpt, Hildesheim, 1976).

Keiser, George R., 'Lincoln Cathedral Library MS. 91: life and milieu of the scribe', *Studies in Bibliography*, 32 (1979), 158–79.

Latham, R. E., *Revised Medieval Latin Word-List from British & Irish sources* (London, 1965).

Lawton, David, ed., *Middle English Alliterative Poetry and its Literary Background: seven essays* (Cambridge, 1982).

——, 'The Diversity of Middle English Alliterative Poetry', *Leeds Studies in English*, n.s., 20 (1989), 144–72.

Letts, Malcolm, ed. & tr., *The Pilgrimage of Arnold von Harff* ... , Hakluyt Society, second series, 94 (London, 1946).

——, ed., *Mandeville's Travels*, 2 vols, Hakluyt Society, second series, 101–2 (London, 1953).

Lewis, Robert E., and Angus McIntosh, *A Descriptive Guide to the Manuscripts of the 'Prick of Conscience'*, Medium Aevum Monographs, new series, 12 (Oxford, 1982).

——, N. F. Blake and A. S. G. Edwards, *Index of Printed Middle English Prose* (London, 1985).

Linguistic Atlas of Late Mediaeval English, see McIntosh, Angus.

Ludolf of Sudheim, *Description of the Holy Land, and of the Way Thither*, tr. by Aubrey Stewart (London, 1897), translation of *De Itinere Terrae Sanctae Liber*, ed. by F. Deycks (Stuttgart, 1851).

MacCracken, H. N., 'Lydgatiana III: The Three Kings of Cologne', *Archiv für das Studium der neueren Sprachen und Literaturen*, 129 (1912), 50–68.

McIntosh, Angus, M. L. Samuels, and Michael Benskin, *Linguistic Atlas of Late Medieval English*, 4 vols (Aberdeen, 1986).

Monneret de Villard, Ugo, *Le leggende orientali sui Magi evangelici*, Studi e Testi, 163 (Vatican City, 1952).

Muir, Lynette R., *The Biblical Drama of Medieval Europe* (Cambridge, 1995).

Neumann, G.A., ed., 'Ludolfus de Sudheim: De itinere terre sancte', *Archives de l'Orient Latin*, 2.2 (1883), 305–77.

Opus Imperfectum in Mattheum, PG 56: 611–946.

The Oxford Classical Dictionary, ed. by N. E. L. Hammond and H. H. Scullard, 2nd edn (Oxford, 1970).

The Oxford Dictionary of the Christian Church, ed. by F. L. Cross and E. A. Livingstone, 2nd edn (Oxford, 1974).

Peake's Commentary on the Bible, ed. by Matthew Black (London, 1962).

Pearsall, Derek, ed., *Manuscripts and Texts: editorial problems in later Middle English literature* (Cambridge, 1985).

Pollard, A. W., and G. R. Redgrave, *A Short-Title Catalogue of Books Printed in England, Scotland, and Ireland, and of English Books Printed Abroad 1475–1640,*

2nd edn, W. A. Jackson, F. S. Ferguson and K. F. Pantzer, 3 vols (London, 1976–91).

Power, Eileen, 'The Opening of the Land Routes to Cathay', in *Travel and Travellers in the Middle Ages*, ed. by Arthur Percival Newton (London, 1926), pp. 124–58.

Pseudo-Matthew, in Tischendorf 1876, pp. 51–112.

Raymo, Robert R., 'A Middle English Version of the *Epistola Luciferi ad cleros*', in *Medieval Literature and Civilization: studies in memory of G.N. Garmonsway*, ed. by D. A. Pearsall and R. A. Waldron (London, 1969), pp. 233–48.

Rice, Joanne A., *Middle English Romance: an annotated bibliography, 1955–1985* (London, 1987).

Robbins, R. H., and J. L. Cutler, *Supplement to the Index of Middle English Verse* (Lexington, 1965).

Röhricht, [Reinhold], and [Heinrich] Meisner, 'Ein niederrheinischer Bericht über den Orient', *Zeitschrift für deutsche Philologie*, 19 (1887), 1–86.

Rooney, Anne, *Hunting in Middle English Literature* (Cambridge, 1993).

Root, Robert Kilburn, ed., *The Book of Troilus and Criseyde by Geoffrey Chaucer* (Princeton, 1926).

Russell, G. H., and Venetia Nathan, 'A *Piers Plowman* Manuscript in the Huntington Library', *Huntington Library Quarterly*, 26 (1963), 119–30.

Schaer, Frank, '*The Three Kings of Cologne*: a diplomatic edition of the unabridged English version of John of Hildesheim's *Historia trium Regum* in Durham MS Hunter 15, with a reconstruction of the translator's Latin text on facing pages based on Corpus Christi College Cambridge MS 275, and a study of the manuscript tradition' (unpublished PhD, University of Adelaide, 1992).

Severs, J. Burke, and Albert E. Hartung, eds, *A Manual of the Writings in Middle English 1050–1500*, 10 volumes published to date (New Haven, Conn., 1967–1998), I (1967), VI (1980).

Seymour, M. C., 'The Early English Editions of Mandeville's Travels', *The Library*, fifth series, 19 (1964), 202–7.

——, 'The Origin of the Egerton Version', *Medium Aevum*, 30 (1961), 159–69.

——, 'The Scribe of Huntington Library MS. 114', *Medium Aevum*, 43 (1974), 139–43.

Skeat, W. W., ed., *The Vision of William Concerning Piers the Plowman by William Langland*, EETS OS 54 (1873).

Smith, Morton, *Jesus the Magician* (London, 1978).

Smith, William, and Henry Wade, *A Dictionary of Christian Biography* (London, 1877).

Stapelmohr, Ivar von, ed., *Ludolfs von Sudheim Reise ins heilige Land, nach der Hamburger Handschrift* (Lund, 1937).

Stern, Karen, 'The London "Thornton" Miscellany: a new description of British Museum Additional manuscript 31042', *Scriptorium*, 30 (1976), 26–37 & 201–18.

Tertullian, *Adversus Marcionem*, in *Quinti Septimii Florentis Tertulliani quae supersunt omnia*, ed. by Franciscus Oehler, 3 vols (Lipsia, 1854), II, pp. 45–336.

Thompson, John J., *Robert Thornton and the London Thornton Manuscript: British Library MS Additional 31042*, Manuscript Studies, 2 (Cambridge, 1987).

Tischendorf, Constantinus de, ed., *Evangelia Apocrypha*, 2nd edn (Leipzig, 1876; rpt, Hildesheim, 1966).

Trithemius, Johannes, *Catalogus Illustrium Virorum*: *opera historica* (Frankfurt, 1601; rpt, Frankfurt a. M., 1966).

Warner, Marina, *Alone of All Her Sex: the myth and cult of the Virgin Mary* (London, 1990).

Wells, John Edwin, *A Manual of the Writings in Middle English 1050–1400* (New Haven, Conn., 1916).

Windeatt, B. A., *Geoffrey Chaucer: 'Troilus & Criseyde', a new edition of 'The Book of Troilus'* (London, 1984).

Worstbrock, F. J., and Sylvia C. Harris, 'Johannes von Hildesheim', in *Verfasserlexikon*, ed. by Wolfgang Stammler, 2nd edn, 9 vols published to date (Berlin, 1978—).

Young, Robert, *Analytical Concordance to the Holy Bible*, 8th edn (London, 1939).

Yule, Henry, *Cathay and the Way Thither*, revised edition, 4 vols, Hakluyt Society, 2nd series, 38, 33, 37, 41 (London, 1913–16).

Zarncke, Friedrich, ed., 'Der Priester Johannes', *Abhandlungen der philologisch-historischen Classe der Königlichen Sächsischen Gesellschaft der Wissenschaften*, 17 (1878), 829–1028.

Middle English Texts

Universitätsverlag
C. WINTER
Heidelberg

17 SARAH M. HORRALL (Ed.)
The Lyf of Oure Lady: The ME Translation of Thomas of Hales' Vita Sancte Marie
1985. 136 pp., ISBN 3-8253-3581-x

18 RODNEY MEARNS (Ed.)
The Vision of Tundale
1985. 180 pp., ISBN 3-8253-3700-6

19 C. WILLIAM MARX and JEANNE F. DRENNAN (Ed.)
The Middle English Prose Complaint of Our Lady and Gospel of Nicodemus
1987. 232 pp., ISBN 3-8253-3963-7

20 MALDWYN MILLS (Ed.)
Horn Childe and Maiden Rimnild
1988. 144 pp., ISBN 3-8253-4042-2

21 GEOFFREY LESTER (Ed.)
The Earliest Translation of Vegetius' De Re Militari
1988. 144 pp., ISBN 3-8253-4057-0

22 VALERIE EDDEN (Ed.)
Richard Maidstone's Penitential Psalms
1990. IV, 144 pp.,
ISBN 3-8253-4269-7

23 PETER WHITEFORD (Ed.)
The Myracles of Oure Lady
ed. from Wynkyn de Worde's edition
1990. 150 pp., ISBN 3-8253-4330-8

24 DAN EMBREE and ELIZABETH URQUHART (Ed.)
The Simonie: A Parallel-Text Edition
1991. 178 pp., ISBN 3-8253-4426-6

25 C. W. MARX (Ed.)
The Devil's Parliament and **The Harrowing of Hell and Destruction of Jerusalem**
1993. 176 pp., ISBN 3-8253-4594-7

26 JOSEPH GALLAGHER (Ed.)
The Doctrinal of Sapience
ed. from Caxton's printed ed. 1489
1993. 266 pp., ISBN 3-8253-0015-3

27 MANFRED GÖRLACH (Ed.)
The Kalendre of the Newe Legende of Englande
1994. 253 pp., 4 Abb.,
ISBN 3-8253-0217-2

28 SARAH MC NAMER (Ed.)
The Two Middle English Translations of the Revelations of St Elizabeth of Hungary
1996. 136 pp., ISBN 3-8253-0385-3

29 KLAUS BITTERLING (Ed.)
Of Shrifte and Penance: The ME Prose Translation of 'Le Manuel des Péchés'
1998. 232 pp., ISBN 3-8253-0586-4

30 CELIA MILLWARD (Ed.) †
La Estorie del Evangelie
A Parallel-Text Edition
1998. 286 pp., ISBN 3-8253-0750-6

69051 Heidelberg · Postfach 10 61 40 · Tel. 0 62 21/77 02 60
Telefax 0 62 21/77 02 69 · http://www.winter-verlag-hd.de